Art and the Absolute

SUNY Series in Hegelian Studies
Quentin Lauer. S.J., Editor

ART
and the
ABSOLUTE

A STUDY OF
HEGEL'S
AESTHETICS

William Desmond

State University of New York Press

TO MARIA AND WILLIAM ÓG

Published by
State University of New York Press, Albany

© 1986 State University of New York

Printed in the United States of America

For information, address State University of New York
Press, State University Plaza, Albany, N.Y., 12246

Library of Congress Cataloging in Publication Data

Desmond, William, 1951–
    Art and the absolute.

    (SUNY series in Hegelian studies)
    Bibliography
    1. Hegel, Georg Wilhelm Friedrich, 1770–1831—
Contributions in aesthetics. 2. Aesthetics, Modern—
19th century. 3. Art—Philosophy—History—19th century.
I. Title. II. Series.
B2949.D47 1986   111'.85'0924   85-9886
ISBN 0-88706-150-8
ISBN 0-88706-151-6 (pbk.)

10 9 8 7 6 5 4 3 2

Contents

Preface

This book tries to respond to the strange neglect suffered by Hegel's philosophy of art. This neglect can be traced, in part at least, to the view that for Hegel religion and philosophy are seen to possess greater ultimacy than art. In part, also, it is due to an often caricatured picture of Hegel's thought as representing an aesthetically insensitive rationalism. Anyone who has studied Hegel with any measure of seriousness soon finds this caricature dissolving. Suspicion, nevertheless, seems to linger longer in relation to Hegel's subordination of art. What has always struck me as perplexing in Hegel's aesthetics, however, is his *continued* ascription of absoluteness to art, even despite the fact that at the same time some subordination to religion and philosophy does occur. The question I found insistent was, how can art be both absolute and subordinate? In this study, as its title perhaps indicates, I have tried to respond philosophically to this question.

Not surprisingly, this issue of art and the absolute turns out to be multifaceted, and as I will indicate in my introduction, I have tried to deal with the many-sided nature of the question. But I need to make the point here that this work makes no pretension to being anything like a comprehensive commentary on Hegel's aesthetics. Undoubtedly there is much room and great need for such commentary. I have rather tried to come to grips philosophically with some of the central issues raised for us by Hegel's philosophy of art. I believe this is essential for the following reasons.

First, without some understanding of art's place in Hegel's thought as a whole, we inevitably end with a seriously truncated picture of his philosophy. Indeed, without some sense of art's place within the whole, it is not always possible to fully appreciate many of the details of Hegel's aesthetics. Second, there is the intrinsic worth of Hegel's contribution to aesthetics, for Hegel was one of the greatest, if not the greatest philosopher of art, both with respect to depth and scope, in the western tradition. Third, there is the fact that crucial issues raised by Hegel's aesthetics still continue to be controversial, particularly the unresolved question of the relation of art and philosophy. This problem goes to the roots of our understanding of the contemporary task of the philosopher, regardless of whether or not we conceive of this task in a traditional manner. Fourth, Hegel's understanding of art provides us with an indispensable philosophical hermeneutic concerning key aesthetic dilemmas of modernity. Yet Hegel also possessed profound historical self-consciousness of the roots of these dilemmas in the artistic, political, religious and philosophical traditions of the west. Finally, the question of absoluteness, perhaps a little like Hegel himself, seems to be impossible to bury, despite the repeated efforts of some contemporary thinkers to shake themselves free of what they imply is the oppressive metaphysical burden of the philosophical past. I tend to see the past of philosophy not as the record of dead answers now discarded, but as the history of essential questions that welcome their own repeated renewal. In this light, I have tried to make intelligible sense of Hegel's ascription of absoluteness to art, and, mediately, of the question of the absolute in some of its wider ramifications. Overall, I have tried to avoid the rhetorical postures and the sometimes stultifying polemics that can attend discussions concerning the so-called tradition of metaphysics.

The above may sound suspiciously like a catalogue of problems for philosophers only. But this, I believe, would be a mistaken impression. The issues I have tried to deal with in this book are not solely of interest to the Hegelian scholar or the professional philosopher. The philosophy of art cannot be pursued in abstraction from the history of culture, a point brought home very forcefully by Hegel himself. Just as Hegel's aesthetics developed in the interplay between art, religion, politics and philosophy, so the present work, at least it is my hope, will have something to say to reflective persons concerned with religion, literature, history and the different arts.

Versions of Chapters One, Two and Five appeared in *Clio, The Owl of Minerva* and *Philosophy and Rhetoric*, and for permission to reprint I thank their respective editors, Clark Butler, Lawrence Stepelevich and Donald Verene. Some material in Chapters Three and Four was read at the 1982 and 1984 meetings of the Hegel Society of America and appeared in the Proceedings, respectively edited by Robert Perkins and Peter Stillman, and both published by State University of New York Press. For institutional support I wish to thank David Roswell, Dean of Arts and Sciences, and also the Faculty Development Committee at Loyola College, Baltimore. For his timely encouragement to continue thinking about Hegel's aesthetics, I want to thank Lawrence Stepelevich. I am grateful to Stanley Rosen for his generous interest in my work. I want to mark my special debt to Carl Vaught for philosophical conversation and friendship over many years. Finally, I must thank Maria and William Óg for their more than dialectical presence. I dedicate the book to them.

Introduction

A revived interest in Hegel has been a noteworthy philosophical occurrence in recent decades. Yet in this revival a peculiar lacuna exists, in that Hegel's views on art seem to have suffered a certain neglect. This indeed is surprising, and it marks not only the recent revival but also tends to characterize older commentary. Full length studies of Hegel's aesthetics in the English-speaking philosophical world have been few.[1] This is puzzling because Hegel's *Lectures on Aesthetics* have a wide accessibility with an appeal not confined to the professional philosopher. Moreover, they reveal the falseness of the common stock impression of Hegel as the paradigm of the turgid, Germanic professor. As even a cursory glance at the *Lectures on Aesthetics* reveals, the scope of Hegel's aesthetic culture was astonishing. His work on these lectures was one of the chief labors of his later years, so one ought not to be surprised to discover them drawing deep from the resources of Hegel's own philosophical maturity. Indeed, the reception of these lectures by his audience did much to confirm and enhance Hegel's intellectual eminence at that time.[2] These often neglected riches call for our renewed attention.

Perhaps one reason why the commentators have not always given full due to Hegel's teachings on art springs from the professional philosopher's caution about art itself: art, after all, might not be serious enough, might not have all the sombre weight of pure logic. Even were there some justice in this debatable attitude, it cannot be seen as a compelling objection in the case of Hegel. Hegel's devotion to logic is well-known, even to the point of his sometimes being labelled a "panlogician." Yet the logical and the aesthetical are not to be seen as antithetical here. For Hegel's concern with art is not just a concession to the more popular consciousness. On the contrary, one of the most startling assertions, perhaps one of the most difficult and striking claims in Hegel, is that art and *absoluteness* belong together. Art has an absolute dimension; indeed, it belongs together with religion and philosophy itself as one of the three highest modes of human meaning. Art is hence no incidental adornment, tacked on at the end of the Hegelian system like a delightful afterthought to the real philosophical labor, the labor of the philosophical concept. An understanding of art is indispensable to a proper understanding of Hegel's concept of the Absolute, and so also to an understanding of his conception of philosophy itself. Since its presence is integral to the systematic totality of Hegel's full point of view, its neglect leaves our grasp of this point of view radically truncated. It is one of the chief purposes of the present work to argue against this truncation and restore art to its appropriate philosophical place within Hegel's thought.

Such an intention might be sufficient motivation for undertaking a scholarly study of Hegel's aesthetics. Yet, in addition to the present state of Hegel scholarship, there are pressing philosophical motivations which might serve to further justify such an undertaking. One of the most problematic questions of contemporary philosophy has been the very nature of philosophical thinking itself. Anglo-American philosophy has sometimes tended to emphasize the relation between philosophy and scientific inquiry, but in European thought the possible kinship between philosophy and art has never been entirely absent. The most influential examples of this are perhaps Nietzsche in his pursuit of the poet-philosopher, and Heidegger's dialogue with key poets such as Rilke and, of course, Hölderlin, Hegel's intimate and one time cultural collaborator. Existentialism generally has tended to emphasize the importance to philosophy of the revelation of concrete existence, as this is effected by the literary imagination, as in, say, Sartre and Marcel. Much of recent literary theory, centering on the concept of "deconstruction," grows out of sophisticated philosophical presuppositions — presuppositions having strong roots in the Hegelian, or rather anti-Hegelian heritage of nineteenth and twentieth century thought — presuppositions, one might add, not always brought to the full light of explicit self-consciousness. Yet many of these contemporary concerns, as I hope to indicate more fully in due course, are already grasped in quite self-conscious terms in Hegel. And where they are not so explicit, the general framework of his thought and many details of his philosophy of art contain richly suggestive possibilities. In brief, Hegel's aesthetics are not lacking in continuing relevance to the contemporary debate[3] concerning the precise requirements of philosophical thinking and its relation to nonphilosophical, nonconceptual modes of meaning. The status of philosophy in a scientific age cannot be adequately explored, I believe, without cognisance of its relation to art. Hegel's aesthetics continues to provoke thought on this score.

But perhaps the most pressing philosophical consideration, as already implied, is Hegel's startling ascription of a certain dimension of *absoluteness* to art. In an age that has witnessed the pervasive presence of nihilism, we tend to be suspicious of, if not to find downright distasteful, all talk of "absolutes." More traditional modes of philosophizing, including Hegel's own discourse concerning Absolute Spirit, are felt to hang under a cloud of suspicion. Yet Hegel was acutely sensitive to difficulties concerning philosophical claims about "absolutes," and in his *Phenomenology of Spirit* took great pains in trying to mediate access to the intelligibility of such claims. In fact there is a strong experiential base to Hegel's thought, as the *Phenomenology* makes clear, and no thinker has inveighed more sharply against the notion of the Absolute as a mere *Jenseits*, an essentially empty beyond. Philosophy cannot be entirely divorced from concrete experience, and its claims concerning "absolutes" must be rooted concretely. Again, as Hegel's *Phenomenology* implies, *all experience*, however rudimentary, entails some implicit relation to absoluteness. Different forms of experience crystalize and articulate this relation in more explicit or fuller manners. But a genuine sense of the Absolute, for Hegel, is not attained by a leap beyond experience, but by an *emergence and unfolding* from within experience itself of its own ultimate dimension. Here two crucial forms of experience, religion and art itself, engaged Hegel's special attention. In conjunction with philosophical thought, art and religion are the forms of experience that most richly reveal man's involvement with questions of the Absolute. Hegel's philosophy of Absolute Spirit is but an effort to articulate this involvement, not in abstract detachment, but in the dialectical interplay between philosophical thought and artistic and religious experience.[4] It is with these that philosophy's kinship lies. It is against them that it confronts some of its greatest challenges. It is out of reflection on them that it often wins its deepest content and wide wealth of concreteness.

Hegel, of course, acknowledges that art and religion have a life of their own, and do not need philosophy in order first to be. Yet they articulate, highly significant responses to the concrete world. They constitute their own peculiar concreteness and do so informed with their own sense of ultimacy and absoluteness. As Hegel readily grants, art makes a claim on man as a whole with respect to his deepest desires and essential purposes. It speaks to what in man is more than the analytical intellect or what Hegel speaks of as *Verstand*. Art only achieves its highest task when, as he puts it, "it has placed itself in the same sphere as religion and philosophy, and when it is simply one way of bringing to our minds and expressing the *Divine*, the deepest interests of mankind, and the most comprehensive truths of the spirit. In works of art the nations have deposited their richest inner intuitions and ideas, and art is often the key, and in many nations the sole key, to understanding their philosophy (*Weisheit*) and religion."[5] These extraordinary, high claims made on behalf of art invite our careful philosophical consideration, especially since Hegel is often fixed in the minds of some as the philosopher who proclaimed the death of art.[6]

My chief purpose in the present study is to try to make philosophical sense of how art might be marked by this dimension of absoluteness. A complete treatment of Hegel's approach to the Absolute, of course, would have to include religion,[7] as well as the complex interplay between art, religion and philosophy. We will not neglect this interplay, but here will rather explore it from the central and organizing perspective of art. When we consider the caution and scepticism that contemporary man displays regarding the question of the Absolute, and when we add to this the fact that religion tends sometimes to provoke strong commitments, be they sympathetic or hostile, art, I believe, offers a fruitful possibility through which we might address again, without corrosive scepticism or merely assertive dogmatism, this issue of the Absolute. For such an approach would have to respect the claim made above, namely, that for Hegel the

Absolute entails an emergence from within experience itself of its own ultimate dimensions. The inescapable experiential rooting of the phenomenon of art in the riches of the concrete order offers us hopeful expectation in this regard.

In centering on art's connection with the Absolute in Hegel, it is not necessary, however, that we isolate art from its relations with other important domains of meaning, and the possible light art might shed on them. For this reason the following study has a double emphasis:[8] first, it attempts to view art as a phenomenon in its own right; second, it explores art's significance through its interconnections with other key forms of experience. We need to see art both in itself and in its relation to other crucial areas within the larger economy of the human spirit. This double emphasis dictates the character of the different chapters. Thus in Chapter One we explore art on its own terms in the light of two chief ways it has been interpreted in the history of western aesthetics: namely, in terms of imitation and creation. We will see how Hegel, while very much stressing the modern emphasis on creation, does not simplistically repudiate the more classical *mimesis*, but seeks to preserve some balance between old and new. In Chapter Two we focus on the tension and affinity between art and philosophy, in terms of the "ancient quarrel" between the poet and the philosopher, and also in terms of the precarious position of art in the modern scientific age. Here we will see that the rich concreteness of the art work is possessed of metaphysical import and sheds some important light on the peculiaries of Hegel's understanding of the philosophical concept. Overall my argument in Chapters One and Two is against the still common view which sees philosophy as displacing art in Hegel.[9] While not denying a certain subordination of art to philosophy in Hegel, this subordination, I will hold, is qualified by a set of complex dialectical considerations which demand that we also affirm the *complementarity* of art and philosophy, and indeed the necessary *openness* of philosophy to art.

In Chapter Three we take up the relation of art and religion in Hegel. Here we return to the issue of "creativity" and the question whether it can be completely "humanized," as has happened in many aesthetic movements coming after Hegel. We will see that Hegel's view of human originality is bound up with an essentially religious understanding of the Absolute, very much removed from any merely aes-

thetic understanding such as "art for art's sake." Our explorations here
will argue that Hegel's view moves against the grain of the "subjectivization" of creativity, a "subjectivization" so widespread since the
Romantic era. Here we will also argue against the complete humani-
zation of the Absolute as developed out of Hegel's own resources by
Hegel's Left wing descendants.

In Chapter Four we approach art and the Absolute from another
angle, intimately bound up with the Left-Hegelian interpretation, this
time in relation to the strong presence of history in Hegel's thought.
I argue that the sense of an end to be found in great art has important
bearings on that much-debated issue of the end of history in Hegel.
Normally this issue is treated in predominantly political terms. The
images of perfection that art originates in the fragmenting flux of time
itself offer us, I believe, very illuminating pointers on this issue. The
general thrust of these two chapters will be to trace out some of the
lines of connection between Hegel's aesthetics and religion, politics
and history, both in Hegel himself and as interpreted, appropriated
and transformed by the Left-Hegelian line of descent. In the main my
argument will be that while the humanism of Left-Hegelianism is a
genuine appropriation of Hegelian resources, it is incomplete and
onesided, and to that extent misleading. Hegel's aesthetic does not
lend itself to a complete humanistic appropriation, and its resistance
to such an appropriation is most pronounced in relation to our central theme, namely, the question of art and the Absolute.

Finally in Chapters Five and Six we attempt to apply to history
some of the consequences of Hegel's coupling of art and the Absolute.
In Chapter Five we relate Hegel's dialectical understanding of the art
work to the recent debate concerning deconstruction. This debate is
directly relevant to the issue of art and the Absolute, since if there is
any one point on which the deconstructionists seem to agree it is in
proclaiming the contemporary *absence* of the Absolute. Has Hegel's
aesthetics the power to make a genuine contribution to this contemporary question? I try to argue in the affirmative. Indeed, in contrast
to the humanism of the Left-Hegelians, the deconstructionists tend to
see themselves as anti-humanistic, and anti-Hegelian. Hegelian
aesthetics has here a relevant point of insertion into the contemporary controversy. Thus in Chapter Five we explore how Hegel is
often a silent shadow to what we might term the Nietzschean-

Heideggerian heritage and some of its recent inheritors such as Derrida. My purpose will be to show how Hegel's aesthetics can be seen to preserve many of the justified emphases of recent developments without sacrificing in the process what we might call *the presence of wholeness*, exhibited by some great art.

In Chapter Six, our final chapter, I take up further this question of the contemporary absence of the Absolute. This time I do so in terms of the eclipse of beauty as an ideal on the contemporary aesthetic landscape, relating this to the contemporary criticism of the so-called metaphysical dualisms of the western tradition, a criticism we again tend to find in followers of Nietzsche, Heidegger and Derrida. My aim is to show how the actuality of beauty, explicated here by a comparison of the views of Hegel and Aquinas, offers us a crucial countercase to the supposed sin of metaphysical dualism that is said to beset and deeply vitiate the western tradition. Here my intentions will be informed by, to borrow a contrast from Paul Ricoeur, a hermeneutic which seeks to recover meaning, rather than a hermeneutic that seeks to demystify.[10] The latter kind of hermeneutic is the kind often practised by the deconstructionists and the followers of the "modern masters of suspicion," as Marx, Nietzsche and Freud have been termed. The dialectical pathway of Hegel's aesthetics does not close a trail of suspicion with a negation, but helps to open, through the struggle with negation, the space for some contemporary affirmation. Though Hegel's aesthetics are firmly planted in the modern context of the expressive self, the full context of this expressive self in Hegel is bound up with a metaphysical affirmation of the beautiful. Without the grounding of this more encompassing context, the affirmation of the aesthetic — whether this be conceived "objectively" in terms of beauty, or "subjectively" in terms of the expressive self — tends ultimately to collapse.

My purpose here, as throughout this study as a whole is not to approach Hegel with the ulterior end of bringing an *accusation* against him — the ulterior purpose too often of thinkers who are taken up with the task of "overcoming" Hegel. A contemporary renewal of the aesthetic may be illuminated by, certainly it will not be obstructed by, Hegel's affirmation of the beautiful. Together these final two chapters, drawing out some consequences from art's link with absoluteness, show the continuing relevance of Hegel's philosophy of art as a rich synthesis of the ancient and the modern.[11] They show us Hegel's philosophy of art as capable of turning to the traditions of the past to enable us to reinvigorate its genuine achievements, and as capable of being directed to the present and future to throw significant light upon some of our immediately pressing perplexities.

Our twofold focus throughout — on art as a form of experience positive in itself, and on art in its interrelations with other forms of human activity, themselves positive in their own right — is dictated ultimately by the *dialectical* nature of Hegel's approach to philosophical questions, including those of art and the Absolute. This brings us to a final important point that has repercussions for the overall interpretation of Hegel. For Hegel, precisely because of the insistent thrust of his thought towards dialectically conceiving the Absolute, is often evaluated negatively as a thinker who ends up with a kind of totalitarian closure, where the accusation of "totalitarian closure" carries a deep rebuke against the distortions worked on reality by the abstractions of philosophical thought.[12] And, of course, this accusation of totalitarian closure against Hegel's philosophical concept is said to work one of its most insidious effects in connection with art, namely, in falsely subordinating it to philosophical rationality, and so violating its essential integrity.

The complex connection of art and the Absolute, however, demands that we counter this onesided picture of Hegel. We need not deny a movement to completion or wholeness in Hegel. We can deny, nevertheless, that such a movement to wholeness must be identified with totalitarian closure. The wholeness of the art work, I will argue, is of central significance here. For the art work makes it possible for us not to deny the importance of some movement to completion, but it does deny that we have to read this movement in a closed manner.[13] The place of art invites a more dialectical as opposed to a more monolinear reading of Hegel. As should be clear, such a reading would be a *double* form of reading: one which views art both as a reality rich in itself, and as related also to other significantly rich forms of activity; one which gives due weight to the kinship between art and philosophy, as much as to their differences, searching for the point of their dynamic interplay and balance.

Perhaps it might be said that any such form of "double" reading inevitably allows too great a degree of ambiguity in Hegel's thought.

The charge of ambiguity is often seen as philosophically damning, and Hegel is sometimes said to be deeply damned on this score. He tends to be damned by Anglo-American analysts because of too much ambiguity, and because of seeming to make a virtue of this fact. He tends to be damned by some of the continental Europeans for not enough ambiguity, or at least for not confessing publicly enough the ambiguity that remains after dialectic does its work. Yet there is an ambiguity of richness and there is an ambiguity of poverty. We have to decide which kind we think is applicable to Hegel. The dialectical approach, I suggest, points towards the rich version of ambiguity (an ambiguity that is not just the indigent equivocalness of propositional imprecision).

And this is all the more appropriate in the present case of art, which so often is the embodiment in imaginative form of richly significant ambiguity.[14] For Hegel's dialectical approach to art it is not a question of, as it were, collapsing into the sticky texture of existential ambiguity. It is a rather a matter of trying to articulate the immanent intricacies of a reality that is initially ambiguous, without in the process impoverishing this initial, primary phenomenon by analytical abstractions. Nor yet, granting the limitations of the abstractions of analysis, is it a matter of reneging upon the quest to make philosophically intelligible and meaningful what in itself is its own richly ambiguous reality. Hegel's dialectic is a form of thinking that tries to respect, indeed preserve the rich ambiguity of the primary phenomenon in the very act of clarifying it or rendering it reflectively articulate. The Hegelian notion of a dialectical *Aufhebung* — a form of thinking that both transcends and preserves — tries to actualize in thought this complex possibility. The inadequacy of the charge of totalitarian closure follows from the fact that the dialectical approach can be seen either as *encapsulating* the structure of a process of articulation, or it can be seen as dynamically *participating* in the process of articulation. A "closed" reading of Hegel exclusively emphasizes this first possibility. With balancing emphasis on the second possibility, the more "open" side of Hegel begins to appear, and in the present case the positive openness of philosophy to art.

The present work, then, involves different attempts at such a more "open" reading of Hegel, revealed significantly to us in the particular case of his philosophy of art. Hegel's joining together of art and the Absolute sets him at some distance from the stock rationalist downgrading of the aesthetic. If art does possess a dimension of absoluteness, this *necessitates* a real openness of philosophical thought to art. Indeed, philosophy might well be seen to presuppose art's concrete richness and ultimacy as necessary sources that must nourish its own more reflective norms. In the end, to negate the dialectical interplay of philosophy and art would be to stifle a significant part of philosophy itself, for it would be to rob it of one of its essential, prereflective roots.

Chapter One

Art, Imitation and Creation

Imitation: Art and the Metaphysics of Image and Original

It is appropriate that we first consider art as a phenomenon in its own right in the light of two interpretations that have dominated western aesthetic reflection, namely art as imitation and art as creation.[1] Art as imitation is more characteristic of ancient views, as in the classical perspectives of Plato and Aristotle. Art as creation has been in the ascendent in more modern times, and particularly since the Romantic era, concepts like "creativity," "originality," "self-expression" have exerted strong influence not only within art but outside of art also in numerous other areas of human activity.[2] Where are we to situate Hegel's aesthetic relative to these concepts? As one might expect from a thinker deeply immersed in the cultural currents of the nineteenth century, Hegel was not the least of those in recent centuries who have attempted to criticize the view that art is imitation in order to uphold a position closer to art as creative. Indeed, in articulating his system of Absolute Spirit, which ranks art along with religion and philosophy at the very highest level of spiritual activity, Hegel explicitly claims to have disposed of the principle of the imitation of nature.[3] This claim invites our attention, especially since some are still wont to think of Hegel, not as the defender of art's creative power, but as the proclaimer of its death.

My purpose here will be to show how Hegel's response to imitation involves an inherently ambitious or "double" evaluation of art,

1

which issues in both a defense of its powers and a criticism of its limits. To make sense of this evaluation, we must first examine his rejection of imitation, both in terms of the shortcoming of classical *mimesis* and its consonance with the context of Hegel's philosophy as a whole. Second, we need to delineate something of the positive, creative view with which he replaces imitation, particularly in its bearings on Hegel's version of art as a form of sensuous self-knowledge. Yet Hegel was not a simple child of his own times. As a great admirer of the ideals of the classical era, he preserved something of its emphasis, such that his positive view of art as creative retains some crucial aspects of the criticized imitation theory. This retention is important for our third and final consideration in this chapter, for it helps define, at least in its initial outlines, the relation of art and philosophy in Hegel. This important relation, as we shall see, is a delicate balance of subordination and openness: a certain subordination of art to philosophy, a clear openness of philosophy to art. Hegel's criticism of imitation makes him to be, at one and the same time, art's defender and critic. Hence we must consider in what sense his subordination of art is merely negative and whether it rather presupposes the openness of philosophy to art. The view defended here is that we must take fully into account the *twofold* character of Hegel's response to art: that he *both* defends it and criticizes it. I will suggest that the ambiguity of this response is not the result of a simple confusion of thought but that it points to the possibility of a positive relation between art and philosophy. This will be the chief focus of the next chapter.

First I wish to offer some broad remarks about imitation to delineate the context which situates the theory and to make Hegel's response to it intelligible. In the course of these remarks I will also make some general remarks about the structure of the imitation relation itself. Art as imitation arises in response to the claim to knowledge often put forward on art's behalf. Art has always purported to be more than sophisticated fantasy, more than pleasurable diversion which helps us while away the boredom of idleness, like alcohol on a weekend. It claims to know and in its best and proper shape to make evident something of profound import. This claim cannot but eventually come under philosophical scrutiny. Socrates, for example, tells us of his examination of the poet and his discovery that the latter cannot give an explicit account of his work's truth; many others, in fact, seem far more capable than the poet on this particular count. Socrates concludes that poetry arises from a kind of instinct or inspiration, the poet being like a seer delivering a sublime message without fully knowing what it means.[4] As a consequence the question of a possible conflict between art and knowledge has to be faced. In response to this arises the view that art is imitation, a view which seeks to articulate a basis on which art's claim might be supported or denied. This view seeks to ground art in an extra-artistic paradigm or model which, if revealed or portrayed by the artistic imitation, might lend its weight to the cognitive claim of art. In the artistic imitation we may perceive what is imitated, in art's portrayal we may recognize its paradigm.

This theory of imitation can assume, of course, more shapes than one. Depending, in the main, on how one conceives the paradigm and its relation to the imitation, one ends up with a different version of the theory. We receive an essentially *negative* version of it in Plato's *Republic* when Socrates criticizes art as the thrice removed copy of the truly real *eidos*.[5] Aristotle, by contrast, attempts to give us a *positive* version when he insists that artistic imitation presents us not with copies of copies but with universal forms devoid of trivial inessentials. In general we may say that a negative version tends to state that imitation distorts or conceals the paradigm, a positive version that it reveals and manifests it.

Granting this, there is nevertheless something common to all versions of imitation: a certain *duality* between the thing imitating and the paradigm imitated. This duality obtains whether one understands imitation positively or negatively, and regardless of what art seeks to imitate. The point I wish to make is not concerned with any particular *content* we might wish to ascribe or deny to imitation. It concerns the very *structure* of all imitation relations. Whether an imitation conceals or reveals the paradigm, there is still a common structure relating imitation and paradigm. This structure demands a somewhat *dualistic* interpretation. For imitation places the art-work in the context of a non-artistic reality, embedding it in a relation which necessarily requires reference to an *external* model.[6] No imitation can stand purely on its own but must relate to an external paradigm. All imitation relations require two constituents ordered in a hierarchical manner. Furthermore, there is a certain *asymmetry* in the structure of this relation: the paradigm cannot be reduced totally to the imitation, but the imitation can be reduced to the paradigm, at least in so far as there is something external to the imitation itself which the imitation seeks (albeit unsuccessfully) to realize. Put differently, there is a core to the imitation which, to be sustained, requires an external paradigm; but the external paradigm sustains its own existence regardless of the imitation. In illustration of this, let us say that Paul imitates Peter. Peter (as the model) has his own existence independently of Paul's imitation of him. But Paul's imitation could not be an imitation at all if it did not have some reference outside of itself to Peter. It is this necessity of an external reference which grounds the asymmetry and duality between paradigm and imitation.

Consequently there is present in any imitation an implicit metaphysics of image and original. The image and the original cannot be absolutely united because, should they be so, the image becomes identical with the original and thus ceases to be an image. There is always a *disjunction* between image and original, imitation and paradigm. Its asymmetry and dualism make imitation to be an image *of* something which cannot be identical with the imitation itself. Even where there is a continuity, this disjunction means that the paradigm possesses a dimension that resists being absolutely appropriated by the imitation. Indeed there can be no such thing as an absolutely pure imitation: if there were, the imitation would be the same as the model and hence be no imitation at all. To preserve the imitation relation, the duality of image and original cannot be totally overcome or reduced to a unity. Though the original may be *immanent* in the image and presented by it, this immanence is only partial and necessitates that the original be also *transcendent*. There is, then, an inherent ambiguity in the nature of imitation itself: the fact that the paradigm can be immanently present in the imitation and hence revealed by it grounds the possibility of the positive version; the fact that the paradigm must be still transcendent in some degree and hence to some extent hidden is the basis of the negative version. In the nature of the case there is an inevitable tension in the imitation between the paradigm's immanence and transcendence, its presence and absence. Relative to whichever pole of this tension we fasten upon, we are tempted to defend imitation as something positive[7] or to criticize it as something negative. In all cases we are forced to acknowledge a duality, disjunction and asymmetry between the image and the original.

Creation: Art and Sensuous Self-knowledge

These general remarks have a direct bearing on Hegel's twofold evaluation of art, his defense of it and his criticism of it, and with them in mind we turn to consider his response to imitation. Hegel's aesthetics is of a piece with his philosophy as a whole, insofar as it seeks a unity which reconciles what are normally considered to be opposites. It is not that he wishes to obliterate the opposites but rather to embrace and resolve their antagonism in a more encompassing unity. And this pervasive preoccupation with the possibility of a *coincidentia oppositorum*, running directly counter to the asymmetrical duality discussed above, is reflected in his treatment of art and imitation.

Hegel's discussion of imitation in his lectures on aesthetics is not very extensive.[8] Though specifically concerned with art as the imitation of nature, it signifies, nevertheless, an attempt to break with the idea of imitation as such. Presently we will see that this break is not entirely successful, but for now it is important to notice that his attack on imitation is chiefly directed on what I have called the negative version of the view. Hegel himself does not make this distinction between a positive and negative imitation. Had he done so, he might well have had to admit that his own position is in important respects a possible form of positive imitation. I will return to this below, but here I wish only to observe that it is not fortuitous that he confines his attack to the negative version of imitation. For in this, the duality of image and original and the paradigm's transcendence are more pronounced than in the positive version. Hence we find Hegel saying that because the nature imitated by art is already present to us in its essential reality, imitation seems not to add anything significantly *new* to his prior presentation.[9] Moreover, imitation risks being presumptuous in being unable to match the diversity and manifoldness of nature: in this respect art falls short.[10] Here we notice Hegel implicitly pointing out the tendency of imitation to draw attention to the recalcitrance of the external paradigm which refuses to be appropriated without residue. Hegel, no doubt, exaggerates the point, even if somewhat graphically, when he compares the imitation of nature to a worm trying to crawl after an elephant.[11] But we must remember that his focus is on the negative version of imitation, with which he is dissatisfied precisely because of its emphasis on the dualism of art and its paradigm and the paradigm's transcendence. Given the central thrust of his philosophy, this dualism and transcendence cannot be solutions for him but are the problem itself. Dualism may well be one's beginning but one's philosophical end, Hegel holds, must be to overcome and resolve the opposition dualism produces.

We can reconstruct the rationale of his rejection of imitation in the following terms. Art as imitation seems to possess what truth it does, not necessarily in virtue of anything in itself as image, but in virtue of something external to it. Hence its value does not reside in the image as such, but depends on an external relation binding image and original. This dependency of imitation seems to make art derivative and of secondary importance compared to the original it imitates. In view of this dependency, we seem to have to deny to art real autonomy and to place it under the dominion of an external norm. If this is so, art has as its end something outside itself and not itself. But if art is defined in terms of something outside itself, art seems to come to nothing in itself. The art image is then spoken of as a "mere" image, where this means that the image, to all intents and purposes, is difficult to distinguish from *illusion* — an expression and instrument of deceit which puts appearance in the place of the real thing. This is, in fact, what often does occur when, with a destructive purpose, we focus exclusively on the negative version of imitation — as we see in Socrates' disparagement of art as a mere counterfeiting appearance.[12]

The above observations relate directly to the negative version of imitation; these further points, not explicitly made by Hegel but demanded by his approach, are relevant to the positive version. The image which imitates (no matter how positive a weight one gives to this) does not *create* its original; it discovers it, finds it already there and must submit itself to it. The question then is: however positive a conception of imitation we have, is it sufficient to do justice to what appears as the *creative* dimension of art? Even if imitation is positive, is it positive enough? Since, relative to the problem of dualism, positive imitation does not totally overcome the disjunction between image and original, must we not instead seek a conception of art in which creation instead of imitation dominates? This is precisely what Hegel attempts to do. Though we can say that there are broad structural similarities between Hegel's view and Socrates' rejection of negative imitation in the *Republic*, there is this essential difference. Socrates attacks imitation to attack art; Hegel attacks imitation not to attack art but defend it in a shape other than imitative. To defend art as creative, Hegel looks to art's creative power to resolve the disjunction between art and what lies outside it.

In response to a possible dualism between art and what lies beyond, then, Hegel is motivated to defend the autonomy of art as containing its own end and possessing intrinsic worth. We must beware of converting art, as do utilitarians and moralists, into an instrument leading to an extrinsic, nonartistic end. Art is only real when free with respect to both its ends and means; and it becomes free when, liberating itself from service to something other, it takes its place in the same sphere as religion and philosophy, the sphere of Absolute Spirit. In other words, for Hegel art is not merely an image but is, in certain respects, its own original. It is not bare receptivity but involves an activity of internal self-constitution which, because it originates its own reality, demands that we resist approaching it in terms of an external norm. Hegel's quarrel with imitation is not intended destructively. It rather seeks to clear the ground of obstacles and make room for a positive approach to art as creative. Of course, he does not claim that external nature has nothing to do with art. Especially with respect to painting, Hegel recognizes that natural form can give guidance and foundation. Yet these given forms do not exhaust the creative power most intimate to art; naturalism is not art's primary concern, and the given natural world does not supply the rule.[13]

In all of this we discern a break with those attempts to naturalize art which overlook the fact that something more is involved than given externality. Just as in the whole of Hegel's philosophy it is imperative to grasp the truth as Subject as well as Substance,[14] so too with art. Hegel's break with imitation is, by implication, a rejection of the static substantialist perspective which fails to see art as a *self-*

articulating activity. As self-articulating activity, art is not primarily concerned with an external object but with *itself* and its own creative resources. Its knowledge, therefore, is self-knowledge, insofar as it produces objects upon which it sets its own seal and in which it manifests and recognizes itself. As self-articulating activity, art is not chiefly directed upon an external domain, separate from and independent of the self. It seeks to overcome any such separation and independence and reconcile the self with the object. This it does by making manifest what is latent in itself as articulating activity and by reduplicating *itself* (instead of an external paradigm) in a higher self-conscious shape. As Hegel sees it, the universal need for expression in art lies in man's impulse to elevate both the inner and outer worlds into a spiritual consciousness for himself, into an object in which he recognizes his own self.[15] Through this self-articulation art becomes something of a creative adventure in which the self brings into being its own self-knowledge.

This break with what is external and this liberation of art's creative resources is of a very definite sort. It is not absolute or final; for art's self-knowledge is achieved only through the externalization of the self in a sensuous embodiment. If Hegel's attempt to dispose of imitation indicates a deficiency of the naturalistic attitude, it also wills a *restoration* of the natural and the sensuous in a new and more appropriate setting. There is an intimate connection between art and the sensuous. The latter is not an empty matter: it is the place where the self takes shape as *Geist* and comes to self-articulation — especially through becoming embodied in the human figure.[16] The self objectifies itself in the sensuous but this is not a loss of self. Rather the self recovers itself in the sensuous; and so only by losing itself does it begin to find itself as articulate. It is not the sensuous *qua* sensuous that concerns art. The sensuous must appear as the semblance of the sensuous, the shining (*Schein*) of the sensuous. What art presents is something freed from its merely material nature without ceasing at the same time to be sensuous. The work of art occupies a mean between pure thought and the immediately sensuous. It idealizes the sensuous, which no longer appears as brute uninformed materiality. The sensuous is spiritualized, spirit appears in sensuous shape, and the two together form a unity.[17]

We can illustrate this last point by briefly speaking of the concreteness of poetry. The only external matter *qua* matter that poetry retains is sound. We discern a movement beyond bare sound. But in this movement concrete sensuousness is not lost but heightened. Such sensuousness is lost to some extent *as* concrete sensuousness (compared with, say, music or painting), but it is retained as *ideal image* of the concrete. Thus the thought of poetry (and it does have thought),[18] is not abstract but concrete and imaginative. Poetry has liberated itself from the concreteness of external matter and produced the ideal concreteness of image and metaphor. In that sense, the ideality of poetry is not remote and unreal but has a compelling urgency which springs from its twofold impetus to make thinking concrete and to render the concrete articulate.

Turning now to art's claim to knowledge, we find Hegel upholding this claim because art is not simply sensuous, and because as the spiritualization of the sensuous it brings to light its own content, namely the Ideal.[19] The nature of the Idea in Hegel is, of course, a crucial issue in his philosophy as a whole and a full interpretation of its meaning would hardly be distinguishable from an extended reading of Hegel's entire philosophy. We will return more fully to relevant details characterizing Hegel's view when subsequently to this chapter we deal with the concreteness of Hegel's concept, and also when we deal with the religious and metaphysical implications of Hegel's aesthetics. For the present the following remarks must suffice with respect to the aesthetic themes of imitation and creation.

The Ideal is the Idea in sensuous shape, the self-becoming of reflective thought in which thought and sensuous shape conform with each other and converge on an immediate unity.[20] The Ideal is not a simple preconstituted content which is externally imposed on the sensuous vehicle of its expression. It rather comes into being in a process of self-articulation, arising from and going forth from artistic self-activity. Thus this artistic content is self-determined, and in this is to be distinguished from the content arising from the external determination characteristic of the imitation. If we compare the content of imitation to an offspring issuing from parents outside of artistic activity itself, we can say that the immanently developed content of art as creatively self-determined makes art to be the father, mother and midwife of its own vision.

Here we reach a clear divergence between Hegel's approach to art's grounding and that of the imitation theory. Again we come across his disagreement with any metaphysics of image and original which too strongly speaks of the original as transcendent. In his view, the image (the sensuous shape) and the original (the Idea) begin to coincide in the Ideal. The sensuous image becomes itself an original by embodying a self-originating content and not just simply reflecting one. Art does not simply mirror or image an already constituted world or original: it itself originates and constitutes a world where the image and the original move towards an identity wherein we cannot absolutely separate the two. The original is not transcendent to the artistic act but comes to embodiment in this very act of articulation. In the Ideal the original becomes immanent by being embodied in the image of art.

And thus in Hegel we do not find that gap or separation between image and original which is so conspicuous in the imitation theory. That separation is transcended since spiritual content and sensuous image cannot be abstracted from one another without violating the integrity of the artistic whole. This does not mean that Hegel forsakes the possibility of giving art a ground. His position, rather, states a possible resolution of the issue. Within the framework of his view art can be seen as contributing to its own grounding; as a sensuous self-knowledge, art seeks to be self-grounding by overcoming the gap between image and original involved in imitation. As sensuous self-knowledge, art creates its own object and grounds itself by doing so. Its object is its own self-articulation. The gap that is present in imitation and that robs imitation of self-grounding is diminished in the Ideal where the original (the Idea) begins to lose its transcendence with respect to the image, and the image begins to immanently articulate the spiritual content of the original.

Art and Philosophy: Openness and Subordination

But with this we confront what is for Hegel the limit and the highest point of art. And so here we are put in a position to understand Hegel's twofold evaluation of art, as both defensive of its creative power and critical of its limitations. Here also we can discern the outlines of a twofold relation of art and philosophy as both the openness of philosophy to art and yet art's qualified subordination to philosophy. Let us then conclude this chapter with some remarks on this double evaluation in the context of imitation and creation. We will then take up in the next chapter the *positive interplay* of art and philosophy still allowed by this double evaluation. The point to be chiefly emphasized now is that the immanence of the Idea in the Ideal is a precarious achievement which is to be found in its aesthetic fullness only in the classical art of ancient Greece. Once attained it gives way to a *new transcendence* of the Idea. The reconciliation of image and original achieved in art is not an absolutely final one. Only in the philosophical concept is the Idea fully immanent for Hegel. The limitation of classical art is the limitation of art as such:[21] it fails to completely reach the true identity of knower and known because it needs a sensuous shape in which to know itself, and hence is still caught in a separation, albeit less extreme than in imitation, between image and original. In the final analysis, the Idea is not fully trans-cendent to art nor yet fully immanent in it. In fact the true *form* of self-knowledge is not the sensuous self-knowledge of art but the rational self-knowledge of philosophy. To attain the rational self-knowledge of philosophy we have to move beyond the image in so far as it possesses a limiting element of externality. From the standpoint of philosophy the limits of art begin to appear.

The upshot, therefore, is that we discover a fundamental tension in Hegel's position. Somewhat ironically, Hegel begins by ascribing to art its end within itself only to qualify this view when he considers that the end of every spiritual activity, including art, can be ade-quately articulated ultimately only by philosophy. From this final perspective art does not receive its complete ratification from itself but from philosophy. While Hegel rejects the transcendent original of imitation in favour of an immanent concretization of artistic truth, he concludes by claiming to overcome in the true original grasped by philosophy what he considers to be the limitations of the artistic image. Thus there is a tension between his acceptance of art's truth and his assertion of its limitations. And so also in a peculiar way Hegel is in agreement with the imitation theory he criticizes. We might say that Hegel, in criticizing a negative form of imitation, not only falls into a new version of positive imitation, but also runs the risk of a new version of negative imitation, in terms of art's relation to philosophy. Hegel, I believe, need not be seen as entirely succumb-ing to this risk, though ambiguous elements in his view sometimes lend themselves to a less subtle reading of the issue at stake. It is not surprising that Hegel had such a strong admiration for the art of classical Greece. Nor is it surprising that there is a similarity between Aristotle's understanding of imitation as presenting pervasive universal forms and Hegel's insistence that the Idea is made sensuously immanent in the embodiment of the art work. Though Hegel gives dominance to the creative dimension of art, he nevertheless returns to stress what we found to be already present in imitation, namely the original's transcendence and the image's limitation with respect to it. Hegel's divergence from imitation consists in the fact that according to the imitation theory the original comes *before* the image, is preconstituted with respect to it, while for him the original in its true, full form only comes *after* the image, being the reflective result that is brought to fullest articulation in the further development of philosophy. In both cases the real original in its proper form is *beyond* the image — even if for Hegel art can contribute to the constitution of the original in final philosophical form.

Summarizing in broadest terms, Hegel rejects a negative form of imitation in terms of external nature, tries to replace imitation with creation in a fashion that reminds us of a positive form of imitation, only then to force us to ask whether he also provides us with a new negative version of imitation in relation to philosophy. Art remains tied to the sensuous image and so fails to give us the conceptual original constituted in proper form in philosophy. This sensuous image can be seen as a positive imitation of philosophy in partially revealing what philosophy alone truly reveals; it can be seen as negative imitation in concealing the form of this reality at the same time. Our conclusion must hence reiterate this twofold attitude to art: art is not solely negative, not exclusively positive, but both positive and negative together.

The issue of the relation of art to philosophy in Hegel, of course, raises the question of his reputed proclamation of the death of art. But the "death" of art must be understood in accordance with the peculiar philosophical fashion in which Hegel understands death: not as sheer negation but as negation which is in turn negated and transmuted into affirmation. We must insist that Hegel's subordination of art to philosophy is not any simple overlordship, as it were. It is a complexly qualified subordination in the sense that art does constitute its own genuine realm of meaning, and to this extent genuinely grounds itself in its own imaginative self-creation. But in this art does not self-consciously account for itself and its own grounding; this is the task for the rational reflection of the philosopher. The rational philosopher attempts to give a reflective account of art in which he must be open to granting art its rights without feeling himself constrained to merely reduplicate what we already have fully in terms of art itself. Art enacts its creative tasks; philosophy reflectively ponders on art's significance, both in itself and in its relations to the larger economy of the human spirit and its other significant activities.

Thus we might venture that Hegel's claim to have transcended art philosophically has often been seen in all too negative a light. Croce, for instance, describes Hegel's aesthetics as a funeral oration in which he passes in review art's various forms, art then being laid to rest in its grave with philosophy left to write its epitaph.[22] But if we recall the affirmative intent of negation in Hegel, what proves more fundamental is not the supposed absorption of art by philosophy but rather the opening of philosophy to the concrete richness of art — an opening which must encourage an ever more inclusive philosophical comprehension. Just as Hegel repudiates an exclusive bifurcation of art and philosophy without denying their difference, so he also, though supremely confident in reason, seeks to avoid falling afoul of the traditional rationalistic disparagement of art. Beyond the sheerly immediate, the power of articulation is present in all forms of experience from the rudimentary to the most complex. Though one might be tempted to give a rigid demarcation of their respective spheres by saying that the philosopher deals purely with concepts, the artist solely with images, such a rigidity runs counter to Hegel's intention. On the contrary, the philosopher must be provided with the reflective counterpart to the artist's imaginative vision, namely *speculative reason*.[23] The speculative reason of the philosopher seeks to realize a conceptual unity to match — but not necessarily replace — the expressive unity offered to us by the artist's imaginative vision. We must now see how this might be revealed in the *kinship* of the art work and the philosophical concept in Hegel, and how each strives for a concreteness that allows them to be complementary modes of articulation.

Chapter Two

Art, Philosophy and Concreteness

The Tension of Image and Concept

It is a philosophical commonplace to juxtapose logic and imagination, reason and sensibility, the concept and intuition, philosophy itself and art. Frequently these pairs are thought of as opposites, one mediated through abstract reflection, the other a more intimate participant in the given of concrete existence. Philosophy does not always come off uncriticized in this opposition. Its reflective, analytical impulse is often thought to abstract us, remove us from the concretely real. Art, by contrast, it is said, serves to keep us closer to the particularities and richness of the concrete, and so to be justified in the greater immediacy of its appeal. Such an opposition is as old as the ancient quarrel of poetry and philosophy, renewed in Plato's exiling of the poets, renewed again but this time reversed in Nietzsche's dictum: Homer versus Plato, this is life's basic antagonism.[1] Hegel too fought in this war. And we might expect, given the common view of Hegel as the rationalist philosopher *par excellence*, that Hegel struggled on one side alone, that of philosophy. Lovers of art have sometimes found it hard to forgive Hegel's disputed imputation that, within his system, art must finally rest in a position subordinate to philosophy. We must now ask, however, whether Hegel fought this struggle in the terms laid down by the old opposition.[2] Hegel, we must admit, knew something of *both* sides of the opposition, as indeed did

15

Plato and Nietzsche also. As we have already seen, it is misleading to think of Hegel in terms of the stock rationalist response to art. To the contrary, the entire thrust of his thought is to dwell with opposition, contradiction, struggle, not with the intent to destroy or eradicate, but to include and reconcile. His central notion of sublation or *Aufhebung* alone should be sufficient to give us pause and enable us to question any stark polarity of art and the philosophical concept,[3] to enable us to inquire whether Hegel furnishes us the resources needed, if not to completely reconcile their opposition, at least to profoundly mitigate their tension. Despite the differences between art and philosophy, we must now see how their affinities also run deep.

Hegel's philosophical practice reveals its own peculiar intimacy with art. This is evident not only in Hegel's thorough familiarity with the art of his day, and in the fact that the *Lectures on Aesthetics* reveal Hegel's astonishing acquaintance with the many different arts from many different periods. More important, perhaps, is the fact that the character of Hegel's own thinking is frequently imbued with a highly metaphorical dimension. Part of the power of Hegelian concepts derives from their metaphorical and analogical underpinnings.[4] The peculiarities of Hegelian style with its jokes, allusions, sarcasms, leaps of fancy, striking metaphors, do not mark it with the kind of abstract sobriety that we might expect from, say, the journal article of today. At the very least we must insist that the character of Hegel's own philosophical language is not that of plain prose. The normal antithesis of plain prose and poetry cannot be straightforwardly applied to this discourse.[5] Not surprisingly the comparison has been made between some of Hegel's works and works of art, as for example when Kaufmann compares Hegel's *Phenomenology* to Goethe's *Faust*, or more generally to the *Bildungsroman*.[6] It is not irrelevant to point out that Hegel himself likened the development of thought in the *Phenomenology* to a *Bildungsprozess*. While a *Bildungsprozess* pertains generally to a process of cultural formation, the presence of the *Bild*, the image, in what ostensibly is an education towards the attainment of the philosophical concept is striking. Image and concept intertwine. The concept, we may suspect, sometimes secretly draws on the resources inherent in the image, even despite the fact that part of one's stated aim is to attempt to transcend the image.

Indeed, Hegel speaks of the many philosophical positions through which we must move as like moving though a gallery of pictures (*eine Galerie von Bildern*).[7] The very multiplicity of philosophical positions, however, need not be a mere collection of items, only externally related, on this view. Each philosophical position might be seen, and in fact Hegel tends to see it, as one work within a total *oeuvre*, in which reason forms a series of articulate and significant worlds. This perhaps reveals something of the significance of Hegel's final words in the *Phenomenology*, words borrowed from the poet Schiller but turned by Hegel to his own use:

> The chalice of this realm of spirits
> Foams forth to God his own infinitude

This also recalls some earlier remarks of Hegel where every genuine philosophical position is compared to an authentic work of art, complete in itself, because it carries the totality within itself. In speaking about the process in which philosophical reason raises itself above mere personal idiosyncrasy and contingency into its proper realm of universality, Hegel very significantly implies that this universality is not antithetical to the rich individuality pertaining to authentic works of art. Thus he says:[8]

> The true peculiarity of philosophy lies in the interesting individuality which is the organic shape that Reason has built for itself out of the materials of a particular age. The particular speculative Reason (of a later time) finds in it spirit of its spirit, flesh of its flesh, it intuits itself in it as one and the same and yet as another living being. Every philosophy is complete in itself, and like an authentic work of art, carries the totality within itself. Just as the work of Apelles or Sophocles would not have appeared to Raphael and Shakespeare — had they known them — as mere preparatory studies, but as a kindred force of the spirit, so Reason cannot regard its former shapes as merely useful preludes to itself.

What might be involved in this coupling of art and philosophy? The suggestion of the present chapter is that art and philosophy together throw essential light on the nature of concreteness, and that this light illuminates their relatedness at a level more fundamental than their supposed opposition. To develop this suggestion we will proceed in the following manner. First, we will survey Hegel's own concern with the issue of concreteness. Second, we will look at some important characteristics of the art work which reveal to us something of the essential nature of concreteness. Third, we will look at the similarities that hold the art work and the philosophical concept together under concreteness. Finally, such similarities will allow us to more fully conceive of philosophy as not necessarily replacing the imaginative unity of the art work but of providing, in the reflective sphere, a conceptual unity that strains to match art's richness.

The Question of Concreteness

Contrary to a common view of Hegel as one of the least concrete of thinkers, the spectre of empty reason always haunted him, and his entire effort might be seen as an attempt to exorcise this barren spectre and restore reason to health. We have some lighthearted testimony to Hegel's concern with the question of concreteness in his *feuilleton* entitled *Wer denkt abstrakt?* (Who thinks abstractly?), where in a cheerful, popular vein Hegel suggests that common sense thinking, seemingly the most concrete, is often a veritable tissue of abstractions.[9] Gabriel Marcel, himself concerned with bringing philosophical thinking back to the concrete, and seemingly an existential antipode to Hegel, recognized Hegel's struggle to preserve the concrete: no philosopher, he holds, protested more strongly against the confusion of the concrete with the immediately given.[10] Of course, Hegel's insistence on concreteness has raised profound difficulties, perhaps most notably the famous, or infamous, question of how Hegel makes the transition from logic to nature. This difficulty, one might add, also posesses an important connection with the present topic of philosophy and art, if we consider the words of a recent commentator on Hegel's *Logic*.[11] These are further ramifications to the issue of concreteness, by no means irrelevant to the present theme but outside our present scope. Yet what cannot be gainsaid overall is Hegel's involvement, in many different forms, with this issue of concreteness.

How might we put the issue here? The question might be put thus: is concrete thinking possible, or is this a contradiction in terms, given that thinking seems to necessitate abstraction? Two responses immediately suggest themselves: for convenience let us call them the "existentialist" and the "essentialist" response. In the "existentialist" response, concreteness is sometimes emphasized in a manner which attenuates the relevance of rational thinking. The opaque "thereness" of the concrete confronts us and thinking alone cannot completely pierce its impenetrable crust. Thinking may even be a block between us and the real. A split between thinking and concreteness seems to unavoidably open up. The "essentialist" response, by contrast, finds much in the concrete that is irrational, capricious, accidental, but it tends to turn away from these as irrelevant to philosophical thought. Instead, thought either occupies itself with its own pure forms, or else with abstract universals stripped of concrete accidentals. Thought thus tends to close in on itself, satisfied to substitute its own formal self-consistency for the vagaries of material concreteness. But once again, as in the "existentialist"response, thinking tends to be sundered from the concrete, only in the case of the "essentialist" the sundering takes place from the side of thinking.

The issue of concreteness, of course, concerns the possibility of whether we can avoid or surpass this split, indeed whether these two above responses exhaust the question. Hegel's response here is helpful. These two above responses, in fact, tend to simply repeat the problem by differently bifurcating thinking and concreteness. Hegel's response represents a further approach, neither exclusively existentialist nor simply essentialist. Thinking must be true to the concrete, and so be both existentialist and essentialist at once. We must, as it were, move between these extremes, and thus attempt to bind them together. Only thus might some conjunction of the logical and ontological orders be possible.

Abstraction is part of any venture of philosophical thinking, Hegel grants, but such ventures are at best incomplete, at worst futile, if they fail to establish contact with the concrete. This necessity assumes its own form in modern philosophy. Thus on this score we find Hegel in the *Phenomenology* comparing his own times to the ancient era.[12] In ancient times the task of thought was to liberate man's mind from immersion in the immediate realities of life, and in rising above the concrete to let thought define itself according to its own appropriate forms. Because of its unfamiliarity and strangeness, the abstract side of thought then required accentuation. But the additional requirement is imperative for the modern era: namely, for thought to descend again into the concrete wealth of the world, thereby to regain a fullness lacking to merely abstract thought. Abstract thought is not true thinking,[13] thinking faithful in the full both to its own internal norms and to the concrete order. Where the ancient world lacked abstraction, the modern world is surfeited with abstraction, and this surfeit, in a way, is its peculiar privation. Acutely sensitive to this question of concreteness, Hegel sought a possible position beyond the alternatives of thoughtless concreteness and unconcrete thought.

The ancient way of posing the problem of concreteness was in terms of the relation of Being and Thinking. The modern way, starting with Descartes, puts the issue in terms of the relation of subject and object, *res cogitans* and *res extensa*. In both cases the issue tends to be posed by means of two terms alone, and the resulting reflection tends to be dogged by a certain dualism. With Hegel we might say that the issue need not be exhausted by two terms conceived of as opposites, the objective and the subjective, Being and Thinking, if you like, the ontological and logical. Philosophical reason must transcend such dualisms. Hegel attempts, as it were, to provide a complex response to Kant's famous dictum: intuitions without concepts are blind, concepts without intuitions are empty. But again, we do not approach the problem fruitfully if we posit concept and intuition as two entirely irreducible powers, as Kant tends to do. To insist only on their irreducible difference is inevitably to fall foul of dualism, whereas the issue of concreteness requires the possibility of their continuity.

How might we approach the possibility of their continuity? Again, the suggestion here is that the relation of art and philosophy provides one fruitful way. Art and philosophy provide us with the modes of human activity corresponding to the epistemological powers we discover in intuition and the concept. Should we discover some continuity between them, then, important light may be thrown on the issue of concreteness. Put somewhat differently: beside Being and Thinking, the ontological and the logical, the *aesthetical* might be introduced as an essential mediating term. As with Schelling, the art work is to be conceived of as possessing some metaphysical significance. Since Hegel places art along with religion and philosophy in the realm of Absolute Spirit, we must say that not only the logical but also the aesthetical has a certain ontological weight. In brief, the art work may reveal something essential about the nature of concreteness. And given the relation of art and philosophy in Hegel's system, it may tell us something about Hegel's own desire to make the philosophical concept concrete. As Hegel himself implies in his praise of Schelling: it is the discovery, by Schelling, among others, of the crucial significance of art *for philosophy itself* that marks an important advance.[14]

Concreteness and the Art Work

Given this focus, what, then, does the art work reveal to us concerning the nature of concreteness? At first the art work seems to present itself to us as an immediate material object, a mere *objet d'art*. Its concreteness seems to be just this, its simple empirical particularity. It seems to be the aesthetical version of the bare "this" of which Hegel speaks in the *Phenomenology* in terms of the object of sense-certainty. To this immediate concreteness is often ascribed art's positive power. The art work it is said, impresses itself on us with sheer unmediated presence. Clearly, however, the concreteness of the art work cannot be identified with such an unmediated particularity. Were it so, it would exclude all internal complexity and immanent differentiation. It would cease to be a *work*, moreover a work of art; for sheer immediacy would not entail the mediating activity of its artistic originator. The art object is more complex and full than a bare "this" because it is a worked thing, a something made, a *poiesis* in the etymological sense.[15] Its concreteness is that of a creation.[16]

As such it involves a reference to the *dynamic activity* that originates it. An art work is the product of a process of origination and never can be fully understood in abstraction from this process. Its dynamic concreteness is just the fact that it is the *sensuous embodiment* of such a process of origination. Moreover, this dynamic concreteness is not blandly homogeneous. Tension is ingredient in its nature. If, for instance, we think of the artist wrestling with his materials, we conjure up the picture of such a struggle with sometimes disparate, sometimes opposing strands. The art work articulates and embodies something of this struggle. In sum, the art work makes concretely articulate a *complex process of emergence* both in the artist and his expressive powers, and in his material and its susceptibility to aesthetic form.

It may indeed be helpful to speak of the concreteness of the art work in terms of its embodying a process of *concretization*. What is made concrete? One point essential to the present theme is that the art work makes concrete some *universal significance*. We can approach this in terms of the fact that no art work can be completely formless. But the form it expresses cannot be something merely disembodied in the manner of a generalized abstraction. The form of the art work arises out of it immanently. Hence its concreteness is neither empirical particularity, nor disembodied universal form. Its process of concretization is a process of active formation. We do not discover a dualism of particular and universal, instance and form, the sensible and the intelligible. On the contrary, the art work tends to rescue particularity from arbitrariness and universality from incommunicability. Again in the etymological sense, the art work might be seen as a *poetic universal*: the coming to emergence and concretion (*poiesis*) of a universal significance, its being concretely embodied. The art work might be seen as what Hegel speaks of as a *concrete universal*.[17]

Many aestheticians, of course, have tended to emphasize the *individuality* of the art work. How does this square with the introduction of Hegel's notion of the concrete universal? We might think that to couple the universal with the concrete is a contradiction in terms, but this need only be true if we confine concreteness to a narrow particularity and universality to a separated ideality.[18] By contrast, the art work is a concrete ideality. For Hegel, in fact, there is no real difference between the true, genuine individual and the concrete universal.[19] Thus the art work is an individual *whole* in which a universal significance comes to concrete emergence. It not only points back to its originating activity, not only sensuously forms this activity and lets a sense of universal significance emerge. As Hegel strongly insists, as one of its fundamental requirements, the art work contains an end. It is an end in itself, or as I will speak of it below, a kind of *perfection*.[20]

Another way we might put this point is by saying that the art work constitutes a kind of *world*. What is universal about it is its nature as an expressive universe, a rich and dense microcosm. As an individual whole, an expressive world, it telescopes within itself a sense of the whole. For Hegel this makes it to be the sensuous manifestation of *Geist*, the making concrete of *Geist*. The individual world of the art work is concrete spirit. It is the gathering into a rich unity of the activity of spirit; and because its resulting wholeness is thus dynamic, again we come across the consequence that its concreteness cannot be congealed. Indeed if we bear in mind the possible metaphysical significance of art, previously noted, and if we take into account what for Hegel is the religious significance of art, we might say that the rich concreteness of the artistic microcosm awakens us to the analogous concreteness of the macrocosm, awakens us, in Hegelian terms, to the universe itself as a concretion of Absolute Spirit.

To summarise then: the concreteness of the art work presents a certain compacted fullness which brings to the fore the following considerations. First, it implicates the idea of dynamic origination. Second, it makes concrete a certain process of emergence. Third, it articulates itself into the shape of a certain embodied formation. Finally, it brings to light a rich wholeness and concrete universality. If we now turn to the philosophical concept, we shall see how very similar considerations apply to it in relation to origins, emergence, forms and ends. Where the art work gives sensuous, imaginative expression to such concreteness, the philosophical concept tries to be its reflective conceptual counterpart.

Concreteness and the Philosophical Concept

Much has been written about Hegel's notion of the concept, but its relation with the art work remains insufficiently explored. Findlay compares Hegel's dialectical practice with the art work, but the analogy is merely mentioned, its ramifications are not developed.[21] Let us now look at the philosophical concept in terms of these essential points we discussed in relation to the art work: origin, emergence, formation and *telos*. First, the philosophical concept essentially implies the idea of origin. We can see this initially if we merely focus on the etymological meaning of concept, conception. Just as, in a sense, there are no mere *objects d'art*,[22] so also there are no mere philosophical conclusions, propositions. The meaningfulness of both dissolves if either is dissociated from its source of origin. Without the latter they become just dead ends, not living completions or wholes. This fact, that the philosophical concept is never to be torn loose from its origins, finds one of its clearest expressions in the central importance of the history of philosophy for Hegel. Indeed, Hegel almost obsessively dwells on the question of the origin of philosophy and repeatedly returns to the question of beginnings, both in the *Phenomenology* and the *Logic*. Philosophical questioning involves a regressive, returning movement in which empty formal abstraction must yield place to concrete comprehension.

What is involved in such comprehension? Hegel's answer is given in terms of the movement beyond *Verstand*, the formal, analytical understanding, to *Vernunft*, or genuine, synthetic reason. Our focus here is not on this complex cognitive process on the part of the knower[23] but on the relation of thought to the concrete, and so consequently on the concreteness of the concept. What we must say is that philosophical thought involves a return to its origin in the concrete but that this concrete origin is itself richly complex and must be understood as the process of emergence of what is genuinely universal. Just as the artist does not just stand at a merely spectatorial distance from his material but grapples with its initial amorphousness, so philosophical thinking involves movement towards the density of the concrete. Something is immediately given and granted to be given, but this fact does not immediately disclose its significance. Rather experience comes to intelligibility as the art work comes to form, that is, through a process of dialectical articulation. The philosophical concept emerges in the interplay between the knower and the known, and without this mediating interplay subjectivity would be an inarticulate blank and objectivity an undifferentiated homogeneity. Philosophical concepts must grasp this process of emergence, for this process is the active formation of intelligibility. Merely asserted doctrines which express bare results separate this process from its results; hence, the results themselves decay in intelligibility. The philosophical concept must articulate the process of emergence that defines intelligibility in the fuller sense.

What emerges is this concrete process and what does the concept grasp? Again, the analogy with the art work proves instructive in that the art work embodies a particular kind of dynamic form or immanent universal. We can make this more plain by comparing Hegel's concept with two other traditional interpretations of the concept: what we can call the empiricist-nominalist and the Platonic-realist positions. The empiricist-nominalist position tends to define the concept as something abstracted from particulars. It acknowledges that we use general terms, but given its belief that all knowing derives from primitive sense impressions, such general terms, "concepts," must be derivative and secondary, not what is primordial in knowledge. From a sample of instances we extract features common to all and collect these features under a common name (Locke, Hume). This, as it were, distilled commonality is named by the general concept. Such concepts, however, have no reality in themselves but are simply more remote variations on the primordial thing itself, the particular impression. Thus, for instance, Hume speaks of ideas as but "pale copies" of the more vivid and basic sense impressions. The main point to emphasize here is that this concept does not express a universal *in* the particular. The general term does not have any ontological weight, for in the main it is the product of the knower's abstracting ability. As with the Medieval nominalists, the universal becomes a mere *flatus vocis*, a linguistic fabrication of the knower, not an ontological constituent of the concrete.

The Platonic-realist, by contrast, reverses the emphasis of the empiricist-nominalist. Particularity is not what is primordial but only has its identifiable being in virtue of some more fundamental principle, namely, the universal, the idea, the *eidos* in Platonic terms. Without some nonsensory familiarity with this idea or *eidos*, we could not even identify the particular, for without this universal standard the particularities of the concrete would remain opaque and undiscriminated. Our approach to the concrete, on this view, is guided by prior ideas which are not themselves derived from empirical particulars. And because of this guidance, there must even be some *separability* (the Platonic *chorismos*) of universals from all particulars. Moreover, again in sharp contrast to the empiricist-nominalist position, these universals have genuine ontological weight. These possess their own reality independently of the particulars of experience and the abstracting activity of the knower. The upshot of such separability tends to be what is termed the Platonic transcendence, with its accompanying dualism: universal and particular become bifurcated into two essentially different realms, the sensible and the intelligible worlds.

The chief difficulty with both these standpoints is their tendency to separate particular and universal, even to set these two in opposition, though, of course, the opposition is set up from different directions. Thus the main consequence of both for the philosopher is *the impossibility of a concrete concept*. The empiricist-nominalist gives us a pandemonium of detailed particulars, a sheer multiplicity without genuine unity. The Platonic-realist gives us a shadow world of separated universals, an abstract unity without concrete multiplicity. One gives us a blind concreteness, the other an empty concept. Concrete and concept become assigned to different worlds.

At this point, prior to turning to Hegel's understanding of the concept, it is important to remind ourselves again of the vital way in which metaphysics and aesthetics intertwine. Plato himself here provides a most illuminating example. The aesthetical dimension of experience is criticized precisely for metaphysical reasons. Moreover, it is disparaged on just these grounds of the separability and transcendence of the Platonic *eidos*. As a *mimesis* the art work fails to represent or render concrete the *eidos* in its true form. As is well known, for Plato the art work becomes a thrice removed representation, a mere appearance, and so liable to deceive and lead to illusion. As such a mimesis the art work does not properly mediate the separation between concreteness and the concept of the universal. With Hegel, however, appearance assumes a more positive modulation. Appearance is the concrete emergence and so disclosure of the universal. And so *already* the gap between concreteness and concept is not such a fundamental separation to be subsequently mediated or bridged. As a genuine sensuous appearance of spiritual content, the art work in its concreteness is already beyond this gap and so can serve to illuminate the relation of the concept to concreteness. Let us now look more closely at this intertwining of aesthetics and metaphysics in Hegel's rendition of the philosophical concept.

Hegel's view of the philosophical concept can be seen as a third way, somewhat reminiscent of Aristotle, which mediates the oppositions of the two above extremes. The universal comes to emergence in the concrete. First, the universal has ontological significance: it is not just *our* construction. On this there is some point of agreement with the Platonic realist. Nevertheless, Hegel gives a different modulation to this ontological significance. Universality is only truly universal when it is concrete. The universal cannot be separated from the concrete precisely because the latter is the very process of its emergence and formation. Concreteness is not exhausted by particularity because the particular is precisely a particular *manifestation* of the universal.

As Hegel tries to show in the opening chapters of the *Phenomenology*, to do justice to the fullness of the *particular itself*, we cannot confine ourselves to a mute "this-here-now." Rather the particular reveals itself as internally intricate, self-differentiated, immanently complex, just like the concreteness of the art work. Thus Hegel is undoubtedly in agreement with the empiricist-nominalist in stressing the necessity of close attention to the detailed particularities of experience. But the universal is immanent in the particular, embodied there. The universal of the empiricist-nominalist, by contrast, tends to be a collocation of properties externally related to each other and not intrinsically embodied in the thing itself. We might say that the empiricist-nominalist, as it were, intervenes a little prematurely, and instead of letting the universal concretely emerge or appear in the particular, he imposes an abstract general concept of his own construction. He does not, in Heideggerian terms, let Being be, or as Hegel might put the point, allow the significance of *die Sache selbst* to come to proper self-manifestation. The philosophical individual must become, as it were, fully rational (*vernunftig*) — that is, capable of being universally open, capable of being universal in himself — in order to become capable in turn of grasping the universal in the real. Analogous to the artist's struggle with his initially recalcitrant matter, the concept of the philosopher comes to articulation in the middle space between the rational self-development of the knower and the coming to self-manifestation of the universal in the real.

Having noted the relation to origins, emergence, and formation, we must now note that the concept for Hegel involves a relation to finality or ends. The concreteness of concern to the concept is not that of a static universe. It is the concreteness of a world in the process of becoming. Consequently, the philosophical concept if genuinely concrete, must be *teleological*. In Platonic terms, the philosohical concept has the aim of making the eros of reason self-conscious. In a sense it might be that only God thinks concretely, only God's concept is a concrete concept. Yet the eros, dynamism of reason has its own participation in absoluteness and consequently seeks an end commensurate with this characteristic of its own nature. The philosophical concept not only refers to origination, emergence and formation; it also refers to completion or wholeness. Our immediate response might be to deny this possibility as setting the target too high, as exceeding the bounds of human limitation. But again the art work illuminates the possibility that a certain fullness, wholeness is in fact sometimes actual for man. The true is the whole, Hegel held. This requirement of wholeness makes itself specially felt in relation to both the art work and the philosophical concept.[24] How we interpret this wholeness is a difficult matter, of course. But the admission of its occurrence is vital. Philosophical reflection, to be genuinely concrete, must direct itself to those concretions of wholeness, making intelligible their possibility, making explicit their frequently opaque meaning. There is not only an analogy of the art work and the philosophical concept here, but rather the latter tries to explicate in self-conscious terms the wholeness that the former makes present to man's consciousness in the form of *Darstellung* or *Erscheinung*.

Given this involvement with the art work, it should not be surprising that when Hegel speaks of the philosophical concept he resorts to the use of an *image*, that of the *circle*.[25] Traditionally, circular movement was an image of divine movement, an image of perfection, a perfection moreover that was a *perfecting*, a dynamic process, not a static product. In this image we can see the desire to gather together the previous moments of concreteness. The philosophical concept emerges in mediating the significance of the immediately given concrete. It returns retrospectively to question its origins. It opens itself to those occasions in experience where the sense of concrete universality is especially manifest. It implicates a movement of thought towards a concrete wholeness. The philosophical concept, in this light, reaches out to both origins and ends and attempts to mediate their antithesis. Thus philosophical thought is circular in the sense of being an articulate recollection. The philosophical concept is *the teleological recollection of a process of origination* within which the concrete world comes to appear as an articulated and rich whole. As a kind of micrososm of articulation that gathers and recollects the significance of such a world, the philosophical concept, like the art work, is itself a kind of world.[26]

The concept of organic unity is one of the chief ideas by which aestheticians traditionally have understood the art work , and it is not beside the point that to illustrate his understanding of the concrete concept Hegel uses an *image* which particularly incorporates this idea of organic unity. To refer to the concept Hegel uses the image of the plant growing.[27] The plant develops itself: the seed grows from its particularity to become not a mere particular, but an individual reality that at the same item is representative of the species. A universality of nature is implicit in its particularity from the beginning. A similar consideration is at stake in the famous metaphor of tree and bud in the *Phenomenology*.[28] What these images invoke is the idea of a rich unity within which there is an immanent, concrete complexity and which the normal oppositions of universal and particular do not properly succeed in capturing or articulating.

For Hegel, as we pointed out in relation to the art work, the concrete is the individual but the individual is a union of particularity and universality. The individual is the concrete universal, and the philosophical concept articulates just that character of immanent complexity illustrated in the above images of unity. The universals of the Platonic-realist and the empiricist-nominalist both tend to be extrinsic to the individual thing itself. Regardless of how we evaluate Hegel's ultimate success here, his insistence on both a concrete concept and a concrete universal represents an advance on the problem which the Platonic-realist and empiricist-nominalist pose but which they make difficult of resolution by the way they pose it. The question is not how we join together a universality and particularity that have been disjoined from the beginning. The question is whether in actual experience there are occasions which right from the beginning wed universality and particularity. Part of the strategy deemed helpful here involves asking: are there real instances in experience which give us some access to the notion of the concrete universal and the need for a concrete concept to express it? If there are, what are they? The art work, I have contended, is one such vitally revealing instance.

Art and Philosophy as Complementary Modes of Concrete Articulation

To conclude this chapter we might return in Hegelian fashion to our beginning and draw some important consequences from these similarities of the art work and the philosophical concept. Our main suggestion must be that art and philosophy work as complementary modes of articulation, one oriented to imaginative concreteness, the other to conceptual concreteness. At the outset we noted the peculiar intimacy of art and philosophy in Hegel. We might now say that this kinship is not just a juxtaposition of two spheres that we as interpreters ascribe to Hegel *after the fact*. Rather this kinship is *already working* in the entire fabric of Hegel's mode of thinking. The philosophical artist in Hegel is as important as the rationalist logician. More, the philosophical artist in Hegel determines something essential in the rationalist logician. It is to give a misleading picture of the spirit informing Hegel's thought if we insist upon separating these two.

If I may put it this way: an aesthetic dimension infiltrates the Hegelian style of logical thought. It is not just that a philosophical system lies at the back of his aesthetics, though this is true. It is that Hegel's notion of philosophical system, particularly in its emphasis upon dynamic form, organic unity and wholeness, has an unmistakeable aesthetic ring. This ring is revealed, for example, in the overall character of two of Hegel's major works: The *Phenomenology* and the *Logic*. We have previously noted the analogy between the *Phenomenology* and an art work. This further point may be helpful here. The art work is always an imaginative venture at articulation, and so always carries some aura of *adventure* about it. Perhaps this is why in art we value originality: it reveals this essential venturesomeness. The *Phenomenology* is undoubtedly original in striking ways, but what is more important here is that it captures the sense that thought itself is a kind of adventure. Consciousness ventures a vast panorama of possible forms; it ventures towards an absolute form of consciousness. All of the ventures fall short, bar the final form — so the *Phenomenology* is a "highway of despair" (*der Weg der Verzweiflung*).[29] But what carries us to the final form is that the essential venturesomeness of thought remains and, despite the despair, will not be extinguished.

The *Logic* seems to provide us with a more difficult example, with a more crucial test. What, if anything, is artistic about the *Logic*? Nothing in the particular details of this work might seem aesthetically attractive, yet if we pause and look at the *Logic* as a whole, and if we consider its characteristic forms and the entire thrust of its development, we see that it has a highly *dramatic* structure. *Logos* and *poiesis* are not entirely antithetical. Where the *Phenomenology* presents the dramatic unfolding of the possibilities of concrete consciousness, the *Logic* discloses the drama of the logical possibilities of pure thought. First, it is presented as a whole or a totality. But within the totality we find the aspect of developing structure, dynamic form. Here the dramatic dimension makes itself felt. Hegel's *Logic* presents itself as a dramatic unity. For it does not just list a mere aggregate of thought forms or enumerate a series of dead categories, like a lifeless table of contents. The logical forms of thought are presented as living powers that come to emergence, that come to increasing articulation, that come to clash with other categories even as they complete themselves, that find themselves visited with transitions, transformations, reversals and reconciliations within more encompassing stages of thought. The possibilities of logical thought drive themselves forward, like characters or powers in dramatic conflict and development. All move towards the final *dénouement* where the Absolute Idea commands the stage and gathers previous possibilities of thought to itself as necessary episodes to the articulating of its own concluding, consummating significance. In presenting the developing drama of essential thought forms, the *Logic* reveals, as it were, the philosophical art of reason itself.[30] It should not surprise us that some of the most forceful and influential of Hegel's views in aesthetics are developed in connection with drama, particularly tragedy.

So also philosophy cannot consist in just *reducing* art to concepts, or of merely using it for the illustration of some more generalized abstractions. Their relation works in two directions. Philosophy explicates and brings to self-consciousness the richness made present in art. But also, the concreteness of art continues as a basic challenge to philosophy, challenge for it to overcome its own tendency to reduce experience to generalized abstractions. The fundamental point is not to conclude to a dualistic opposition, an exclusive "either/or" between them. Without denying their tension, the fundamental struggle is not so much between art and philosophy as between the initial obscurity of the concrete order and man's exigency to bring it, the concrete, from its obscurity into the light of articulation. Philosophy and art alike share in this common struggle to make articulate, each in their respective ways, this initial, undifferentiated tangle of the concrete.

One is tempted to rigidly demarcate their respective spheres by saying that the philosopher deals purely with concepts, the artist solely with images. But put in this way, while getting at something of their difference, we are tempted to set up too exclusive a relation between them. Their difference, however, is not one of simple opposition, but rather, one might say, a difference of orientation. That is, both philosopher and artist, as it were, stand in the middle between the concrete and its articulation. The speculative, reflective *logos* of the philosopher tilts in a more intellectual direction; the imaginative expression of the artist tilts more towards the sensuous. But both the rational explication of the philosopher and the imaginative expression of the artist establish a genuine relation of reflection and sensation. Both reflection and imagination manifest alike the same thrust for articulation which gives original power to thoughts and sensations equally, and which supplies a center to ground their affinity. This struggle for the articulation of the concrete becomes the root out of which stem art and philosophy as distinct, though related, modalities of meaning.

And given this fact, it is too simplistic, I think, to conceive of the relation of art and philosophy as merely the linear subsumption of the first into the second, or as just an omnivorous incorporation of the sensuous image into the rational concept. We are pointed more towards a dynamic interplay, perhaps one might call it a *dialectical balance*, between different modalities of meaning, both of which issue from the same exigency to make the concrete articulate. This dialectical balance, in allowing for the positive interplay between the two, also does not exclude the possibility of their *permeability*. Art and philosophy may thus act upon and react to each other in ways that are profoundly provocative. Indeed if we confine ourselves to but one challenging aspect of art for philosophy, it is that art struggles to preserve a real concrete sense of the emergence of articulation in a primordial way: it participates in the struggle for articulation, as Hegel well recognized, in a bodily way. In this regard, art for the rationalist philosopher might be compared to a Trojan Horse. We seem to have left a wooden and lifeless work into the center of our citadel, a thing that in no way seems to threaten our defenses. But in the night its hidden resources of power flow out from it, with the result that the Trojans, previously secure within the circle of their city, finally find their defenses breached. In analogous fashion, the temptation of the rationalist to use the philosophical concept to secure himself in a circle of abstractions is destroyed, or rather reason itself is made open once again, by the richness harboring in the concreteness of the art work.

Chapter Three

Art, Religion and Absoluteness

Art, Religion and Absolute Spirit

The power of articulation comes to imaginative emergence in art, making art a realm of meaning in its own right, and binding it to philosophy in relation to concreteness. Our question now is how we are to interpret further this artistic power of articulation, whether indeed we are to confine it to a solely aesthetic rendition. We are brought back to the concept of "creativity" and are forced to ask whether this for Hegel has exclusive aesthetic connotations, or whether, and how, it opens on to the religious dimension of experience. With this question we must attempt to face the metaphysical significance of art (already briefly mentioned) in connection with Hegel's ascription to art of a certain *absoluteness*.

This ascription of absoluteness to art is perhaps *the* central problem of Hegel's aesthetics, so it might be helpful to summarize and refocus the difficulty once again here. There are two chief reasons why the precise place of art in Hegel's philosophy of Absolute Spirit has always been controversial. One is the implication that philosophy is "higher" than art, as also is religion: philosophy is *the* ultimate activity which, it seems, supersedes art and places it below itself in a subordinate position. The second is Hegel's proclamation of the so-called "death" of art: art, Hegel implies, is a thing of the past, given particularly the scientific culture of our age. We should be wary, however, of thinking that these two views, stated thus, adequately represent Hegel: that he was concerned, on the one hand, to philosophically reduce art, and on the other hand, to supersede or leave it behind. The inescapable obstacle to these two possibilities is Hegel's continuing insistence on the absolute character of art. This absoluteness does not square with the intention of reductionism or supersession. For how can something with an absolute character be either reduced or superseded?

The effect of this is not only to make us question the reductive view but also to return us to the complexity in Hegel's position. How, in effect, are we to understand Hegel's insistence on art's absolute character? We must acknowledge in Hegel this insistence, but its precise nature remains unclarified and requires further elucidation. Can art preserve its absolute character, if religion and philosophy are also said to be absolute? How are we to place art relative to the absoluteness of these other two? The approach suggested here is that we look at the connection of art with religion. All too frequently Hegel's commentators tend to initially separate art, religion and philosophy too strongly. Then subsequently the relation of different *pairs* of these three activities are explored. These pairings tend to confer a certain predominance on philosophy. Philosophy is coupled with religion and their relations and tensions detailed. Philosophy is coupled with art, whether in a manner which emphasizes their kinship, as we have just done, or one that more strongly stresses their antagonism. But the pairing of art and religion does not figure strongly. Yet it should, not only for its overall importance in Hegel's thought but also for aesthetical reflection in general. Our attempt to rectify this omission here will throw light, we hope, on art's absoluteness for Hegel.

To focus on this pairing of art and religion has the added advantage of inevitably extending us to the full Hegelian triad: philosophical reflection simply cannot be left out of the picture. An understanding of art and religion will facilitate, I believe, a more discriminating view of the interplay of all three activities belonging to Absolute Spirit. I hope to make good on this promise below where I suggest that the relation of art and religion has important implications for the overall interpretation of Hegel's thought, particularly on the recurring, thorny issue of Left and Right readings. For this issue has reverberations not only in contemporary politics and religion, but also in contemporary aesthetics. Indeed, as we shall see, aesthetics itself is very important in the politics of such diverse thinkers as, Sartre, Marcuse, Camus, all of them heirs to some aspects of the "Left-Hegelian" heritage.

A helpful way to elucidate art's absoluteness is through this question: is art for Hegel an exclusively aesthetic or a religious phenomenon? What is meant by art as exclusively "aesthetic" and as "religious" will be clarified as our discussion develops.[1] Our brief answer for now is that art points beyond exclusively aesthetic considerations to a further religious significance. Moreover, this "pointing beyond" and the transition it generates, I will argue, are rooted in the character of art itself as reflected in Hegel's view. Properly understood, there need be nothing artificial in agreeing with Hegel that the significance of art is religious. This need imply no super-imposition of a falsifying religious meaning, nor any theological violence to the art work, nor any diminution of the need to consider art on its own terms. Precisely to treat art on its own terms reveals the further thrust to the religious, indeed its implicit presence there. To explicate this claim we might proceed thus. First, we need to ask what marks art as an exclusively "aesthetic" phenomenon. Next, we need to examine art as "religious" and its contrast with the "aesthetic" conception. This we must do in two stages: first, historically in terms of Hegel's conception of Symbolical, Classical and Romantic types of art; secondly, in terms of the systematic, philosophical issue of whether "creativity" is to be understood in an entirely humanized manner. Finally, this comparison of the "aesthetic" and the "religious" will allow us to make some suggestions of the kind mentioned above concerning the overall reading of Hegel, and particularly the continuing importance of art in the Left-Hegelian reading.

Art as "Aesthetic"

What, then, might be involved in art considered as an "aesthetic" phenomenon? Historically the point might be made by recalling how, proceeding from the Renaissance, art sought to liberate itself from the constraints of religious subservience and increasingly to assert its own autonomy with respect to ecclesiastical control. Especially in the nineteenth century art came to be seen as an exclusively aesthetic sphere. That is, it came to be seen as a self-contained expression of the human spirit, generated by powers of its own, particularly the imagination, distinguished by certain characteristics that set it apart from other areas of human significance, like history and science.[2] These are very broad considerations, I realize, but the nineteenth century movement of *l'art pour l'art* is indicative in its own exaggerated way of just this strong will to make art entirely self-contained. Of course, this did not prevent the poet, say, from conceiving of himself as a new kind of secular priest, an aesthetic *vates* worshipping, ministering at the shrine of beauty.[3] For the essential point consisted in art's assertion of its own independence, even sometimes to the point of the artist setting himself apart from the common run of men by his special, "poetic" garb.

Why might the artist thus assert himself with such strong distinctiveness? A key element here is that to understand art as an autonomous aesthetic activity is to judge as essential to it the idea of human expressiveness.[4] What does the art work as expressive reveal? Most basically it seems to reveal the fact that it originates in the creativity of the artist, and that, on being completed, it presents itself for the aesthetic contemplation of its audience. As an aesthetic phenomenon, the art work is something made by man, albeit individuals of special genius, and something made for man's appreciation. Man is to be seen not just as one thing of nature lost in muteness among its other silent things. As Hegel himself implies: man, like the Absolute in its truth, is not just Substance; he is also and more importantly to be seen as Subject.[5] As such man can give articulation to his own reality. In the aesthetic realm he struggles with the initially amorphous character of his own sensuous being.[6] In his aesthetic production he tries to imaginatively articulate himself and his sense of being. Hence the aesthetic object reveals that man is not just a simple imitator, or a passive mirror of a given external nature. It rather reveals the expressive powers of man whereby his creative potentiality is actively realized. Man as aesthetic does not just mirror external nature; he also externalizes his own nature, and particularly its plastic, originative, imaginative powers. In the aesthetic products he brings into being, he realizes, he recognizes and he confirms his own creative powers.

When we here speak of art as an "aesthetic" phenomenon in this sense, what is most noteworthy is a tendency to humanize art in its entirety. Man becomes the beginning, middle and end of art. Beginning: because *qua* artist, he is an originating source. Middle: because in the art work he gives expressive form to himself, and thus mediates with his own initially inarticulate reality. End: because the aesthetic products he brings into being are for the essential purpose of man's own self-contemplation. Art emerges from and goes out of man, passes through him and returns to man once again, now with the gain of aesthetic articulation. In becoming conscious of the aesthetic object as the expressive outcome of his own work, of the art work itself as the product of his own activity, the artist becomes conscious of himself, aesthetically self-conscious, in and through the work he has created.[7] Indeed such a view is very persuasive in making art a form of man's self-knowledge, albeit a self-knowledge embodied in and mediated through the variety of sensuous objects comprising the aesthetic realm. Moreover, man's own nature seems so rich in latent resources that the task of giving it creative expression allows of an open-ended future. Thus art as "aesthetic" seems to offer a fertile understanding in terms of man itself, and in this to assure art's future through its appeal to the hitherto unrealized, unexpressed, as yet unimagined wealth of man's being. If we recall the question of art's absoluteness, then the burden, indeed glory of this absoluteness would here rest completely on the shoulders of man. A version of this view might be, for instance, Nietzsche's glorification of the artist-creator as the supreme human type, bearing also in mind his doctrine of man as the unfinished animal, that is being with an opening onto infinite promise.[8]

How does the above general view relate to Hegel? Undoubtedly we must admit that Hegel subscribes in significant measure to this understanding. His insistence that art be treated as a genuine spiritual realm in its own right makes him a forerunner, even adherent of this view. This may be confirmed not only from the general orientation of his large systematic works, but also by the details of different discussions in the *Lectures on Aesthetics*. Thus Hegel insists that art reveals the plastic powers of human imagination, that art shapes an articulated image of humanity itself, that art provides man with a sensuous self-knowledge answering to his deepest needs and highest aspirations. Likewise, his aesthetics places a strong accent on the creative, expressive powers of man, in contrast to the merely imitative. As we saw already, all of this is clearly granted by Hegel. The fundamental question, however, is whether we can restrict our considerations to man's creative power. Or rather, since Hegel does not deny the artist's creative powers, the question is better put: how are we to interpret the full significance of such powers? Is art to be subsumed under an entirely humanistic aesthetic? Must we make a model of Feuerbach's anthropological reduction of the religious realm, only now applying this model to the aesthetic realm in the form of the question: is the creative power of the artist also to be completely anthropologized?[9] Or, granting the real truth of the humanistic aesthetic, must we rather understand its meaning in the light of a further consideration, an added complexity? Art as aesthetic phenomenon reveals it as the dialectical self-mediation of man in imaginative form. The question is whether humanistic self-mediation is adequate to the artist's creative power, whether this points to a more complex mediation where the dialectic is not just between man and his own self. In that Hegel holds to a transition from art to religion in his philosophy of Absolute Spirit, I think we must answer this question in the affirmative. We must grant, Hegel seems to imply, an absolute dimension to man, but the meaning of this absolute dimension directs us further than man. We must grant the essential truth of art as "aesthetic" but a philosophical examination of this truth, Hegel seems to say, points us further to art as a religious phenomenon. Let us now look at this second approach to the matter.

Art as "Religious": Symbolical, Classical and Romantic Art

In treating here of art as "religious" we need to bear in mind the following preliminary points. First our focus in not on religion in any sectarian sense, and so also not on art as subordinated to some ecclesiastical yoke. Nor is our focus on a special category of art called "religious art" as opposed to secular, profane art, that is, art dealing with subjects generally sanctioned as "religious." So also we are not concerned with art used as a means for a religious purpose or end, as it might be used for religious propaganda or in some forms of liturgical art. With Hegel art is not to be used merely instrumentally: its activity is an end in itself, a value of intrinsic worth. Granting this, the issue is whether the intrinsic worth of this activity calls forth a religious interpretation.

Nor is the question here one of art and religion as two irreducible cultural categories, essentially distinct yet capable of different combinations.[10] The question rather concerns the metaphysical meaning of art's creative expressiveness. A creative articulating power runs through all forms of expression as a *continuous* power: the same power, what Hegel calls *Geist*, articulates itself in a plurality of different forms. Consequently we do wrong to excessively sediment these forms and separate them irrevocably. The issue is not whether the artistic *form* can be reduced to the religious *form*, or perhaps both to a third form, for instance philosophy;[11] but, whether this creative articulating power expressed in art and in other forms can be completely characterized in aesthetic terms, whether the religious form brings out something essential that the exclusively aesthetical form does not fully manifest. In Hegel what *unites* the three highest activities, art, religion and philosophy, is not one particular form, but the very power of *Geist* itself, for it runs through all three. Our attention on art as "religious" is not, therefore, on one form alongside other forms, but on *the forming power itself* which indeed is conspicuous in the creative expressiveness of art but which, because it can never be set apart simply as art's privileged possession, calls for a more than aesthetic interpretation, even in the sphere of art itself.

If we now consider Hegel's view more closely, we need to notice an historical consideration and a systematic, metaphysical point, as is so often the case with Hegel. The historical consideration has to do with the fact that even down to Hegel's own era we tend to discover a conspicuous intertwining of art and the religious.[12] Thus we may recall that in the final movement to Absolute Knowing in his *Phenomenology of Spirit*, Hegel's focus is not on art as "aesthetic" but on *Kunstreligion*, the religion of art. Here Hegel's discussion is complex, but in the main he plots a somewhat tortuous emergence of increasingly self-conscious artistry: expressing itself through inanimate nature, through plant and animal life, to the highest self-conscious literature of a people; from the abstract, through the living to the spiritual work of art. The important point here is that this emergence is essentially religious. Normally we think of inspiration, rapture, dreams, the unconscious, to be more amenable to religious interpretation in terms of the "pathos" of the artist who receives the divine *afflatus* of the Muse.[13] Hegel is not unmindful of this; but he also affirms that a more complex, fully religious significance develops with the development of self-consciousness. Religious significance does not drop from sight with the development of self-consciousness, as if the divine could only emerge in the darkness of night. Rather this significance is progressively appropriated by man, inwardized, interiorized, revealing most fully the true nature of the human and divine, and their essential relatedness. Again, Hegel's discussion of *Kunstreligion* shows how little art is "aesthetic" in the sense of a specialized, self-sufficient activity. Instead of this compartmentalized *l'art pour l'art*, art here permeates the entire life of a people, in its ethical, political and religious manifestations. *Kunstreligion* reveals the *world* of a people, and so as art is a certain articulation of *the whole*.[14]

An equally significant intertwining of religion and art is to be found in Hegel's schema for elucidating the historical development of art, namely in terms of Symbolical, Classical and Romantic art. Given our present intentions we might briefly note how the religious enters into all three types. Thus when Symbolical art is characterized as permeated by an opaque sense of the indefinite and the sublime, the religious note of reverence before mystery, of awe before the infinite, is unmistakeably present. Hegel's own examples of Symbolical art are through and through the carriers of forms of religious consciousness, for instance the Pyramids and the Sphinx. Though for Hegel Egypt is the "land of symbol" and the Sphinx is the "symbol of symbols," the religious note is equally present when he connects Symbolical art with the pantheism of the Orient, with Arabic mysticism, and the sublime poetry of the Israelites in the Old Testament.[15] Similarly with Classical art, expecially the art of ancient Greece, once again we are not in the presence of an "aesthetic" object, in the sense above defined. Certainly we find here Hegel's special interest in the human figure, but the vital religious note is not lacking here either. We discover the perfection of Classical art in the statues of the Greek gods, but this aesthetic perfection springs from the consummate balance with which they make present the gods in physical form. They reveal an immediate sensuous unity between the human and the divine in which all disproportion and discord between the two is banished. We might note also that Hegel implies that the defect of

Classical art is just its tendency to limit the expression of spirit, *Geist*, to the human spirit and figure. As with the perfection of Classical art, so also with its limitation, we come across a clearly religious import.[16]

Finally, in the third kind of art, Romantic art, the religious note is perhaps the most insistent of all. There might seem some irony in this for, historically speaking, Romantic art makes its most pervasive appearance at the threshold of that humanistically oriented modernity that defines art as an "aesthetic" phenomenon. Yet right at this threshold, certain considerations imply that it is this form of art, in contrast to the Symbolical and the Classical, that is marked by the most explicit and complex religious import. Why so? In Romantic art we come across what can be called an *inwardizing* in man himself of the sense of the infinite. Hegel explicitly calls our attention to this in his *Aesthetics*.[17] The infinite is not just "out-there," as it tends to be in Symbolical art. Nor is it completely proportioned to the human figure as physical, as it tends to be in the aesthetic perfection of Classical art. Deep down within himself man is a kind of world. *Grande profundum est ipse homo*, St. Augustine had exclaimed in his own religious exploration.[18] A similar thought is not uncharacteristic of many nineteenth century Romantics, nor of Hegel's own exploration of the self, particularly in the *Phenomenology*.[19]

Subsequently to Hegel, this "inwardized infinite" will tend to be progressively construed in a more exclusively humanistic manner; indeed such a humanizing of the infinite tends to go hand in hand with "creativity" theories of art, an essential ingredient to art as an "aesthetic" phenomenon, as we saw. But in Hegel himself, this inwardizing of the infinite entails the struggle to bring to light, within the interior recesses of man himself, the ultimately religious significance of experience. Not unexpectedly for Hegel, Romantic art only becomes possible *after* the human spirit has been percolated historically through the Christian religion. For in this religion, man himself, particularly in the depths of his inward subjectivity, becomes the most rich disclosure of the meaning of divinity, namely of God as spirit or *Geist*.[20] It is this disclosure of *Geist* in its true form that Romantic art struggles to effect; and we must add, with the increasing realization that the sensuous embodiment essential to the aesthetic side of art may not always be completely adequate to this task. Unmistakeably with Romantic art, we are witness to a transition beyond art, or better, witness to art pointing beyond itself to a significance which calls for a fuller religious form. Hegel explicitly indicates this when he speaks of Romantic art as "the self-transcendence of art but within its own sphere and in the form of art itself."[21] In this complex utterance we see laid bare the constituents of Hegel's view: that art is its own sphere; that nevertheless within its own sphere the transcendence of the "merely aesthetic" is already at work; but also that this transcending is not the simple negation or supersession of art but is rather tied up with its highest attainment and fulfillment. Art itself, as it were, sacrifices its own exclusively "aesthetic" form to open out upon a fuller religious configuration.

Art as "Religious": Creativity and Geist

These historical considerations concerning Symbolical, Classical and Romantic art bring us directly to the philosophical point with regard to art's metaphysical meaning. The last citation from Hegel concerning Romantic art particularly requires more systematic elucidation. For Romantic art allows us to affirm man's creativity, but how do we reconcile this with the purported religious import of the same art? To respond to this question we are pointed to the necessity in Hegel, I suggest, of conceiving man's creativity in other than exclusively humanistic terms. In Hegelian terms, man's creativity must be seen to participate in and disclose a "creativity," an "expressiveness" that in the end is more than man as a finite individual:[22] the power of Geist understood in an absolute sense. Seen thus, the crucial point is not to reduce art to religion but rather to elevate art as "aesthetic."

This we can see more explicitly if we constrast art construed as "aesthetic" with art as "religious." Art as "aesthetic" insists on man's creative powers; art as "religious" concurs, but goes further — these powers themselves point to a more fundamental creative expressiveness, that of Absolute Spirit. Art here has metaphysical significance because the powers it expresses are not private or subjective in the pejorative sense. Nor are they simply man's possessions. They are rooted in the nature of actuality itself and of a piece with its most fundamental essence. For art as "religious" cannot be completely characterized as man's sensuous self-knowledge. Nor is the outcome of the artistic act solely a human product, a human artefact. The artist struggles with his material and gives it form. His material is not only external matter but also his own self. But in his struggle with his external and internal matter, he is really wrestling with a power that is not simply external or internal, neither just the external things of nature, nor his own finite self. For Hegel this power is Geist. It too becomes ingredient in art's self-knowledge and in the embodied product of creation. Art as "religious" attempts to effect for man the imaginative articulation of this power. It strives to capture in the art work some conjunction of finite man and this power. It is the struggle for this conjunction that confers the added complexity on art as "religious."

This complexity, moreover, makes more intelligible Hegel's insistence on the absolute character of art. For in this complex view, art is absolute in the mode of its activity: man's creative powers are grounded in and reveal the absolute power of Geist. Art is absolute also in the actuality with which it deals, the actuality of Geist which it seeks to present in its imaginative articulations. And indeed, all great art might be seen as attempting to realize this double aim: to reveal the dignity and glory of man in his original and creative powers; and to strain to display the bond between these powers and what is absolute. Great art, as it were, strains both inwards and upwards towards a limit difficult not to call religious. If the play on words will be allowed, great art both gives us images of the divine in man, and thus in man gives us images of the divine.

The point might be further developed in this way. The Romantic and modern emphasis on "creativity" and "expressiveness" points to a norm immanent within art itself. This immanence sometimes tends to be counterposed to the transcendence characteristic of the more classical, imitation theory of art. Imitation involves the relation of an image (the imitation) to a transcendent original (the model or paradigm external to the image). Thus it might seem that this imitation theory is more consistent with art as "religious" in this sense: the transcendent original seems to guarantee the difference between man's creativity and something further, and also seems to justify the reference of artistic activity to some reality other than man. A chief difficulty with imitation, however, is its tendency to produce dualism, which may lend itself to a diminution and subordination, even denial of art's immanent creative powers. Hegel rejects such a diminution, yet how is he to justify art as "religious" without falling back on imitation or something like it, and thus falling into the unacceptable dualistic consequences that seem to necessarily follow?[23]

A way out of this impasse, I suggest, is to conceive the contrast of "creativity" and "imitation" less starkly, not so strongly as a pair of opposites. For Hegel does not completely repudiate imitation, but might be seen as attempting to incorporate it within art in a non-dualistic way. That is, ancient Classical imitation, as it were, refers the art image to an external god, and so tends to appear as antithetical to modern, Romantic creativity. Hegel's view represents an attempted synthesis of the justified emphasis of both these possible positions. But the Hegelian "imitation" does not chiefly refer outside to an external god; art, we might put it, is rather a kind of "interiorized imitation" where the god of its reference is most properly discovered *within* the self as an originating source of creative power. After all, imitation is in fact a relation of appropriation, and so as a mode of representation always involves some inwardizing movement of spirit. The norm of this "interiorized imitation" is an immanent one, and so joins up with the notion of "creativity." It is a most interesting fact that the more accomplished an imitation becomes the more it begins to present itself as a creation in its own right. At a certain point of accomplishment they begin to shade into each other. At this point imitation and creation cease to be merely opposites.

All of this can be rendered more explicit by reference to the analogous problem of religious representation in Hegel.[24] For Hegel the most adequate religious representations do not try to unmoveably fix the divine in sensuous externality. Rather they point to spirit in the medium of sense, representing the divine as "indwelling." Thus again their representing, "imitating" intention is an interiorizing movement, not an exteriorized one. For their intent is to represent *Geist*, and this cannot be effected without this inward turn. Man discovers himself most fully in this turn, but not just as representing an external divinity, but as creatively taking part in the process of *Geist* itself. Maritain puts a similar point well when he says that the artist does not just copy creation but continues creation.[25] On the present view we do not have to jettison "creativity," as perhaps Classical *mimesis* might suggest. Nor need we inflate man's creativity into the fullness of the Absolute itself, as some extreme Romantics have been tempted to do. It is not a question of either this mere diminution of man nor yet of his simple divinization. It is possible to affirm man's creativity while still seeing this in the context of a "creativity" more ultimate than man.

Of course, "Classical" and "Romantic" are notoriously ambiguous categories and are not always used with any proper precision.[26] But it is helpful, I believe, to think of Hegel's view of art as religious as somehow bringing these two together. For apart from the triadic categorization touched on in the last section, the Classical and Romantic, in Hegel's rendition of the concepts, might be seen to emphasize key elements in the religious and the aesthetic conception of art. Thus the Classical (here drawing on Hegel's usage) focuses on representations of the divine in human statues of the gods, while the Romantic imaginatively explores the enigmatic recesses of the self. When I suggest that for Hegel art might be seen as religious, I mean to imply that ultimately art points beyond any simple antithesis of these two possibilities. There is no question here of returning to Classical representation or *mimesis*. Rather we must move beyond the exclusively aesthetic rendering of the Romantic self — the sense of divinity must be incorporated as an immanent norm. This is perhaps just the religious significance of Romantic art previously noted: the inwardizing in man himself of the sense of the infinite. This revelation of an immanent norm is precisely what is at stake in the "interiorized imitation" that comes to expression in human creativity.

Let us now sum up the contrast of the "aesthetic" and "religious" reading of creativity. In the "aesthetic" interpretation man is involved in an imaginative conversation with himself. This conversation is complex and rich, and indeed its internal intricacy can be conceived dialectically: man is *both* sides of the conversation, the speaker, the spoken and his own listening interlocutor. The discords, clashes and contradictions within man generate this conversation, just as the conversation sometimes yields to man's own agreement with himself, unity with himself, peace with himself. Yet for all this, the dialectic of this conversation makes it ultimately to be a humanistic monologue. In the contrasting "religious" interpretation of creativity, a further complexity is inherent in the dialectic which makes the conversation into a different dialogue. In this dialogue, of course, man comes to hear himself, but always within the context of a conversation with what is more ultimate than the finite individual, something that cannot be completely "anthropologized." Perhaps this also throws some light on why, for Hegel, art must make way for religion in an even fuller way. As lending itself to an exclusively "aesthetic" reading, art tends not to always bring out the full dialectical interplay of the human and the divine. Moreover, tensions between the two may not be entirely resolved on artistic grounds alone. That is, man's finite creative power may not be fully known for what it is in the context of the infinite power of the divine. Outside of this context, we always risk an inadequate conception of human power.

In religious terms, God is at work in the artist,[27] but the artist, as a finite individual, may fail to see the significance of this. His failure may take the form of asserting: this work is mine and mine alone, as modern, individualistic doctrines of originality tend to imply. Or it may take the opposite form: the artist then says, this work is not mine at all but the outcome of some completely other agency, some foreign force which invades me with inspiration. One view may elevate self-activity to an unsurpassed degree; the other may stress the receptivity of the self to a point approaching sheer passivity.[28] With Hegel, I think, neither alternative ought to be asserted exclusively or as they stand in their onesidedness. The creative power of art reveals a complex conjunction of self-activity and receptivity to what is ultimate, or what religious representation depicts as the union of the human and the divine. Hegel would insist on avoiding a humanism making man foreign to the power of the divine, and also any alienating religion which makes the divine power completely foreign to man, as say in the estranged form of worship of the unhappy consciousness. Both these views come down to competing dualisms which, though they seem to face in opposing directions, are actually complementary.

Perhaps something of the point might be suggested in the following way. What is chiefly at issue is how we are to understand the riddle of *Geist* itself which, it seems, cannot be simply reduced to either God or man, nor to the competing theological and humanistic dualisms. Rather man and God *both* are *Geist* which is, as it were, the energy that dynamically articulates their distinct reality and their inseparable continuity. As articulated in man, as creative in man, *Geist* is not reducible to more normal humanistic terms. It is more than the finite individual. This perhaps is part of the point of Hegel's way of exploiting the more than finite connotations of the religious representation of "God." At the same time, since the riddle turns on the enigma of Geist, we ought not to get bogged down in the representation "God" in a manner which simply "reifies" or "objectifies" Geist as an infinite being over against man. The competing theological and humanistic interpretations sometimes do bog down in complementary dualisms, such that it is forgotten that it is the reality of Geist and what this means that is at stake. We might even see both "man" and "God" as two "representations," that is, concrete articulation of Geist, which itself is not reducible to one or the other in a dualistically exclusive way. Though again, the language of religious representation, in its acknowledgement of both the infinite *and* the finite is ultimately more adequate to the absoluteness of Geist, than is the humanisitic interpretation.

The Aesthetic and the Religious: On Right- and Left-Hegelian Readings

These last remarks provide us with a context to discern some relevance in our present theme for the overall interpretation of Hegel. A number of possibilities present themselves here, but our discussion of art as aesthetic and religious throws some suggestive light on that perennial issue of Right and Left readings of Hegel. Very broadly, these Left and Right readings are thought to epitomise respectively a humanistically oriented and religiously inclined view of Hegel, corresponding, again very broadly, to the two possible interpretations of art developed above. The complementary dualisms in relation to art mentioned above can be seen to clarify many of the differences thought to separate Left and Right readings. Let us first ask how these two possibilities link us with the Right-Hegelian reading.

Those who are sympathetic to the defense of the religious dimension of Hegel are sometimes classified as to the "right," even though this classification is not always discriminating enough with respect to the *differences* between possible religious interpretations, ranging along the spectrum from the orthodox to the heterodox. Frequently, however, the religious reading of Hegel is thought to emphasize God to the point of the attenuation of finite man, precisely as finite.[30] Man risks becoming absorbed in God. Indeed some claim that this absorp-

tion of the finite so proceeds that traditional theism yields way to pantheism. The issue of pantheism, of course, is complex in Hegel, and
much discussed. There are many instances where the implication of
his thinking does seem to attenuate the difference of the finite and
the infinite, yet also it is to be recognized that it is no part of Hegel's
deepest intentions to eliminate this difference. The interpretation
developed above of art as religious, I suggest, strengthens rather than
weakens the view that Hegel does *not* seek to commit us to the eradica-
tion of this difference. For the artist, on his own terms and as a finite
individual, is a real center of creative power. He is not, as it were, the
mere passive puppet of a domineering divine power. Yet within the
realization of his power, his participation in the divine power is disclosed. While the difference remains, it now ceases to be a mere
dualistic opposition between Absolute *Geist* as infinite and the
creative expression of *Geist* in finite man. Hegel's own remarks on
pantheism in the *Encyclopaedia* indicate his refusal to destroy that difference, in a manner quite compatible with criticizing the relation of
finite and infinite conceived as one of dualistic opposition.[31]

There is some irony here in the fact that art as "aesthetic" and
"religious" reveals a real point of contact between Hegel and the individual taken to be one of his most trenchant religious critics, namely
Kierkegaard. Kierkegaard saw himself as religiously set against Hegel
precisely on this supposed attenuation of finiteness within the
Hegelian system. The irony here centers on their common attitude to
the merely "aesthetic": despite its indispensible role in human existence, both deeply agree on the insufficiency of the exclusively
"aesthetical" to meet man's fullest demands for absoluteness.
Kierkegaard, it is true, understands this demand as most fully realized
in religion, while Hegel ultimately gives the palm to philosophy. Yet
both, regardless of their differences, seem to concur on this essential:
if it is not to ultimately atrophy and perhaps deform its own inherent
seriousness, the "aesthetic" must be open to the "religious" — in
Kierkegaard's case in terms of the different stages of life's way, in terms
of his disclosure of the inner tensions of the purely aesthetical and the
necessity for it to yield to the ethical and the religious; in Hegel's case
in the self-transcending of art as "aesthetical" with the emergence
through it of *Geist* in its religious and philosophical forms.[32]

These very brief indications must suffice with regard to what we might call Right-Hegelian aesthetics. Reflection on Hegel's view of art, taking seriously art's claim to absoluteness, does illuminate the possibility of, as it were, dialectically balancing the artist, as a finite creator, with Absolute *Geist*, as infinite creative power, without causing to vanish the difference of the two. In the Left-Hegelian aesthetic, by contrast, this difference tends to vanish in a contrary way. For here it is man himself who tends to become *the* creative power, the absolute creative power. The Promethean proclivites of Left-Hegelian humanisms are well known. This Promethean proclivity finds its expression here in the reinterpretation and transformation of any religious reading of "creativity." In this regard, it is the Left-Hegelian view that bears more directly on the fate of art as an aesthetic and religious phenomenon after Hegel. After Hegel art tends to lose much of its religious implication, and the aesthetic conception, in so far as it puts the emphasis on man's expressiveness and originality, comes to dominate.[33]

On this we need but cite Marx, the most powerful and influential of the Left-Hegelians. It may be incidental that the youthful Marx was stirred to write some poetry. Yet Marx's more mature emphasis upon the *productive powers* of man, on his ability to make himself in and through his productions, can be seen as but a more proletarianized version of the aesthetical conception. *Homo aestheticus* becomes *homo faber* who, in turn, is inseparable from *homo oeconomicus*. Throughout we find the humanistic emphasis upon man's self-activity, now however materialized and made sensuously actual through the historical process of production. Indeed Marx speaks of man's ability to produce according to the "laws of Beauty," and links this with what makes man's productive powers specifically human. Indeed the discovery of the manuscripts of the early Marx, the "humanistic" Marx, served to reawaken some of the aesthetical dimensions inherent in the Marxist vision. Nor is the aesthetical entirely absent in the "mature" Marx. In *Grundrisse*, for instance, the true realm of freedom is said to lie beyond simple material production. And Marx cites the case of the composer to illuminate what is involved in genuinely free activity: this is more than mere amusement, involving as it does the serious discipline and intense exertion of self-realization.[34] The aesthetical is inseparable from the full active realization of the human and in its own way epitomises man's self-realization.

Undoubtedly the line of this Left-Hegelian heritage extends deeply into our time, and what is more, in its specifically aesthetical form. Here the work of Lukács might be mentioned. We might also recall the importance of art for many of the Frankfurt school, for instance the importance of music for Adorno, and Benjamin's view of "the author as producer." Perhaps Marcuse provides the most striking example of a Left-Hegelian effort to reassert the essentially liberating power of the aesthetic: free society requires free senses and imagination; aesthetical freedom and political liberty are inextricably linked.[35] Even among the French existentialists, notably Sartre, we find the aesthetic conception coupled with aspects of the "humanistic" Marx. Literature particularly is revealed not only as the reproduction of man's drama in society; it displays, indeed participates in the self-production of historical man.[36] Examples might be multiplied instancing the extent of the aesthetic influence of the Left-Hegelian heritage.[37] The crucial point concerns the shift of the centre of absoluteness to man himself. This is bound up with the entire modern philosophic problematic of subjectivity: whether the creativity of the self is completely independent and self-sufficient, or only intelligible in relation to something more ultimate. Obviously art as "religious" points to this second possibility, though, as we have seen, it is the first possibility that has been most prominent since the historical disintegration of the Hegelian system. As Taylor rightly points out, the self has been loosed from its anchor in cosmic *Geist* and made absolutely creative on its own account.[38]

This development is related to the fact that in the nineteenth century art as "aesthetic" itself sometimes tried to assume a kind of religious character. Art as "aesthetic" made its own claims to absoluteness, as in the "aesthetic" man of the nineteenth century for whom art is all, or the whole. The question is whether this represents an adequate response in relation to art's claim to absoluteness. When Hegel grants art a place in Absolute Spirit I do not think that this was any anticipated endorsement of the exclusively aesthetical view in this nineteenth century sense. Hegel, I suggest, would concur with the position implied by Heidegger *vis à vis* Wagner's effort to turn art into a kind of religion:[39] rather than art's completion, this may be a sign of decline, in that the effort to make the artist the sole creative absolute represents an attenuation of the sense of the absolute. We require a sense of the absolute stronger than the merely aesthetical can supply. The aesthetic man of the nineteenth century might seem to signify a reaching out of art to the totality of life, but often there is a paradoxical reversal in this. The "aesthetic" man, motivated by artistic "purity," is rather tempted by the "ivory tower" and so towards isolation from that totality. Against the mediocrity, crassness, philistinism of life, the "aesthetic" man exaggerates this separation to the point of wearing a special "artist's" uniform, almost, one suspects, in imitation, perhaps parody, of the priest's special garb. Art is turned into a totality itself demarcated from other cultural fields. This is only partly an index of the supposed poverty of common life; more importantly it is a sign of the separation, alienation, estrangement of the artist, and a struggle against the waning powers of art to affect the whole of life, that waning of art's power which in Hegelian terms would be discussed under the heading of the "death of art."

When Hegel touches on the so-called "death of art," it is his alertness to this waning power of art in the contemporary era that we must keep in mind. If there is a "death of art" it partly lies in the inappropriate centering of the absolute completely in man, or as we can put it, the loss of art as "religious" event. That art becomes separated from the totality of life and sets itself up as a totality is very significant here in being tied with the loss of the "religious" dimension of the "aesthetic." For it is this dimension which might support art's claim to absoluteness, and so give it some power over the whole, the totality of life. The "aestheticising" of art seems to reveal the highest glorification of art; yet this "aestheticising" reveals art no longer immersed in but cut off from the sense of life's wholeness. The "aesthetic" glorification of art might be thus seen as an attempt to stem the internal haemorrhaging of art which results when its intimacy with a religious sense of the totality goes. Art itself erected into a kind of religion might be seen as an effort to reassert the old, true powers of art. But cut off from the wholeness of life (a separation perhaps justifiable in reaction to the spiritual poverty of aspects of nineteenth century life),[40] any genuine religious inspiration becomes increasingly difficult and both art and religion begin to wither together. Art as "aesthetic" loses its ground in the religious opening to powers of being more ultimate than finite man. And if Nietzsche is correct, the self of modern subjectivism finally runs itself aground on to the rocks of contemporary nihilism.

Of course, the Left-Hegelian, recognizing the ultimate bankruptcy of sheer "aestheticism," particularly in its nineteenth century form, does attempt to further radicalize the substitution of the "aesthetic" for the "religious" of the sort just described. Here we come across the reverberation in contemporary politics of some themes of Hegelian aesthetics, as mentioned at the opening of this chapter. Put simply, the Left-Hegelian ushers the artist out of the ivory tower and onto the barricades, out of the holy temple of contemplative art and into the raw struggle of the practical world of action. The image of the creative artist shifts from the solitary, secular "priest" to that of the socially engaged engineer, or a member of the elite avante-garde of revolutionary praxis. Revolution itself becomes a new religion with a concept of creativity originally borrowed from aesthetics but now called upon to perform its work in the real, material world. Before the aesthete was content to dream up imaginative worlds in the art work; now the revolutionary in the artist insists that the dream be realized in fact, that through action it be translated from ideal image into material reality.

This move mirrors in art Marx's own effort to shift philosophy itself from contemplative thought to revolutionary praxis, where the point is not to rationally interpret the world, as Hegel did, but to actively change it, as Marx hoped to do. The point becomes not just the aesthetic creation of works of art but the political creation of a new society as itself a kind of work of art. Not surprisingly, there exists a widespread sympathy among twentieth century artists for revolution and revolutionary figures in politics. This sympathy, we now see, has its roots in a Left interpretation of Hegelian aesthetics, where it is not just a question of the "aesthetic" versus the "religious" conception of art, but also of the "revolutionary" versus a "religious" interpretation. Or better, the "aesthetic" conception has been radicalized in its vision of creative originality into an inspirer, an expression and sustainer of revolutionary politics.[41]

Let us now conclude this chapter by attempting to gather together the overall direction of its discussion, and placing these last reflections more firmly in the perspective of Hegel's aesthetics. As I hope to have made clear, if the argument presented here concerning art as an aesthetic and religious phenomenon in Hegel holds good, then neither the Right nor Left alternative is adequate. Art cannot be completely humanized in a manner which makes irrelevant the question of the contribution of something more than man. Nor can what is more than man be so emphasized in art that the real creative contribution of the human individual is neglected. A sheerly aesthetical view might put man in the center, but into man the Hegelian absolute would vanish. A sheerly religious view might put the absolute at the center but into its power the creative contribution of man would be absorbed, and so man as artist would vanish. By contrast with both these alternatives Hegel's view of art as religious incorporates the aesthetic, but art does not vanish into religion, nor is religion reduced. Rather we find a complex balance of aesthetic and religious considerations such as we have tried to adumbrate. The aesthetic points beyond itself to the religious but the creative contribution of man is not thereby jeopardized; while the bond between art and the religious safeguards art's own participation in what is ultimate. When Hegel affirms art's absoluteness within the realm of Absolute Spirit, it is just such a complex balance that is in question.

Because of its complexity and indeed its internal tensions, this "balance" is easily upset. We saw this in the Left-Hegelian stress on the "aesthetic" rather than the "religious": here just as the "aesthetic" and "religious" tend to be assimilated in a certain fashion rather than balanced, so also do the "political" and "religious" become assimilated rather than balanced. It is true, of course, that just as art and religion were deeply intertwined for Hegel, so also were religion and politics.[42] But here a distinction essential to the Hegelian balance is banished in the Left-Hegelian appropriation. In this latter, putting the point in Hegel's own terms, Absolute Spirit tends to be collapsed into objective spirit; or rather objective spirit, in the shape of the "political" is elevated into the absolute and comes to possess something of the ultimacy and centrality previously possessed by art and religion. In Hegel art and religion may be deeply rooted in the political but they are marked by a dimension not entirely reducible thereto, as we must grant if we acknowledge some truth in his distinction between objective and Absolute Spirit.

This "politicizing" of art and religion goes hand in hand with a turn to human history acknowledged by Left-Hegelians to have been initiated by Hegel but "mystified," that is, distorted and left incomplete by him, because of his religious and speculative concerns. This turn to history, it is said, must now be completed through a more thoroughgoing, anthropological, entirely immanent appropriation. In this turn to history, the "completion" of history figures as one of the central controversial questions. Given the present remarks concerning the tangled relations possible between the "aesthetic," the "religious," and the "political," we might well ask if Hegel's philosophy of art can throw any light on this so-called "end" of history. This question can be seen as bearing on a further essential dimension of art's tie with absoluteness in Hegel. We will concern ourselves with it in the next chapter.

Chapter Four

Art, History, and the Question of an End

Art and the Question of History

Many of Hegel's successors, most notably the Left-Hegelians, do him the honor of being one of the first to underscore man's historical nature, albeit, it is quickly added, in a manner "mystified" by Hegel's deep concern with man's religious essence. Many thinkers, not always Marxists, share some such view of Hegel. In broad terms this is how it tends to run: because of his religious "mystical" bias, Hegel spoke of Absolute Spirit, particularly stressing the intimacy of man and God. But nevertheless in this he brought to the fore that aspect of becoming, development, process, all notions converging on the reality of historical manifestation. This intimacy of man and God is disclosed in the dialectical identity of man and *Geist*. Hegel, it is said, was right to identify man and spirit, but wrong to hypostatize spirit into some power transcending man. In fact, *Geist* is nothing other than, nothing but, human activity developing itself and coming to determinate articulation through the dynamism of the unfolding historical process. There is no *Weltgeist* other than man. Rather man is just the *Weltgeist* of the historical world in that his active power brings it into being and moves it as a world. Man's power is the agency of history and man's power alone. History is the domain of man's work, not the product of God's power. History and the development of humanity are all but synonymous.

It is certainly true that Hegel took history very seriously, a fact now widely admitted. Moreover, for Hegel, history and the development of humanity are deeply intertwined. As we saw previously, even a religious viewing of art in Hegel in no way serves to diminish the intensity of his central focus on the human. The issue still remains, however, of what, more precisely, it means to take history seriously. Part of Hegel's answer is that the seriousness of time is manifest from a standpoint that is not always completely identical with time as frequently comprehended. To take history seriously is to try to determine the meaning it might disclose. But the ultimate principles of temporal genesis are not for Hegel exhaustively characterized as but the products of temporal genesis. Rather temporal genesis is for Hegel ultimately to be comprehended as the production of eternity and is meaningful as the disclosure of this.

What this might mean is, admittedly, extremely difficult to explicate satisfactorily. However, we can say here that once again Hegel himself was intent on avoiding those two extremes subsequently serving to define Left and Right-Hegelians. For the Left-Hegelians reduce eternity to history and in doing this tend to narrow Hegel himself. Now to argue against this reduction is not, in a contrary fashion, to advocate the negation of history, where this means the dissolution of history into eternity, a view sometimes imputed to religious interpreters of Hegelian thought. Hegel himself cannot be confined to either extreme. Such dualistic bifurcations feed on one-sided interpretations of his approach, each alternatively playing one side of his rich complexity off against the other. The problem is neither the reduction of eternity to time, nor the annihilation of the historical in the transhistorical. The problem for Hegel is whether we can make intelligible sense of the possibility of a mediation or reconciliation between these seeming extremes, whether a meaningful meeting or conjunction of the two might prove to be a viable possibility.

We need to confront, as it were, a dialectic between a wrong absence of history and a wrong excess of history, between a kind of escape from history and a kind of drowning in it. For there are two opposite poles that might sometimes tempt us here. First there is possible an absence of history that produces an approach so atemporal that it can offer no real point of insertion into the concrete world wherein we actually find ourselves. Alternatively, there is possible an excess of history that produces an approach so historicist that we may again fail to find ourselves properly in the concrete world, now instead staggering rudderless from relativity to relativity. My purpose in this present chapter is to inquire whether art, and Hegel's understanding of it, can provide us with some pointers towards a meaningful middle way between these extremes, whether it can provide a significant balance between the inescapable demands of history and what Dostoievski termed "those accursed eternal questions," questions no less inescapable than history. We should be alerted to this possibility already, I believe, given our previous discussion of art as aesthetic and religious. Here the question we ask is this: can art provide man with a crucial instance of meaning that emerges in the flux of time itself, but which yet struggles there to bring to birth a reality that rises above the dissolving, corrosive relativities of time? Does art manifest man's genuine need to articulate and embody something unconditional, or at least approaching the unconditional, without denying his own inescapable rootedness in the conditions of history? The fact that Hegel assigns art to Absolute Spirit must again cause us to seriously consider this possibility. We must ask how art's absoluteness might be related to history.

More specifically still, we must ask if Hegel's view of art can throw any light on that controversial issue in Hegelianism generally, namely, the question of the end of history. Often Hegel's concern with history tends to be restricted by commentators to political issues, or to the problems encountered by the historical scholar in his specialized discipline.[1] Thus the issue of the end of history tends to be treated in conjunction with, for instance, some of Hegel's startling assertions about the state being the divine Idea as it exists on earth.[2] Of course, the precise issue of the end of history continues to be controversial, and Hegel's own words are not devoid of ambiguity. Yet I think it fair to say that discussion of Hegel's view of history often tends to remain on the level of what for him is objective spirit — the world of political power and social institutions and their development through time. While any full discussion of history cannot avoid considering objective spirit in this sense, the strategy suggested here is that we cease to confine the problem of history in Hegel to this level exclusively. As should be expected by now, for Hegel the matter can be adequately handled only if we are willing to consider how history appears in relation to Absolute Spirit.[3] It is true that Hegel's treatment of history is generally recognized to be incomplete without reference to the importance of religion. Marx was one of the first in a line when he spoke of religion as revealing the secret history of a people. This claim, in fact, is only a restatement of Hegel's own view as expressed in the *Encyclopaedia* when he says: ".... the history of religions coincides with world history."[4] Of course, in Marx we find the above-remarked tendency to treat of history in terms of objective spirit — in his case this implies the reduction of the significance of religion to social and economic processes, the result being what Marx describes as the "putrescence of the absolute spirit." Nevertheless, it remains true that the relation of history and religion has received some genuine attention by Hegel's commentators, even by those not sympathetic to religion.

The relation of history and art has not received similar attention. Adapting the remark of Marx, I would like to suggest that art too reveals a secret history for Hegel, one that is not altogether explicable in terms of objective spirit. Once again, our focus here on the relation of art and history must take into account the precise place of art in Hegel's system as a whole. Hegel himself points to art as itself an historical phenomenon when he details the phases of its development in terms of Symbolical, Classical and Romantic art. Our attention here, however, is not primarily on the historical development of art in this sense. Rather we are concerned with the manner in which art, taking into account Hegel's ascription of absoluteness to it, might provide man with the sense of an ending, and how this sense of an end might shed important light on the question of the end of history.[5] This question, we might add, is not unrelated to the religious issue of the "fulfillment of time" and "the end of days." To fully explore the connection of religious eschatology and the sense of an ending in art is beyond the present scope, though the connection is genuinely implied in Hegel's aesthetics, interwoven as this is with man's historical efforts to articulate the sacred.[6]

Art and Time: Dialectic in Imaginative Form

A dialectical view of history is frequently credited to Hegel. What in the fullest sense is involved in this view would take us beyond our present scope.[7] What is of interest here is how art is related to time, how art exhibits the nature of dialectical process in a way charged with temporal significance. In Hegel art might be seen to effect a certain dialectical appropriation of the significance of time, and to do so in a specifically imaginative form. What is meant by this? We might first recall Aristotle's famous assertion and link this with Hegel: poetry is more philosophical than history.[8] Poetry is more philosophical than history because it discloses a universal import that is purified of trivial inessentials. Because history is often cluttered with insignificant contingencies, there remains always a side to it that tends to fall short of full intelligibility. Poetry gives birth to something less contingent for Aristotle, something essential and necessary. Hegel's view of art here displays a strong kinship with that of Aristotle. Art for Hegel delivers man close to full intelligibility, and for this reason is assigned a place in Absolute Spirit. The issue, I add, is not however a matter of pitting art against history in terms of rival claims to belong to Absolute Spirit. Nor is it a question of simply substituting an artistic fiction for an historical narrative of fact, nor of depreciating the importance of accurate historiography. On the contrary, for Hegel art involves an imaginative effort to gather up from history an essential meaning. It is not opposed to history. Rather it is one of man's central ways of appropriating the significance of his own history, in a manner uncluttered by distracting contingencies and in a manner allowing him to contemplate his own character, that is, in a manner which affords him some self-knowledge. Art is not anti-historical or a-historical. It is rather an imaginative appropriation of the essential strivings of historical man.

To develop this view further it is necessary for us to examine some of the dialectical characteristics of art, or rather of the art work which makes it to be such an imaginative appropriation.[9] Those characteristics of the art work most relevant to the theme of history are these: its concrete uniting of spirit and sensuousness; its dialectical wholeness; its attempts to make present a unification of freedom and necessity and of individuality and universality; and most especially its being marked by an intrinsic end. We have touched on some of these characteristics before, but we must look at them afresh, only now more closely in relation to history. This will bring out an essential element of their significance.

The chief characteristic of the art work for Hegel is that it is the concrete, sensuous presentation of spirit, of *Geist*. This means that though the art work may present itself as a material object, it is not exhausted by its sheer materiality. As we saw in Chapter Two, the art work is not just a simple empirical "this." Instead its concreteness indicates a richer, less bare existence. The external aspect of the art work is not identical with the art work in its fullness, for this fullness is only intelligible by reference to *Geist*. For the art work, let us say a sculpture, is a material existence already worked on by human activity. So its presence contains the mediation of spiritual activity. Even as a material object the art work reveals and expresses concrete spirit as creative in man. When Hegel speaks of the beauty of art as a beauty higher than nature, that is, as a beauty born again, reborn of spirit, it is just this point that is at stake.[10]

In addition to this unavoidable reference to spiritual activity, the art work also gives form to this activity. The art work articulates human activity in order to guard it from fragmentation and dissipation. In other words, the art work gathers together human activity into a unity or a whole. The true is the whole, Hegel held. Part of the truth of the art work is just this, its wholeness. Moreover, this gathering of activity is not blandly done, as it were. It is performed against the grain of opposition. Struggle always enters into the creation of the art work. If the art work is a whole, it is one which incorporates some reminder, some recapitulation of the pathway of its own struggle with opposition. For this reason we might say that the type of wholeness the art work exhibits is dynamic, dialectical wholeness. The art work is not a simple, univocal unity but an internally intricate unity, held together despite the opposing strains it seeks to accommodate.[11]

The most noticeable dialectical character of the art work for Hegel is revealed in its uniting what often are taken as antagonistic poles, namely, sensuous existence and spiritual significance. Against any dualism of the sensuous and the spiritual, the art work involves the sensuous presentation of spirit, a presentation which is concomitantly a spiritualization of the sensuous.[12] This emphasis on the sensuous and its being informed by spirit, this attention to their conjunction in the art work, might be said to link art and history in this sense. The sensuous realm is the realm of appearance, the realm of time. Now art remains tied to this realm of becoming, but with it sensuousness, appearance, time take on a significance that is more than their bare facticity. The art work shows the sensuous appearance of time to be significant beyond brute facticity. When Hegel speaks of the art work as spiritualizing the sensuous it is to some such significance that, I think, he points our attention. We might add too that when he speaks of the sensuous presentation of spirit he repudiates the opposite extreme. He repudiates that dualism, traditionally ascribed to Platonic thought,[13] which places the significance of time utterly beyond time, in an all but unavailable eternity. Art's conjunction of spirit and sensuousness is the aesthetic version of what for the religious consciousness, especially the Christian consciousness, is incarnation, or what for the philosophical mind, at least in its Hegelian form, is the manifestation in history of Absolute Spirit.

Hegel ascribes this rich sensuousness to art in his *Lectures on Aesthetics* when denying that the mode of appearance of art is a mere deceptive semblance. He puts the point, in fact, in a manner highly reminiscent of Aristotle's view which we previously noted. He does so in a very important passage which contrasts art with historical narrative, a passage which, if only for its echo of Aristotle, deserves to be quoted in full. Hegel puts it thus:[14]

> Just as little can the representations of art be called a deceptive semblance in comparison with the representations of historical narrative, as if that had the more genuine truth. For history (*die Geschichtsschreibung*) has not even immediate existence, but only the intellectual presentation of it, for the element of its portrayals, and its contents remains burdened with the whole mass of contingent matter formed by common reality with its occurrences, complications and individualities. But the work of art brings before us the eternal powers that hold dominion in history, without any such superfluity in the way of immediate sensuous presentation and its unstable semblances.

We can see this exclusion of the superfluous in the way the art work brings to the fore an issue unavoidable in any treatment of historical process, and which figures prominently in Hegel, namely, the interplay of freedom and necessity. The artist, if you like, finds himself subject to the cunning of reason in aesthetic form. For Hegel the art work is defined by a certain internal necessity. The artist himself indicates this necessity when he speaks of his work having to be this way and no other. He may tell of his initial freedom either to undertake or leave undone the work. But he will also tell how, once freely undertaken, that it is not simply he who does the work, but rather that the work itself imposes a certain necessity on him. His self-determination determines the work, but in turn the self-determination of the work determines him. In a word, there occurs a dialectical interplay between freedom and necessity. So also the artist may perhaps speak of his *new*, realized freedom in terms of just this dialectical interplay, when he and the work coincide in a complex unison of intention and achievement.

Even subsequently the beholder experiences the same dialectical interplay with the work. Initially, the details of the work seem to be just there, and we may seem free to conjoin them this way or that, whichever way we please. Yet if we dwell with the art work, and if this work is genuine, it comes to crystallize into a whole: the parts fit together and we discern a certain necessity in their cohesion. And since we are now guided by this sense of necessity, we are forced to discard our "old" freedom. But we do not experience this necessity as a mere external constraint. Rather it comes to us as a liberation, a release: we are freed from the fragmentariness of mere detail and come to be at home in a rich whole. It is not that we discard or obliterate the details, but in standing beyond their fragmentariness we ourselves are freed from fragmentation. Such a "standing beyond" which unites and preserves the internal details of a complex whole, in fact, makes the art work an aesthetic concretion of Hegel's general principle of *Aufhebung*.

Let us note this further important characteristic of the art work which links it with the theme of history, namely, the manner in which it joins individuality with universality. Above we drew attention to Aristotle's assertion of the more philosophical character of poetry, more philosophical because more universal than history. With Hegel, however, we find an emphasis upon the individual character of the art work. The art work does not classify experience according to abstract categories but thoroughly individualizes it. Hegel's insistence on this individualizing side of art ties art with history, for history is inextricably bound up with the individual. At the same time Hegel retains the Aristotelian insistence on universality. The individual art work even as individual does exhibit its own universal-

ity. The art work in this respect is an actuality of great significance
for philosophy itself in that it helps us concentrate on individuality
without having to exclude universality at the same time. Reflection on
the art work, that is, helps us make intelligible Hegel's idea of a
concrete universal. History, too, converges on the emergence of such
a universality, most especially concentrated in the person of man
himself, the most highly individualized of beings in nature. Not surprisingly, as we have noted before, the human figure occupies a central
position in Hegel's reflection on art.[15] As an illustration of how an art
work might present this conjunction of the individual and the universal, this convergence on concrete universality, we need only think of
the portrait. A portrait is something entirely individual, yet a great
artist may sometimes show us a universal face emerging in the particular face. We might think of the later self-portraits of Rembrandt.
In these we find a completely individualized face that epitomizes
something universal. This individual face is at the same time a universal face, the face of humanity itself, it its suffering, in its sympathy,
in its self-knowledge.

But by far the most important characteristic for the issue of art
and history is that the art work presents itself with the character of
an end. Hegel very strongly draws our attention to this characteristic
of art.[16] He goes so far as to say that it is by dwelling on this character
of art that we pass towards a true conception of art. Consistent with
this emphasis Hegel rejects, for example, those utilitarian theories
which evaluate art in terms of its usefulness for practical life. Art is   –
not a means to an end, an instrumental object we exploit for purposes
beyond itself. Art is marked by being an end in itself, something that
is intrinsically an end. In this sense art frees us from the desires of
sensuous appetite. It releases in man a freer, more universal, more
contemplative comportment towards things. This understanding of
art is anticipated, of course, by Kant's earlier concern with the dis-
interestedness of art, just as subsequently Schopenhauer was to
exploit a similar point when he spoke of art, especially music, as
liberating man from the tyranny of the will.

We enjoy the art work for itself. And we enjoy it for itself because
it is not a simple imitation. For an imitation, as we saw before, tends
to borrow its content from elsewhere, from sources external to itself.
The art work, by contrast, is productive of its own content, a content   –

which belongs intimately with the art work itself, not a content parasitical on other things. Moreover, this end character of art causes
Hegel to reject moralistic and propagandist theories of art. Art is not
fully itself, not fully free, when it is in subservience to interests extraneous to itself, whether these interests be moral, political, religious.
Indeed, Hegel's insistence on art as marked by its own intrinsic end
should make those commentators a little bit more cautious when they
say that art for Hegel is merely a provisional stepping stone on the
way to philosophy. Hegel's rejection of any instrumentalist theory of
art makes his position on the relation of art and philosophy much
more complex.

But in what sense is art an end? I think it is helpful here to speak
of the art work as an end in somewhat Greek terms, terms indeed
which Hegel incorporates into his entire philosophical outlook, as
many commentators have pointed out. Though there is a "Christian"
aspect to Hegel's sense of an end,[17] the art work here can be said to
be an end in a somewhat Aristotelian sense of "*telos*." That is, it is the
completion of a process of becoming. In this particular case, the art
work is an actuality emergent out of the productive power of the
artist. The artist's work is originative, dynamic, formative, and his
end product always incorporates such dynamic origination within
itself. The art work gathers together a process of origination, giving
form to an initially amorphous power, actualizing a latent potency.
The art work is an end not only as completing a process of origination. More importantly, it is an end as *perfecting* such a process. In
that sense, we might say that the great works of art are man's images
of perfection.

We might say that for Hegel at every level of experience and
being, the operative presence of some kind of perfection is to be discerned. In Hegel's terms, at every level of experience the Absolute is
at work; but not every form of experience *knows* that this is so. With
art, as with religion and philosophy, this knowledge comes to
emergence, and does so to seek progressively more articulate forms. So
perfection may be pluralistically realized in the world, but it only
comes to be so known as pervasively present, as struggling for full
emergence into self-consciousness, with art, religion and philosophy.
The art work, as it were, catches this struggle for emergence as it articulates itself, and embodies it concretely for the contemplation of

man. Art participates in this struggle and expresses it in the form of imaginative self-knowledge. The wholeness embodied in the art work carries some mark of this self-consciousness of perfection. It discloses not just any instance of wholeness or perfection — for things in nature might attain without self-consciousness their own appropriate perfection — but one stamped with man's own self-knowledge.

Art, History and the Embodiment of an "Open" End

In the light of the foregoing we might now try to make more explicit how the end character of art might illuminate the problem of how we find an end in history. Obviously this does not exhaust the problem of the end of history, but it may shed helpful light on it. Often we tend to think of history as merely a parade of random stories, a succession of "nows" or temporal instants strung out in a line, with only external connection between each moment, between before and after. Such a history would be an endless succession in which it would be absurd to speak of any possibility of completion. For Hegel, of course, such an endless temporal succession is not properly human history at all. History properly appears when man tries to appropriate such endless succession, giving form to the meaningless supersession of moments. Time becomes historically meaningful when through recollection, *Erinnerung*, man thoughtfully gathers his past to his present, in a manner which gives the past a meaningful place in the formation of the present, and which gives the present a measure of ballast and articulation in order to make a meaningful future possible. Mere endless succession comes down to being a "bad infinite," that is, a process of becoming that never comes to any genuine realization of itself. Hegel's claim, however, is that against the "bad infinite," history manifests a true, genuine infinity; or as I put it just now, a process of becoming that does come to a genuine realization of itself. The reason why Hegel's claim about this genuine infinity is controversial is, of course, because of the future. If time and history have a future, can we say that any process of becoming ever genuinely realizes itself? If the future is the not yet, and thus open in some degree, is not all of human history ineradicably infected with some element of the "bad infinite"? The future is the yet unrealized side of endless succession, and we cannot be completely assured that its realization will overcome the meaninglessness of mere endless succession. Something may remain of the "bad infinite" never to be appropriated. How might art relate to this "bad infinite"?

Now it seems to me that the kind of completion and perfection exhibited by the art work can serve as a means for making intelligible, at least in some measure, Hegel's claims about the end of history, and in a manner wholly consistent with his consigning art to the realm of Absolute Spirit. If, as I said, the art work is a certain completion of an originative process, it displays an appropriation of time that cannot be characterized in terms of endless succession, the "bad infinite." All the characteristics of the art work we have delineated — its active nature, its wholeness, its dialectical nature, its interplay of freedom and necessity, individuality and universality, its character as an intrinsic end — all point towards a process of becoming that does come to a genuine realization of itself. The art work gathers together such a process of becoming, and is not altogether unlike the philosophical concept itself in being thus recollective. In a word, the art work brings a process of origination to perfection.

The attractiveness of this suggestion in relation to history resides, I think, in the character of this perfection. For this perfection we find in art displays, even in its completeness, an open-ended side. So, for instance, perfection in art is not something achieved just once, where prior to perfection there was only a long ascent, mere stepping stones to this point, and where subsequent to the point of perfection all that awaits us is a long decline or decadence. Perfection, once achieved, is something to be achieved again and again. Its realization is open to a plurality of possible actualizations.[18] The perfection of this art work, or even of that artistic movement, does not preempt the possibility of other future instances of perfection. Perfection is not a univocal concept; within the Hegelian perspective it must be seen as dialectical. Part of what this implies is that the perfection of the art work gives us historical instances of a process of origination that may genuinely realize itself here and now, without exhausting future efforts at different but equally genuine self-actualizations. So we could say that the highest art of a people helps it to be at home with time without the need to deny the unexpected or devouring character of time future. Perfection in the art work gives us, if the phrase will be allowed, a kind of "temporal eternity," or alternatively an "eternalization of the temporal." Such a perfection is implied by Keats, to take but one example, when in response to the singing Nightingale, now metamorphosed into a symbol of all art, he says: "Thou wast not born for death, immortal Bird!"[19]

Various examples of some such "eternalization of the temporal" might be cited from Hegel's *Aesthetics*. We might just mention one very significant instance: that is, Hegel's reflections on the meaning and nature of Flemish painting.[20] Here we have the extreme of the mundane and the temporal, bourgeois worldliness with all its attentiveness to the daily details of ordinary life. Yet this temporal ordinariness gets caught up and arrested for contemplation, and thus presented to the gaze of the beholder as immensely rich and meaningful. Hegel is especially insistent on the powers of painting to rescue from oblivion the absolutely evanescent moment, to hold it still for the eye, and without, it must be added, freezing its inner vitality, without destroying the interior motion of its temporal dynamism. Again it is not a question of stopping the evanescent moment, of distorting what is essentially dynamic by forcing it into a falsifying stasis. It is a question of articulating in a rich image the significant presence of this temporal dynamic, of embodying it for contemplative perception. The rich image, though it may be a still presence in contrast to the tumult of the raw flux of time, itself, as it were, shimmers with the energizing dynamism which emerges with time itself. And such "energizing dynamism" would appear to be one of the central meanings of the "eternal," of "eternity," of the very activity of the Absolute itself for Hegel.[21]

The importance here of the concept of perfection is intimately related to the unity of the art work already mentioned. But again we need to remind ourselves that such a unity is not any static identity. On the contrary, it is the very process itself of concrete unification. What time as endless succession works to scatter, art tries to perfect through unity. Art has always been one of man's chief weapons in his war with decay for just this reason. Man likes to think that his existence springs from some internal principle, but instead finds himself at odds with an external Fate. He turns to art and the unity it gives in order to alleviate this opposition or at least make it more tolerable. For the unity of the art work, as we implied in previous remarks, tries to present itself as something effortless and free, yet also as something which at the same time is only manifesting an internal necessity, what Hegel speaks of as a *Selbstzweck*. As aestheticians and critics often remind us, the true art work exhibits a kind of organic unity, not just a mechanical unity, a unity determined from within, not one imposed from without. Against the metallic click of the clock and its refusal to be stayed, art's unity becomes a kind of substitute for Destiny.

The relevance of these reflections for the theme of history becomes clearer if we acknowledge that art tries to condense what is significant in "strung-out" time in order to give man an ideal image of historical significance. We might go so far as to say that art reveals spirit in history in a far more concentrated form than is often found in the random contingencies of what we might call "newspaper" history.[22] This need not entail any advocacy of an aestheticism that would flee the contingencies of history. The aesthete uses art either as a means of escape or as a means of entertainment, but in either case he instrumentalizes art. The aesthete is only an elegant instrumentalist. Again this runs counter to Hegel's insistence that art contains an end. Art is not a medium for fleeing history but an actual imaginative struggle with the initially hidden significance of man's historical existence, a significance that may fail to come to sufficient definition if human consciousness is confined to "newspaper" history, that is, history for the utilitarian or purely pragmatic spirit. As Newton Stallknecht puts it: ". . . art is seen to offer a realization of value that history . . . seems forever to postpone. So interpreted, the contemplation of beauty in whatever form appears as a sabbath of the human spirit . . . Such enjoyment may be thought of as a personally disinterested admiration that is not far removed from thankfulness. . . ."[23] It is because there is in art something beyond the pragmatic mind that its full significance is not to be found for Hegel on the level of objective spirit. We could say that where objective spirit exhibits the prose of actuality, Absolute Spirit, in one of its guises, reveals the poetry of actuality, in this sense of language, *logos*, approaching its most concentrated and significant form.

Let me point out that there is another sense in which the perfection of the art work gives us some glimpse into the genuine infinity of which Hegels speaks.[24] The art work exhibits a certain wholeness, but if we attend to this we find there is a kind of compacted fullness which seems to be inexhaustible in terms of finite analysis. For this compacted fullness of the art work is not just a recollective gathering up of the past. It is also a kind of implicit spanning of the future. The art work is always a promise of repeated reinterpretations, repeated resurrections. When great artists sometimes speak of creating for posterity, some intimation of this peculiar futurity of the art work is present. They hope that their work will be a perfection even for the future, something ageless, something immortal in time. The inexhaustibility of the art work is a heritage of past spirit that secretly reaches forward to as yet unborn appreciations.

This inexhaustible character of the art work has often been pointed out, but we may here underline one significant implication that follows from it: namely, the resistance of the art work to finite analysis. For we cannot say that *this* is the meaning of the art work, or that *that* is. Every such assertion which tries to fix the significance of the art work to finite predicates may indeed get at one important meaning about it, but only to find itself missing another. In this sense, the compacted fullness of the art work tends to chasten any excessive claims made on behalf of finite analysis, or what Hegel would speak of in terms of *Verstand*, the analytical understanding. This inescapable sense of the presence of something "more" makes the art work a kind of meaningful infinity that is not a *Jenseits* elsewhere, but one there, actually before us for our continued contemplation. In this once again we come across another reason why art is assigned to Absolute Spirit along with religion and philosophy. For in its ability to chasten finite analysis, art manifests its kinship not only with religion but with philosophical reason, *Vernunft*, as Hegel conceives of this.[25] The noninstrumentalized form of aesthetic consciousness that we discover in the imaginative recollection of art finds its counterpart in the equally noninstrumentalized form of conceptual consciousness that we come across in the speculative recollection that marks Hegelian philosophizing itself. In both we find a dialectical opening of consciousness, aesthetic and conceptual, and an effort to gather together its gains, beyond the boundaries of finite analysis.

Art's Wholeness and the Problem of Closure

Let us conclude this chapter with the following reflections which serve to carry us forward to the theme of the next. As attempting to understand art as making present some sense of the genuine infinite, Hegel's aesthetic has implications for two of the chief conceptions of time, namely the linear and the cyclical notions. Here we might begin to glimpse something of the religious dimension of the issue. The linear view is said to mark the historiography of the Judaeo-Christian tradition: time leads directly forward from a beginning to an end, and the story is an unrepeatable, unique narrative. By contrast, the cyclical, circular view is thought to characterize the pagan, more mythological world view: time is marked by the recurrence of essentials, the most obvious being the round cycle of the seasons, though rational philosophers also have given their exalted versions of a similar outlook, say, in the Greek speculations concerning eternal return. Hegel's view of art might be seen as trying to do justice to both these emphases, the mythopoeic and the more plainly historical.[26] First, the uniqueness stressed in Judaeo-Christian historiography is captured in Hegel's affirmation of the art work as an individualizing concreteness. But uniqueness in art becomes mere eccentricity without the infusion therein of the essential. Hegel's dialectical unification of individuality with universality in art speaks to this Greek "essentialism." Once again Hegel reaches out both to the "universalism" and sense of the eternal of Classical art and to the "individualism" and the sense of the crisis of the temporal within Romantic art. He attempts to include both in the perfection of the aesthetic synthesis.

Moreover, as an imaginative recollection art tries to prevent the disintegration of linear time into the "bad infinity" of mere successive duration. Art stays the relentless *progressus ad indefinitum* by creating a rich, significant whole, a finite individual that reverberates with the sensuous presence of the infinite. The genuine infinity for Hegel is not one which dissipates itself in linear duration; it returns to itself, gathers its temporal productions to itself, perhaps analogously to the way God, the cosmic-artistic creator of the religious *Vorstellung*, is said to gather his creation, the finite world, back into his embracing, inclusive divinity. Here, in fact, it seems again all but impossible to avoid some reference to the religious dimension. Thus here too we might see, in fact, the imaginative recollection of art in Hegel as sometimes straining towards an attempted dialectical synthesis of the Greek and the Judaeo-Christian, the Classical and the Romantic, without omitting the sublime presence of the power of the infinite which Symbolical art or the different pantheisms of nature try to see as sensuously pervasive.

Of course, with respect to any recollective enterprise, whether in art or philosophy itself, there can easily occur something like the following dissatisfying, as it were, dissolving dialectic. The linear concept of time tends to point forward to futurity, often emphasizing such ideas as "originality," "novelty," "creativity"; the cyclical concept of time tends to stress the repetition of the past, the recurrence of the perennial essentials in relation to which there seems nothing new under the sun. Now if, on the one hand, we *remember too much* we can easily be crushed by the burden of a weighty past. Too much memory sometimes paralyses. Just to remember everything is really to remember nothing, for to remember everything is to lack discrimination with respect to the genuinely memorable. On the other hand, if we *forget too much*, the result may be a bland contemporaneity wherein the latest superficiality comes to be branded as absolute originality. Old truths turn tedious and forgetfulness allows us the feeling of exciting novelty. But since the object of our contemporary interest may not possess abiding significance, our excitement may amount to much ado about nothing. In forgetfulness we unknowingly repeat the past, perhaps with contemporary "coloration," marvelling at this "coloration" as if it were some supreme invention. To have something "new" to do, we make a virtue of amnesia. In the first case, we numb ourselves in immersion in the past; in the second case, we agitate ourselves in isolation from it. Both these extremes are not unrelated because both float over the present as something to be surpassed, one retreating to the past, the other rushing ahead into the future. For one the past is the tedious history of what is true; for the other it is the tedious history of what is in error, the present being a mere springboard to the future. One reverently mummifies the past in antiquarian devotion; the other turns on it in the spirit of negation, dissolving everything past and present in a orgy of debunking. If we might use this image: one is a sterile old man, supped on a jaded memory; the other is a thoughtless child, enthusiastic and lively yes, but infatuated with every groundless novelty.[27]

We have here a dissolving dialectic between "oldness" and "newness," where one side might be called "reactionary" and the other "revolutionary," adding that each extreme is finally necessary to the definition of its opposite. For Hegel these extremes are not ultimate and we must guard against this dissolving dialectic.[28] The choice is not, as it were, between being old guard and being avant-garde, between, if you like, kneeling in a church and shooting from the barricades. For in the metaphor we have used, the senile old man and the facile child are not entirely different: they each lack living judgment as to what is essential, the robust memory that discerns the *genuinely memorable*. The genuinely memorable, whether in art or elsewhere, for Hegel cannot be said to derive from exclusively historicist considerations. In a frequently quoted statement, Hegel held that philosophy was its own time comprehended in thought. What is sometimes overlooked, however, is that what philosophy thus comprehends in time is not itself just time. For in those famous words which we find in the preface to Hegel's *Philosophy of Right*, the twofold requirement of time itself and the eternal as emergent in time are clearly set forth by Hegel. Thus on the one hand, he forthrightly says:

> Whatever happens, every individual is a child of his time; so philosophy too is its own time apprehended in thoughts. It is just as absurd to fancy that a philosophy can transcend its contemporary world as it is to fancy that an individual can overleap his own age, jump over Rhodes.

There is no escape from our conditionedness, our rootedness in a certain time and place. On the other hand, the dimension of the unconditioned is not gainsaid; rather it is to be discerned as emergent within the conditions of time itself, as the eternal that is to be apprehended within time, immanent within the present itself. Thus Hegel very significantly says: ". . . . the great thing is to apprehend in the show of the temporal and the transient the substance which is immanent and the eternal which is present. . . ." Again he says: "To recognize reason as the rose in the cross of the present and thereby to enjoy the present, this is the rational insight which reconciles us to the actual, the reconciliation which philosophy affords."[29]

Similar considerations can be applied to Hegel's view of art. If we recall our opening remarks about Hegel's desire to steer a middle course between an historicist excess of temporality and an eternalist absence of history, we might venture that the art work in its "open" wholeness may represent an imaginative rescuing and preservation of what is genuinely memorable for man. The imaginative recollection of art is a struggle for significance within the flux of temporal relativities, but in that imaginative struggle the essential for man comes to emergence and articulation. For the essentially memorable is what Hegel calls (to recall a crucial previous citation) "the eternal powers that hold dominion in history."[30] Past, present and future may here be held together in a certain balance by art, a balance which may — gather what has been great, which may make richly manifest a presently occurring manifestation of ultimate meaning, and which may offer no bar to equally significant future articulations of man's sense of the ultimate. Indeed the peculiar perfection of past and present art welcomes the further process of repeated, even intenser exploration of this sense of the ultimate.

The sense of an end that art may offer us, then, need not force us into any spurious "closure" of history. Hegel has frequently been attacked as offering such a closure. The wholeness of the art work, in its gathering of past greatness, in its rich presentness, in its openness to futurity, undermines any such closure. The "open" wholeness of the art work need not be identical with "totalitarian closure." The story is not finished in this closed sense. But this need not entail the denial of any possibility of the sense of an end: the end "opens" out precisely because what its wholeness makes manifest is the sense of the presence of infinite inexhaustibility. On this point it is much less misleading to speak of the art work as a "whole" rather than a "totality," in that the latter concept more easily lends itself to wrong connotations of "totalitarian closure." "Wholeness" is a conception that can be freed of such restricting connotations. Wholeness and infinity — conceptions that correspond very broadly to the Classical and the Romantic, the Greek and the Judaeo-Christian — are not ultimately antithetical for Hegel, but may be held in some contemporaneous balance, as the perfection of great art sometimes serves to indicate.

This theme of art and the end of history has important implication not only for the different conceptions of time but also for cultural currents in our own time.[31] Accepting the view of Hegel as a philosopher of "totalitarian closure," some contemporary thinkers, instead of developing the Hegelian heritage in a humanistic direction as do the Left-Hegelians, *repudiate* entirely the Hegelian heritage on just this issue. Following Nietzsche and Heidegger, they set out to "deconstruct" the tradition of western thinking, and Hegel as perhaps one of its greatest representatives. Their anti-Hegelianism and their efforts to "overcome" Hegel, especially since these center on the question of art and philosophy, now invite our attention. In the next chapter we must see how this sense of an end, this sense of art's wholeness, has implication for the current, purportedly "post-Hegelian" notion of "deconstruction" and for the approach to art implied by this notion.

Chapter Five

Dialectic, Deconstruction and Art's Wholeness

Deconstruction and the Absence of the Absolute

The dissolving dialectic between "oldness" and "newness," rear guard and avant-garde, mentioned at the close of the last chapter, tends to be resolved in favor of the "new" and the "avant-garde" by "modernist" approaches to art, and even more so by various strains in contemporary culture now often dubbed "postmodern."[1] This resolution finds many different expressions in contemporary culture, but, relevant to present purposes, we need but mention its aesthetic and philosophical manifestations. Aesthetically, it is revealed in the pervasive repudiation of imitative, mimetic ideals in art, coupled with a contrasting glorification of notions like "originality" and "creativity." Philosophically, it is to be found in the critical, often debunking attitude to traditional philosophical ideals, present, for instance, in the rhetoric of some of Heidegger's epigones in their purported "overcoming" of the tradition of western metaphysics. Does Hegel's philosophy of art have anything of significance to contribute to this contemporary situation? We have already seen Hegel's complex concern with imitative and creative views of art. I now wish to argue that Hegel's view of the art work as a rich end, as what we previously called an open whole, presents a countering positive balance to some of the culturally corrosive results that have sometimes sprung from the critical approaches of modernist and postmodernist thought.

Undoubtedly, Hegel's sense of art as such an end is at odds with the modernist and postmodernist view of the waste and desolation of contemporary history, what T.S. Eliot speaks of as "the immense panorama of futility and anarchy which is contemporary history."[2] It is foolish, however, to think of Hegel's affirmation of art's wholeness as proceeding from some bland metaphysical complacency. Hegel's awareness of what he terms the "slaughterbench" of history,[3] makes him extremely sensitive to the possibilities of vast meaninglessness often encountered in history. We need only remind ourselves that already before Nietzsche, it was Hegel who strongly pointed to the absolutely crucial significance of the experience of the "death of God," and who in his account of the "Unhappy Consciousness" already delved deeply into the pivotal importance of the absence of the Absolute for all human consciousness and history.[4] The question, of course, is: acknowledging, as Hegel clearly does, the possibility of this extreme desolation, how further are we to respond to it? Do we just acknowledge it *simpliciter*, only then perhaps to succumb to it, to finally surrender to it in the very act of conceding its presence, indeed in the very act of articulating its character? Or encountering it, do we then work to counter its power? Hegel's defense of the wholeness of art must point us to this second direction.

The relevance of Hegel's aesthetics for the perplexities of contemporary culture should be sufficiently established by this defense, even if only in some provisional manner. But Hegel's relevance here is not just an importation of his aesthetics *ab extra* for purpose of an admittedly interesting scholarly study in contrast. There is a line of direct cultural continuity here which carries us from Hegel to today, though in this case not towards the reappropriation of the Left-Hegelian heritage, but to those contemporary cultural critics who are deeply *anti-Hegelian* in their repudiation, not only of the Hegelian heritage, but of the entire tradition of thinking characteristic of western metaphysics. Once again our chief stress throughout this study on art and the absolute receives another modulation here. The descendents of Hegel on the Left take up Hegelian themes, preserving and developing them in a humanistic way, particularly themes connecting aesthetics with religion, politics and history. In contemporary cultural criticism anti-Hegelianism is represented by certain descendents of Nietzsche and Heidegger who presently tend to mass under the banner of "deconstruction." What exactly "deconstruction" is — a matter sometimes seemingly as enigmatic to its practitioners as to its opponents — I will attempt below to clarify. Speaking very broadly for now, however, deconstruction clearly represents an "anti-humanistic" stance which does not seek to return to any nonhuman, i.e. religious Absolute of the Hegelian sort. Rather it tends to deny any absolute at all, regardless of whether this is conceived of as human or divine. The face of the human is made the object of question but any road to a nonhuman absolute seems barred. To long for any such road is to be guilty of "nostalgia" for metaphysics, a feeling, it would seem, that it is not respectable for twentieth century intellectuals to entertain, for reasons that these same intellectuals do not always explain or perhaps even feel the need to make intelligible.

In short, deconstruction tends to present us with an anti-Hegelianism of an anti-humanistic sort.[5] Left-Hegelian Marxists and existentialists might here be seen as attempting the deconstruction of Hegel's religious absolute in a favor of man as the only historical absolute. By contrast, these more recent deconstructionists attempt a more throughgoing anti-Hegelian deconstruction of even man considered as making any claims to absoluteness. We are left with no absolute. Or rather, we seem to be left with deconstruction itself as the only possible claimant to absoluteness — a peculiar paradox, we must grant, since as we shall see, the activity of this "absolute" is to subvert, to dissolve all absolutes. There is indeed a certain affinity between Left-Hegelians and these anti-Hegelians in relation to this common intention of subversion. Where the Left-Hegelians are concerned with "political subversion," the post-Hegelian deconstructionists might be said to be concerned with "cultural subversion" — particularly with respect to more traditional mimetic and organicist theories of the aesthetic. The Hegelian affirmation of wholeness is called into question and immediately the question of art and the absolute arises again. Only in this case the question put to art, particularly contemporary art, turns on the complete *absence* of the absolute. Art's wholeness and the question of this absence will be of concern to us in the present chapter.

I should make clear at the outset the limits of my purpose in this chapter. My purpose is not to pit Hegel against, say, Derrida in an extended study of their relations and contrasts. Derrida himself has made Hegel an object of his interest and a full account of his often elusive views would involve too large an undertaking here. In addition, Derrida displays an ambiguity towards Hegel, mixing, it seems, criticism for metaphysical closure with praise for Hegel's openness, perhaps not always intentional, to difference.[6] Clearly I have been arguing against the excessively closed view of Hegel throughout this study and have no quarrel with the opening up of some important, overlooked intricacies in Hegel's texts. What I would like to do here, however, is to stand back from what Trilling has called "the adversary culture" of which, I believe, deconstruction is an expression, and to offer some general reflections from the viewpoint of Hegel's aesthetics. Undoubtedly this may mean painting a picture in somewhat broad strokes, too broad some might think. Yet given Hegel's own stated view that the true is the whole, there is some justification for at least attempting to see the larger picture. For the importance of Hegel's aesthetics does not lie solely in the detailed intricacies of textual exegesis (though this is not to be neglected) but, relevantly here, in its contribution to the self-knowledge of western, and especially modern culture. By now we are sufficiently familiar with some key aspects of Hegel's aesthetics to venture some reflections in that direction.

The issue here is not the charge sometimes brought against Hegel, and indeed traditional philosophy generally: that the primacy of the concept (Begriff) hides or tries to efface figurative underpinnings which, mirabile dictu, deconstruction now exposes. I believe Hegel was well aware of the dialectical interplay of philosophy and art (as I indicate in Chapter Two) and that his philosophical practise is not unmindful of its own origins in the metaphors of art and the representations of religious consciousness. I think there is less shattering "news" here for Hegel than his critics seems to think. The issue here is rather the nature of articulation itself in art: what justice there is in Hegel's dialectical understanding of this; whether as this understanding implies, this articulation has a teleological thrust; whether indeed this teleology of articulation yields a kind of wholeness which is, nevertheless, not an unacceptable totalitarian closure. We have already seen something of the complexity of the articulating power of Geist in relation to art, philosophy and religion (in Chapters Two and Three) and something of the "open" end of art in relation to history (in Chapter Four). Since deconstructionists seem to be deeply suspicious of all teleology, the issue can be further developed here, and moreover with our sights on the importance of Hegel's aesthetics in the context of the contemporary absence of the absolute. Of course, the literature on deconstruction is large and still growing. My purpose is not just to add to it. But since much of it is written from a perspective which is non-Hegelian, if not anti-Hegelian, my remarks from a Hegelian perspective may prove helpful. In the context of Hegel's aesthetics, they may help us see how Hegel might view the forces of a dissolving negativity that is often at work in contemporary culture, and that Hegel himself clearly recognized as a mark of modern culture generally.

Literary Theory and the Question of Wholeness

The issue of the absence of the absolute is very much at the center of recent critical theory. Deconstruction, if you like, reminds one of the Hegelian negative, but now exploited primarily for its negativity, not as for Hegel for its power to positively determine. Negation for Hegel, as is well known, means determinate negation, and hence is said to have some positive import. With deconstruction we find a tendency to undermine all determinacy, in order thus to reveal the ultimate *indeterminacy* thought to characterize art, language and especially literature. We can see here the shift wrought by this negative dialectics as first from God to man, and then from man to language itself as the cunning, indeterminable power that eventually mocks all simple humanistic pieties. This shift, in fact, might serve as a metaphor for the history of modern consciousness after Hegel. First God is dialectically negated by the Left-Hegelians, but still with the constructive purpose to positively determine human reality — to open the full space for self-determination, man's own human determination of history. Now, however, at the latter end of this arc of dialectical negation, it is man himself who is negated by the anti-humanistic, anti-Hegelians, and not to further consolidate humanistic self-determining, but to show the human as itself determined out of some more basic indeterminacy.[7] Relative to this more basic indeterminacy there can never be, it is claimed, any genuine unifying sense of absoluteness. We might think here of Foucault's mocking Nietzschean laughter at the "death of man" that follows the "death of God."[8]

Given these provocative perspectives, it is not surprising that deconstruction is one of the most controversial, if not the most controversial issue in recent literary theory. A measure of this controversy is the manner in which advocates of deconstruction and its antagonists tend to square off against one another, each confronting his opposite with highly combative rhetoric. The very term "deconstruction" itself carries something of the agonistic spirit. Traditionalists, nondeconstructionists, tend to respond with a matching animus. Yet what is at stake in the controversy is not always adequately spelled out. The deconstructionists do not always present a clear account of the character of their critical strategies. The traditionalists, themselves not always sure of the precise theoretical presuppositions of deconstruction, grow uneasy with the practice of the deconstructors. Whatever else is obscure, one thing seems clear on both sides: theory has invaded the sphere of critical practice, in a manner which demarcates this forking of the ways: some exult in the new theoretical liberation; others groan under an excess of theory that they claim carries them from a balanced experience of the literary work itself. The controversy, however we further refine its character, is precipitated at the point of conjunction of philosophical theory and literary, critical practice.

What is further noticeable is that many of those uneasy with deconstruction often refuse to counter it on a full theoretical level.[9] Theory, the implication seems to be, is precisely what perennially risks violating the original integrity of the literary work of art. Better to put Satan behind one, than to sup with this devil, however long one's spoon. The command to Satan, however, does not seem to carry much efficacy. This Satan is not a docile boy. We have to sit down to dinner with Lucifer. For deconstruction is a critical strategy that grows out of a set of complex philosophical presuppositions, and only some clarification of these presuppositions will effect any fruitful encounter with it.

We might approach this clarification in the following stages. First, we need to indicate some of the historical antecedents of deconstruction. Many critics are not sufficiently familiar with the philosophical influences that shape the aesthetics of deconstruction. I propose first to look at what I will call the Nietzschean-Heideggerian heritage. Many deconstructionists work in the shadow of Nietzsche and

Heidegger, but we also need to notice a great, let us call it, "anti-shadow," namely, Hegel. Here Hegel, as we already implied, is the great ancestor and the great antagonist. Much of contemporary European philosophy has reacted to Hegel, but also lived off the supposedly *disjecta membra* of his system. The historical repudiation of Hegel will provide us with a crucial focus for defining the character of deconstruction. Secondly, we need to indicate something of the precise character of deconstruction which links it to Hegel and separates it from him. Thirdly, we need to present Hegel's own view in relation to this issue, particularly his notion of dialectic as a fruitful foil to deconstruction.

My purpose will be to argue that there are profound affinities between dialectic and deconstruction, though there is a decisive parting of perspectives on this central issue. This central issue, which we have already indicated as the problem of the wholeness of the art work, will occupy our final reflections. Here I argue that Hegel's dialectic, not only helps to do justice to the complexity of the literary work as rightly emphasized by deconstruction; it also tries to defend the aesthetic ideal of wholeness. The suspicion that this essential wholeness dissolves at the hands of the deconstructionists is one of the chief sources of the sense of unease with deconstruction. The notion of dialectic, I will argue, points to the great work of art as an inherently complex whole, yet still a whole which entails no denial of its *dynamic* dimension. Dialectic, to anticipate, facilitates a joint or double affirmation of the wholeness *and* dynamism of the art work. Deconstruction, by contrast, tends to accentuate dynamism in a manner which sometimes risks dissolving wholeness. Let us now see in more detail what this might mean.

Art and Post-Hegelianism: The Nietzschean-Heideggerian Heritage

Thinkers who determine the discourse of the decontructionists are many, ranging from Marx to Lacan, from Freud to Saussure. Since our focus here is on the conjunction of philosophy and literary theory, two important figures stand out: Nietzsche and Heidegger. Both of these in turn define an important attitude to Hegel, and the entire tradition of western metaphysics. Each also is a key thinker in contemporary reflection on art, and relevantly here, connected to Hegel through Hölderlin.

Let us first look at Nietzsche. As is well known, Nietzsche exploits the Dionysian and Apollonian principles to understand Greek tragedy, and indeed the whole of art and life. The Apollonian principle defines that dimension of harmonious beauty where form, perfection and wholeness predominate. The Dionysian principle refers us to the promiscuous energy of life itself, the Bacchanalian formless intoxication which destroys the limits of form, surpassing every stabilized perfection or fixed unity. Initially, Nietzsche conceived of art as the balance of these two principles, roughly corresponding to Schiller's *Formtrieb* and *Stofftrieb*, or what above I called art's wholeness and art's dynamism. In time, however, the Dionysian, it seems, comes to predominance. Dynamism, Dionysus, or more abstractly, the Will to Power, is not just one principle alongside another equally fundamental principle. Dionysus, the Will to Power, becomes the basic character of all being, as Heidegger points out.[10] The Will to Power becomes the Whole.

Why should this be important? Its importance here lies in the implication for the notion of form generally, and artistic form particularly. How so? Artistic form can never be ultimate, and becomes a provisional stabilization of the basic energy of being, the Will to Power. Nevertheless, we are always tempted to treat provisional forms or structures as if they were ultimate and insurpassable. We tend to fix the form. But this is to forget what cannot be completely encompassed or concretized in any form or structure, the Dionysian Will to Power. Form, therefore, may serve to hide as much as it serves to disclose. Or stronger, it represses what it cannot directly, consciously embrace. Form, looked at this way, inevitably contains a drift towards a denial, towards a falsification. To counter this drift, we need to "break the form," in Harold Bloom's phrase.[11] We need to let the repressed return and reassert itself. (The connection with Freud is strong here.) We need to let the energy of Dionysus dissolve the excessively congealed structures of Apollo. Applying these philosophical ideas to the literary work, we need to engage in a deconstruction of its seemingly obvious meaning, and expose the lacunae, the repressed, unspoken elements that a more simple reading glosses over.

Mention of the "obvious meaning" brings us to a second element in the Nietzschean legacy, namely, its antagonism to traditional metaphysics, said to be epitomized in the person of Plato.[12] Plato versus Homer: this is life's basic antagonism, Nietzsche exclaimed, and sides with Homer.[13] The viewpoint here is that the artist is closer to the Dionysian truth of things, while the metaphysician, Plato, exaggerates the Apollonian to the point of poisoning it. How so? Nietzsche holds that Plato's resort to the ideal entails a flight from, an evasion of the real. The *eide*, the ideas, the forms, then become an attempt to substitute an eternal world of pure Being for the visible world of Becoming. What characterizes eternal Being is pure stasis: the Forms are dead. Consequently, the Platonic transcendence devalues Becoming, the very ground out of which grows art, for Nietzsche the chief affirmer of life's will to power. Platonism is nihilism,[14] for in substituting the fixed unity of eternal form for the pulsing multiplicity of the here and now, it reduces, negates the wealth of this given world.

Once again, the forms must be dismantled, deformed, deconstructed, or in Nietzsche's phrase, the "Innocence of Becoming" must be restored once again. Becoming is without structure, a diversification without any absolute unity, a play of energies that never finally rests in any one definitive form. The dualisms of Platonic metaphysics, the oppositions it creates between body and soul, matter and form, time and eternity, art and philosophy, must be unmasked for their cowardice before purposeless becoming. The forms are not just there eternally; man, as will to power, puts the structure, the purpose into sheer becoming.[15] Acknowledging this his own authorship of fixed structure, he must also be courageous enough to undo his work, to deconstruct what he has constructed and so undermine the illusion of an eternal permanence. As Nietzsche repeatedly asserts: creating and destroying are always found together. We have it in an immortal phrase (full with a sleeping irony) in which dynamism is exalted over definite form, and its explosive, that is, destructive power disclosed, when Nietzsche proclaims in *Ecce Homo*: I am not a man; I am dynamite!

The obsession with fixed form, or the "obvious meaning" leads to this further consequence. Put succinctly, in the hands of the Platonists, it replaces art with logic. Discursive *logos* comes to predominance over *poiesis* and *mythos*. Logic particularly, Nietzsche implies, lends itself to a certin kind of illusion of unity, or unitary meaning.[16] That is, the ideal of logic tends to be that of a *univocal language*. Logic insists on either the repudiation or resolution of contradictions. Opposed meanings either must be reduced to one single univocal sense, or else the opposition in question rejected as a transgression of meaning. In insisting on the ideal of univocal meaning, logic seems to seek to reduce language to a manipulable system, a lawful and rule-bound system, a total, ordered structure within which everything has one definite place. Since the language of poetry is conspicuous by its lack of univocal language, it becomes logically suspect, indeed suspect to the point of being exiled from Plato's ideal city. The nonunivocal language of poetry is now held secondary, parasitical on the ideal logical language of univocity. For Nietzsche this is another reversal of the true situation. It is poetry that is the more primordial. Univocal language is an impoverished version of this more primordial utterance. If we can adapt the title of one of Nietzsche's works, we need a *Genealogy of Logic* which will restore language from its deformation by the logic of univocity. What is concealed in the univocal ideal must be brought out. The concealed equivocations and contradictions must be coaxed into the open. To make clear a new space for the play of poetry, we need a critique, a taking apart, a deconstruction of this logical ideal.

Heidegger carries forward into the twentieth century and develops further some of these themes.[17] The tradition of the west, he puts it, is essentially logocentric, but this logocentrism tends to forget the source of truth. Primordial truth is not the simple, referential correspondence between definite propositions and a fixed external reality, but an event of disclosure, an unconcealing in *aletheia*. The Presocratic philosophers were closer to primordial truth, but with Socrates and Plato, and borne on by Aristotle and other great metaphysicians, a narrowing of the notion of truth occurs under the aegis of the logical ideal. The result is a forgetfulness of Being. The Platonic *eidos* or form secretly contains a will to power which determines the subsequent history of occidental metaphysics, which now devalues its grand heritage and ends in nihilism. But this end, nihilism, is implicit in the logocentric beginning itself, for both logocentrism and nihilism define different but joined extremes along the spectrum of the forgetfulness of Being. To recover, uncover again what is thus covered in this forgetting, we require a "destruction" (*Destruktion*) of metaphysics, and its overcoming (*Überwindung*).

The Heideggerian "destruction," of course, has been the focus of intense debate, and its defenders have denied that it is an essentially negative enterprise. The tradition of metaphysics, they insist, must be dismantled, to allow what is "unsaid," "unthought," and "unspoken" in it to show itself.[18] The tradition of metaphysics thus becomes a vast text for deconstruction, as is made plain in Heidegger's own dialogue with so many thinkers from that tradition. The hidden tensions in the tradition must be brought to light, and particularly the dualisms and complementary oppositions of soul and body and so on that mark the western tradition since Plato. In the tension of these oppositions, a forgetfulness of Being may be detected. Hence the interrogation of these metaphysical oppositions may help us to renew the question of Being, and so alleviate and perhaps surpass the result of this forgetfulness, namely nihilism.

We will turn to Hegel's dialectic later, but here it is appropriate to note that Hegel functions as a kind of antipodes to some of the Nietzschean and Heideggerian emphases. What is the received picture of Hegel relevant here? Hegel develops, it is said, to the highest degree possible, the themes of western metaphysics, and by so developing them rounds off this tradition in an insurpassable way.[19] In many of his utterances Hegel himself seems to concur with this assessment. First, Hegel seems to be the logocentric philosopher *par excellence*. The real is the rational, the rational is the real, he asserts. Is not this to carry western *logos* further than Plato or any other? Indeed, Hegel's link with and transformation of the rationalist-idealist tradition is revealed in its extremity in that the highest category in his *Logic*, or Being in its richest determination, is the Absolute Idea.[20] Moreover, Hegel holds to the necessity of grasping truth in the highest form, that is in the form of system. Between system and Dionysus stands an absolutization of the Apollonian imperative, it would seem. Again, the Hegelian system seems to throw its order over things in a totalizing manner. No region of being seems to be exempt from its imperious sway. The ambition of the system seems exhausted only before the totality. Does not Hegel attempt to encompass the entirety of history as essential stages of a dialectical progress? More pointedly for present purposes, does he not subordinate art to philosophy? All these points are interpreted by critics of Hegel as showing forth the will to power in its most exalted and extremist form. The suspicion seems to be confirmed when Hegel implies that with him philosophy comes to a completion or an insurpassable closure. As I have implied before and will indicate again later, I believe that a more "open" reading of Hegel is possible. Nevertheless, the above account is perhaps the received, I almost said, frozen picture of Hegel. Given this, and given Hegel's purported propensity to ensnare himself in every trap that the Nietzschean heritage claims to expose, what great thinker seems more ripe for deconstruction?

Identity, Difference and Deconstruction

Before we come to this question, we now need to state as succinctly as possible what is involved in deconstruction itself, given the guidelines of our historical remarks. We can summarize what is at stake here by confining ourselves to four main points: firstly, concerning the nature of language; secondly, concerning the character of critical analysis; thirdly, concerning the limitations of the univocal ideal; fourthly, concerning the inescapability of the equivocal. As I said at the outset, the issue of dialectic has to do with the question of the teleological thrust of articulation. As will be seen from these four main points, deconstruction is also inextricably tied up with the nature of articulation. Indeed aspects of the issue have echoes which go back to ancient dialectic, to Aristotle's view that being is not univocal but spoken in manifold senses, to the medieval question whether human language about the divine, man's articulation of the ultimate is more than univocal or equivocal.

First, deconstruction is a critical strategy consonant with a particular interpretation of language. On this interpretation language functions as an autonomous power. Thus, following Heidegger, deconstructionists are often fond of saying that man does not think with language, rather language thinks with and through man. Through this autonomous power more is meant than any particular speaker intends. Likewise, more is contained in language than any particular interpretation can comprehend. Every effort to pin down the strict meaning of language runs against a limit of failure. As Derrida puts it: the field of language lacks a center; rather language is defined by a free play of substitutions.[21] Language is an endless "dissemination" of itself, a diversification without absolute integration, a plurality of elusive signs that cannot be encapsulated within an encompassing totality. Consequently, in the interpretation of literary texts, there is no one definitive meaning which one definitive interpretation can exhaustively articulate. Indeed the inexhaustibility of language, should we be attentive to it, invariably presents us with a recalcitrance, an impasse, an *aporia*, a breakdown we cannot transcend. Any reading of a text which intends to be an *absolute* reading is not only a misinterpretation of language in its free play. Any absolute reading is an impossibility.

This is related to our second point: deconstruction as a strategy of critical analysis. For the naive temptation of the reader is precisely to think that his reading of language has, in fact, genuinely succeeded in its grasp of meaning. Deconstruction, by contrast, is a technique for disillusioning the reader with regard to this naive faith. The "naive" reader, trusting the surface of language, erects his partial interpretation into a total interpretation. Deconstruction exposes or attempts to expose, the partiality of the partial, not by itself giving an absolute reading, but by attempting to show that no absolute reading at all is possible. On the positive side, the intention is to return the interpreting reader to the text, open to it, as it were, more humbly in his disillusion. It is important to reiterate that deconstruction is a strategy of *analysis*, albeit a form of subversive analysis. What "analysis" does is to confront an initially complex phenomenon which we tend to think we have mastered. In setting out more explicitly the elements of its complexity, this faith in our mastery is questioned and undermined. By "taking apart," "breaking down," the spontaneous and naive response, we open up this complexity in what seems to be its inherent richness. The poetic work especially lends itself to the revelation of this inherent richness of language.

This inherent richness might be granted by many who do not practise deconstructive strategies, and so might seem innocuous. However, it is in relation to the limits of the univocal ideal, our third point, that the deconstructionist attempts to specify the peculiarities of this richness, and this tends to produce a reversal of this richness into poverty. For deconstruction, the univocal ideal of language, said to be intimately lodged in the logocentrism of western metaphysics, is what primarily bars the interpreting consciousness from freely entering the Aladdin's cave of language. Logocentrism, univocity are ingrained so deeply in the texture of western consciousness, that it is all but impossible to acknowledge its presence. The univocal sense, logocentrism, works through us, ferments in the western mind, like a Heideggerian destiny. Our interpreting powers are determined in that direction, and only by a kind of hermeneutical wrench — the violent interpretation of deconstruction itself — can we free ourselves, or if not free ourselves at least become self-conscious, of this pervasive orientation. Even the deconstructionist himself does not claim complete liberty from this determination of the mind. As himself a product of the history of a western metaphysics, the logocentric ideal nests also in his own involvements with language.

The bewitching spell of univocal logocentrism, nevertheless, can be partly dispelled through deconstructive analysis. Univocal language, if subject to close scrutiny, will invariably show its limitations, and moreover let this limitation emerge from within language itself. This brings us to our fourth point: the inescapability of the equivocal.[22] For if treated with deconstructive analysis, univocal language shows itself to contain an entire world of ambiguities, and ambivalences. The univocal word seems to have one meaning and one only. But it often hides a plurality of meanings, some of which are antagonistic and contradictory. The univocal word, the deconstructionist indicates, is a word divided against itself, and against other words. The Apollonian surface of calm, unitary significance yields to a Dionysian tumult of warring words. Again, also reminiscent of the Nietzschean-Heideggerian critique of metaphysics, the deconstructive critic is a virtuoso at discovering in language hidden polarities and oppositions, inversions and reversals, doublings and mirrorings. Indeed, the impression is often created that the poem, say, becomes a disconcerting hall of distorting mirrors; we have nothing but a plurality of images without a fixed or stable original. There is no original — no author, or fixed subject that can be solidly represented, no final, finalizing representation that will restore all to stability. We have the scattering of images, related and unrelated, one image developing into another image, another distorting and subverting the first, an incessant flux of metaphors in ceaseless transformation and reversal.[23]

Difference, sheer difference, or multiplicity without an enjoining unity, is the keynote of this world. In this case sheer difference means the reduction of univocity to the equivocal. Univocity reduces the differences of multiple meanings to one central, determinate sense. Equivocity scatters again this one central meaning into a multiplicity without center or unity. Since, as Derrida says, the field of discourse lacks any center, deconstruction must aim to bring home to us this lack. It does so, one is tempted to say, by satiating us with an excess of equivocations. This may seem perverse to those supped on the more sparse economy of univocity. But this is the deconstructionist's whole point: it is the inherent intricacy of language itself that throws up this equivocal fare.

Identity, Difference and Dialectic

We now turn to Hegel's dialectic, again confining ourselves to those points relevant to the issue of deconstruction. The suggestion here is that many of the themes implicit in the strategy of deconstruction are articulated in Hegel's view of dialectic. Indeed both display close affinities, even if in the final analysis, as we shall see, they diverge in response to the crucial question of the wholeness of the art work. This divergence we will take up in the concluding section.

What then is dialectic? Dialectic is a major and wide-ranging concept, meaning a number of things to different thinkers. However, one theme seems fairly constant: namely, that dialectic has something to do with *conflict*. This we find, to name just some instances, in the conflict of opinions in Socratic dialectic, in the disputations of the Medieval Schools concerning controversial questions, in Kant's antinomies of *Verstand*, in Marx's class war. This theme of "conflict," "antithesis," "opposition," we also discover in deconstruction's emphasis on the equivocal.

The theme is central also to Hegel, tied up with the fact that for Hegel dialectic has to do with the principle of articulation itself. In Hegel, the process of articulation involves reference both to the character of the real and man's own linguistic acts. Dialectic is something both in the order of thinking, or "logical," and in the order of Being or "ontological."[24] What flows from this? Immediately dialectic situates us in a world of process or Becoming. And at least on this preliminary count, the Hegelian world is not unrelated to the universe of Nietzsche. We cannot fix the real into frozen form, or congeal it into lifeless substance. We are greeted by a world in development in which dynamism, to recall previous terms, is a dominating dimension. The difference, however, from Nietzschean becoming is that this dynamism for Hegel cannot be characterized in terms of formless flux. It rather reveals itself essentially as an active process of forming, formation, rather than formless flux or frozen form. For Nietzsche becoming tends to be devoid of *inherent* structure, as when he speaks of the world as a monster of energy[25]; structure tends to be a comforting, necessary grid that *we* humans throw over chaos. With Hegel becoming is inherently a process of structuring, a self-structuring, again in a fully active sense. Dialectic is the principle of the articulation of this structuring. Hence dialectic from the outset implicates the notion of dynamic structuring, as if the energy of Dionysus were ultimately indistinguishable from the process of Apollonian formation, the first driving the process, the second giving this process shape, but the process itself being neither one nor the other but *always both*.

In addition, dialectic is related to the principle of articulation inherent in language itself. This is perhaps where Hegel's affinity with the deconstructionist most comes out. For Hegel, language at its richest is dialectical, but to hold this view entails some subordination of the normal logic of univocal propositions. In formal logic, a proposition ought to articulate a state of affairs in a manner which clearly separates it from its opposite state. A and not-A are mutually exclusive. As a linguistic unit, a proposition ought to have one definite meaning. And should we affirm this one meaning, we exclude the possible affirmation of the opposite. Hegel's dissatisfaction with this exclusionary logic follows from his view of the nature of being as Becoming. If the real is in process, its articulation cannot be fixed to one frozen form. What we find instead is a process in which a thing in time becomes *other* to its former shape, while yet in this process of differentiation remaining itself. Butler, canonizing the metaphysics of common sense, held: Everything is itself and not another. For Hegel, everything is itself and also other. Put somewhat differently: everything has some determinate identity — here Hegel would agree with Butler. But this identity is complex and defined by an inherent process of differentiation. This process of differentiation makes it differ from itself as a simple identity, to become other than such (a similarity with Derrida's *différance* strikes one on this point). Reality in becoming is both itself and not fully itself, and the process of articulation moves towards the fullest determination of what the thing can become but is not yet. To do adequate justice in articulate language to these developments and transformations inherent in becoming, language must itself become more fluid.[26] The notion of univocal propositions fixes language into an excessively rigid norm, fostering the exclusionary mentality of the "either/or" rather than the inclusionary perspective of "both/and." To comprehend, to embrace the structuring process of becoming, the articulation of language must approach this latter possibility or itself become dialectical.

We can develop the point further if we remind ourselves that dialectic implies that an excessive reliance on univocity, if left to its own devices, tends to break down. We can put the point in terms of Hegel's understanding of *Verstand*. *Verstand*, the analytical understanding, tends to abstract from the flux of immediate sense experience, with the aim of stabilizing and differentiating this flux. Its aim is to differentiate, discriminate this flow, but it does so by asserting definite and fast distinctions. It abstracts but also separates, and so introduces some degree of structure, form, into the initial promiscuous tangle of experience. We might think that this analytical separation exhausts the work of reason, but this is not so for Hegel. The clarity and discrimination born of abstraction and analysis is a gain but it is also incomplete. In fact, what the analytical understanding fixes into hard and rigid separation, dialectic, or the continuing flow of articulation, tends to break down again. One of the chief advances of Kant's philosophy, Hegel thought, was to show just this: *Verstand* marches itself towards a series of fundamental antinomies or contradictions that it cannot resolve on its own resources. Put in the terms of the present discussion, fixed univocity deconstructs its own rigidity, and ends in a situation of antithesis and ambiguity which *Verstand* mistakenly believed it had completely overcome. The equivocal returns. For through univocity the analytical understanding tries to conquer a given equivocation; but its conquering categories are themselves conquered by equivocation on the *other side* of the established univocity. Dialectic, for Hegel, simply follows the flow of this development by which an initial unity, seemingly simple and hard set, breaks itself up into polarities, contradictions, antitheses, oppositions.[27]

The comparison with deconstruction is striking. Thinking makes war upon itself.[28] It generates itself and drives itself forward by contradicting itself, creating itself anew out of the destruction of its own previous, partial forms. Indeed, Hegel insistently uses the language of "negativity" to bring forth this dismantling side of dialectic. In fact, it is for such reasons that Hegel incorporates the sceptical principle as an essential ingredient in all genuine philosophical thought. The sceptical principle, particularly as found in ancient, "noble" scepticism, we might say, confronts the experience of "nothingness."[29] Everything we try to affirm with absolute fixity falls in time. Its fixity dissolves and comes to nothing. Thus Hegel's *Phenomenology of Spirit* can be seen as an extraordinarily complex, all but epic working out of this sceptical negativity of the dialectic. Here Hegel warns us that we must stare the negative in the face.[30] And in the *Phenomenology* we discover consciousness trying to assert itself with complete certainty in a plurality of different forms, each of which it tries to fix as absolute. None proves absolute, each form breaks up out of its own inherent tension or strain. Each configuration (*Gestalt*) of consciousness disfigures itself, each form deforms itself, every construction deconstructs itself under the relentless power of the "negative."

Opposition, antithesis, then, is unavoidable in every effort to posit or fix a unity. War is the father of all things, Heraclitus says. The negativity of dialectic, for Hegel, is generative of the process which contructs the forms of reality, or of consciousness, or of language, but it is also what deconstructs such forms in their partiality or limitation. For such reasons, perhaps, Hegel in his *Logic*[31] explicitly praises the German language for containing words capable of directly contrary meanings. This is no index of the German language as a seat of confusion. It is rather a measure of its positive, embracing power. It articulates itself dialectically. As Hegel implies in his famous discussion of the *Speculative Satz* in the *Phenomenology*,[32] the normal propositional form is not completely adequate to articulate philosophical truth in the fullest measure. Richer language, language which contains a whole world within itself, a world inclusive of opposites, is required. The dialectical language of Hegel's own philosophical discourse is his effort to live up to this requirement.

Granting these comparisons with deconstruction, we now come to the further point concerning dialectic. Put most briefly, the power of negativity does not completely exhaust the process of articulation, but rather is itself completed by its balancing positive. At the heart of the "negative" we must affirm a positive. For Hegel reason in its negative dialectic flows into reason as speculative, or reason in its richest positive power.[33] The process of dissolving, of negating, is itself only possible on the condition of something that must be described in positive terms. The confrontation with the negative releases a positive power itself not capable of being characterized in negative terms alone. For Hegel, after deconstruction, dialectic opens up to a moment of reconstitution. This is perhaps most explicit in Hegel's notion of *Aufhebung*: something or some position is negated or cancelled; we transcend that something or position in this act of cancelling; but in that act of surpassing, what is cancelled is also preserved, contained as a necessary condition of the transcending move. *Aufhebung* entails the three dimensions of negation, transcendence and preservation. The limitation from which dialectic frees us, also binds us to it, as a necessary condition without which the fuller release would be impossible, and so as something which we must *newly affirm* from the standpoint of the liberation. In more popular terms, terms which Hegel himself did not employ, the breakdown of the thesis and its simplicity by its antithesis points further again to the synthesis of these two previous antagonists.

This emphasis upon a dialectical *Aufhebung* or more embracing synthesis distinguishes Hegel's dialectic from deconstruction. Both concede the breakdown of the simple unities of univocity; for univocity yields a simple identity without inherent differentiation or complexity. Both trace the process of antithesis emerging from such simple unities. But the deconstructionist interprets such antithesis as sheer difference or equivocation — opposition without unifying meaning. Difference dissolves identity. Hegel, by contrast, interprets the difference dialectically, not equivocally — this involves the claim that the many opposites are in fact capable of being held together, not indeed in any univocal unity, for that is impossible, but in a complex unity immanently differentiated, a dialectical unity. Equivocal difference dissolves univocal unity, but for this "dialectical identity" there is a reintegration of these differences beyond sheer equivocation. We are capable of thinking of the "togetherness" of these differences, of embracing a unity of opposites. Equivocal differences may dissolve

univocal identity, but a dialectical unity seeks to embrace equivocation and go positively beyond its negating, dissolving power. Hence
Hegel gives as a definition of the Absolute: the identity of identity
and difference. That is, there is a complex unity, a dialectical identity
which embraces both univocal unity and equivocal differences. This
unity is absolute because it is *absolving*, freeing, not just dissolving. It
absolves us, as it were, from the sense of difference as sheer hostile
opposition, the animosity of the mutually negating dualisms said to
beset the western tradition.

To summarize then: the process of articulation for Hegel does not
just form and deform, construct and deconstruct. It reforms and
reconstructs. It reintegrates into its fuller developments the partial
articulations it has previously surpassed. Indeed, it is this reintegration which gives discourse its inherent density, its immanent intricacy, its rich and compacted fullness. Like the deconstructionist, the
dialectician may point to this "overdetermined" wealth of discourse,
but to interpret this wealth in terms of the equivocal is to fall radically
short. It must be interpreted in a manner transcending the univocal,
but also on the other side of equivocalness. A dialectical interpretation is one such interpretation which tries to do justice to the rich
ambiguity of language without allowing this ambiguity to fall away
into the sheerly equivocal. Reverting to Nietzschean images,
dynamism and form, Dionysus and Apollo, need not be mutually
exclusive opposites, but rather form emerges dialectically from
dynamism, harnessing its power but not necessarily stifling it, shaping
its discordant strains into a new whole.[34] Form need not be superimposed by the violence of an extraneous force. It comes to articulation
immanently out of the originally undeveloped dynamism; genuine
form is the articulation of the original dynamism. Without this the
original energy would be dissipated without outcome. Through the
process of dialectical formation the original dynamism is shaped and
set forth into its different stages and gathered together into a rich
whole.

Dialectic, Art and Wholeness

Let me now make some remarks concerning the upshot of this
philosophical discussion, in its bearing on the art work. My sugges-

tion is that the dialectical way represents an approach to the art work which preserves what I have called the principle of wholeness, while not necessitating us to discard the deep complexities and polarities disclosed by deconstruction. As should be clear, dialectic points further than its own negativity to a reconstitution within a whole of the separated and sometimes opposed parts. While deconstruction does awaken us often to the latter, thus disturbing our easy sense of the familiar simple unity of the art work, dialectic represents a desire to do justice to a more complex sense of unity. Undoubtedly the deconstructionist tends to repudiate such a unity, and so also repudiates what he claims is the Hegelian effort to bring the work to a closure. The matter is not so simple, however. First we have to ask: does a great art work communicate to the reader something of the experience of complex wholeness? In answer it must be said that what frequently draws us to the work is the anticipation that this will be so. Experience of the art work does often confirm this expectation, in opening consciousness to the experience of a dense and compacted fullness. Second we need to ask: granted the possibility of its occurrence, how are we to make intelligible the experience of this rich wholeness? The dialectical approach is one such way. The deconstructionist way, while feeding on the compacted fullness of the work, risks finishing with a plurality of equivocations without connections. The suspicion arises that the art work in its integrity has disintegrated or even vanished in the process. Instead of the full compacted presence we are left with the trace of an absence.[35] One grows uneasy precisely because this outcome, while it wrenches us out of a too-dulled familiarity, seems sometimes to be at odds with our experience of encountering the art work.

Put differently, the deconstructionist begins with a poem, say, having it seems a certain unity, presenting itself as something marked by a significant synthesis of experience. Deconstruction analyses this unity or synthesis, and discovers it riddled with contraries, oppositions and so on. Dialectic does exactly the same. But where deconstruction seems to give us analysis without synthesis, dialectic insists that we return again to the original synthesis, now with the enrichment of having passed through the analysis. As a strategy of criticism, deconstruction has difficulty in making intelligible the possibility of this original synthesis. As a critical practice, it rouses the suspicion that this original synthesis is simply dissolved. Dialectic, by contrast, allows the strain toward dissolution in every synthesis, but the given experience of the synthesis indicates that contraries are already contained within this original unity. The art work itself is already a dialectical whole, already a unity of opposites within itself, regardless of how we subsequently analyze and take apart its constituent elements. Our subsequent interpretation of it must do justice to both the inherence of opposites within it and its wholeness.

Having analyzed the original unity into its inherent oppositions, the deconstructionist then goes on in practice to deny the possibility of bringing together these oppositions. But such an analysis merely denies its own starting point. Opposition within the art work is not an absolute exclusion; the art work is already a significant *relation* of polarities in tension, a coupling of opposites which are now no longer merely dualized. As Hegel argues throughout his *Aesthetics*, and as we have discussed it variously in previous chapters, the art work is original aesthetic testimony to the significant *togetherness* of these poles in tension. Deconstruction sounds extraordinarily like *Verstand*, or the analytical understanding, gone to equivocation: the polarities are frozen into hard and fixed opposites, and of course, as such they cannot be brought together. But the dynamic fact of the art work already denies this fixation into irreconcilable opposition. The art work as an original unity is already such a movement towards reconciliation, however partial. The dialectical approach, granting the original synthesis and the inherent differentiation of the art work simply traces the process of this movement.

What is at issue here is the appropriate balance between analysis and synthesis. Without proper synthesis, analysis is unbalanced towards sheerly decomposing thought. The original whole dissolves into a deconstruction of the parts of the parts .... But to analyze something so intricate and dense, we must first recognize or identify that something as a whole. Such an act of recognition or identification is not itself an instance of analysis. Something about the art work seems to remain *recalcitrant* to deconstruction as critical analysis. It is an old platitude that the whole is greater than the sum of the parts. Analysis or deconstruction alone cannot tell us what this "more" is, though they can illumine us about the complexity of the parts. Inevitably the feeling surfaces that something essential has been missed, that deconstruction itself represses our experience of this "more," our experience of concrete present wholeness. Obviously we need not entirely jettison deconstructive analysis. What we do require, however, is its balance with a synthetic thinking, not merely deconstructive. Dialectical thinking, I have claimed, represents an attempt to provide such a balance.

One of the fears of the deconstructionist, however, is that the Hegelian insistence on synthesis *closes off* our experience of the art work. Fear of closure is pervasive throughout their writings. My account of dialectic need not turn it into such a prison. Dialectic itself is perhaps capable of a double interpretation, one tending to closure, the other more openended. For dialectical thinking can be seen as either grasping or *encapsulating* the *structure* of a process of becoming, or creation. Or it might be seen as *participating* itself in the active *structuring* of such a process. The former side tends to lend itself to closure, the latter need not. And it is the latter, I believe, which reveals more about the links beween dialectic and dynamism, as spoken of above. On this interpretation, dialectic *moves with* the dynamic process of structuring itself, in both its deconstructing and constructing moments. We might venture that Hegel, like dialectic itself, contains a "double" within his thought, reveals himself as open to a double reading. Indeed, the present chapter might be seen as contributing to a positive "deconstruction" of the deconstructionist's often too closed and fixed view of Hegel. Hegel, on this double reading, turns out to reveal an inherent complexity more challenging than the picture of the stock logician who tries to devour everything in the empty unity of abstract concepts. The "open" Hegel demands that even Hegel's Absolute not be seen as this empty conceptual unity of totalitarian thought. As above implied, the Absolute might be seen as *absolving*, as releasing rather than *dissolving* or *enclosing*.

When Hegel places art in Absolute Spirit, it is to this ultimately releasing wholeness that I think he points. As I have argued before, wholeness need not be closure but may be "open." An "open" wholeness may seem like a contradication in terms, a violent yoking together of absolutely heterogeneous categories: an impossibility in formal logic. But aesthetic experience brings home to us the possibility of such a seemingly absurd coincidence of opposites. The inexhaustibility of the art work reveals just one expression of such "open" wholeness. Hegel's dialectical aesthetics simply represents an effort to acknowledge this and render it intelligible. The deconstructionist sometimes strikes one as uneasily juxtaposing the sensitivity of the aesthete with the virtuosity of a kind of formal, logical analyst. We are reminded of Schlegel's characterization of Romantic Irony as mingling *clear consciousness* with a sense of infinitely rich *chaos*.[36] The deconstructionist plays with this infinite chaos in Nietzschean fashion with a clarity of consciousness almost Cartesian. Not surprisingly, we sometimes find the deconstructionist speaking about oscillating between nihilism and logocentrism.[37] Hegel, however, is neither a Platonist or Cartesian (logocentrism) nor yet a Nietzschean (nihilism),[38] neither freezing the form nor dissolving all form. Form is in motion, fluid and dynamic: not just static form, nor sheer process, but the formation process itself. There is, I believe, a world of a difference between an infinitely rich chaos and an infinite richness. This reference to Romantic Irony is not fortuitous since Hegel derides the ultimate emptiness of its negativity, while relentlessly excoriating Schlegel.[39] To return to the "open" wholeness of the art work, its inexhaustibility, its infinite richness rather than infinitely rich chaos, we must take a step beyond negativity, and in Hegel's phrase, reminiscent of the critic's effort to "deconstruct deconstruction,"[40] we must "negate the negation."

Of course, the deconstructionist sense of negativity is connected with the many obstacles that stand in the way of affirming any ideal of wholeness in the modern era.[41] To properly deal with Hegel's efforts to defend the ideal of wholeness requires us to openly acknowledge the recalcitrance of these obstacles. Hegel, in fact, is one of the most searching critics of the forces in modernity that often work against any ideal of aesthetic wholeness. Because of these countering forces, the temptation is sometimes simply to jettison the ideal. Hegel's response, based on an unblinking awareness of the fragmenting forces of modernity, amounts to something more. Already in his own time, Hegel discerned the dissolving strains at work in modern aesthetic culture, strains that sometimes sound very similar to more contemporary forms of aesthetic scepticism. Hegel's aesthetics, like his philosophy generally, though unblinking when it sees the negative, always tries to advance further towards the possibility of some affirmation. This, as we have seen in the present chapter, is a reflection of what Hegel's thinks of as the teleology of dialectic. In traditional aesthetics the central concept that has articulated the teleology of the aesthetic has been the notion of the beautiful. Hegel's aesthetics also contains a complex affirmation of the beautiful. Granting Hegel's clear consciousness of the fragmenting forces of modernity, let us now look at Hegel's further advance towards the ideal of aesthetic wholeness in relation to this question of the beautiful.

Chapter Six

Beauty and the Aesthetic Dilemma of Modernity

Beauty and the Absolute

In this concluding chapter I propose to undertake a final exploration of our theme of art and the absolute in terms of the significance of Hegel's concept of the beautiful. A number of reasons can be offered for thus focussing on the beautiful, all of which will be examined in more detail later, but which it would be helpful here to outline in advance. Reflection on the beautiful is a justified aesthetic theme in itself, if indeed it is not the major theme in the history of aesthetics. Yet it can also be seen to facilitate some summation, some gathering up of the substantive themes centering on art and the absolute in Hegel's aesthetics. First, while calling to mind the essential motif of classical, Greek aesthetics, Hegel's concept of the beautiful is firmly placed in the modern problematic of the expressive artistic self and art's positive, creative power (themes discussed in Chapters One and Three). Second, the concept of the beautiful is ultimately related to the issue of art's metaphysical concreteness (the theme of Chapter Two). Third, beauty helps us to make further sense of art's effort to sensuously concretize man's sense of absoluteness and ultimacy (the issue of Chapter Three). Fourth, beauty relates to the concept of art's open wholeness and its synthetic power to accept and include within itself the divisive forces of complex dualisms (issues touched on especially in Chapters Four and Five).

103

Finally, the concept of beauty in Hegel cannot be abstracted from the religious motif of making sense of evil, man's experience of suffering, death, the negative — well recognized by Hegel in all its devastating power. Nor can it be separated from the religious and philosophical motif in Hegel's thought of affirming the worth of what is, the ultimate value of the actual itself. Indeed, here we might suggest that Hegel's aesthetics is in many aspects a peculiar theodicy, a theodicy which through art stresses the actual manifestness of *Geist* through the significant sensuousness of beauty. Hegel's own philosophy of history, explicitly put forward by him as a theodicy in the face of the "slaughterbench" of history, reveals many characteristics of an aesthetic theodicy, that is, one which affirms the beauty of this world as a concretion of the harmony of the whole. What these ideas mean in detail we must analyse below. Yet it is clear from this initial, cursory review that they cluster around our concern with art and the absolute.

To treat of beauty's place in this cluster of ideas in some orderly way, it may be helpful if we proceed in the following stages. First, I propose to look at the ambiguous position of beauty for Hegel and his era, how beauty evoked both enthusiasm and scepticism. Second, we need to remind ourselves of what is generally involved in what we might call the eclipse of beauty in the contemporary aesthetic landscape — an eclipse not unrelated to the absence of the absolute previously discussed in relation to deconstruction. Third, we might give some account of certain key features of the ancient and more modern approaches to beauty, approaches I will summarize under the titles of Platonic and Kantian aesthetics. We must do this in order to make sense of Hegel's aesthetics as trying to render justice to both sides, as he tries to embrace together each approach in its different, often complementary strengths.

Fourth, I propose to explicate Hegel's affirmation of the classical ideal of beauty in the context of his acknowledgement of the problematic of the modern self, be it Christian or secular Romantic, indeed be it "post-Christian," "post-Romantic." In fact, Hegel's aesthetics of beauty is not irrelevant to the so-called "postmodern" self. Hegel is as much postmodern as pre-modern, not by any repudiation of the modernist way, but by his philosophical grappling with the deepest perplexities and most estranging contradictions of that way. Here I want to anchor my remarks in a contrast between Hegel's notion of beauty and that of Aquinas. Fifth, this contrast will suggest to us this fruitful possibility for understanding a very crucial characteristic about beauty, namely, that beauty is not an abstract universal in a normal sense, nor yet is it just reducible to sensuous pleasure in the more ordinary hedonistic sense. As Hegel repeatedly insists, it is both sensuous and supersensuous, universal yet not abstract. It pleases with more than "pathological" passion, yet its universality is not just the formalistic universality of Kant's aesthetic beauty.[1] The suggestion here again is that beauty is what Hegel calls a concrete universal, and that, moreover, beauty as a concrete universal bears some important resemblances to beauty considered as a transcendental concept in the Aristotelian-Thomist tradition. These important likenesses shed further significant light on the metaphysical concreteness of art and beauty.

Sixth, this notion of beauty as a concrete universal or a transcendental concept leads us to consider in what sense Hegel's teaching on beauty constitutes equally an aesthetic theodicy and a theodicy of the aesthetical. In this regard we need to raise what we might call the theme of transfiguration, namely the power of idealization embodied by beauty, especially in relation to man's experience of estrangement from being, here articulated in the aesthetic guise of the ugly. The ugly provides us with the aesthetic counterpart to the religious and ethical problem of evil. It helps us once again to consider Hegel's relevance to the modern, or postmodern experience of alienation and fragmentation, Hegel's relevance (again to exploit explicitly aesthetic terms) to contemporary man's encounter with "the noise of the world" in contradistinction to ancient man's intent to attune himself to "the music of the spheres."[2]

Finally, I would like to conclude with the theme of the future of beauty. The future, in whatever form, is always problematical in Hegel's thought. Here we must ask if his aesthetics of the beautiful keeps the door ajar to the possibility of some contemporary affirmation. We need not deny perhaps a certain nostalgia, say, for the beauty of the Greeks in Hegel, as with so many others in his time. Nietzsche remarks that German Idealism and Romanticism might be understood as a tremendous homesickness for the Greeks.[3] And often, we must grant, we can detect a plaintive note of elegy sounding throughout Hegel's aesthetics of the beautiful. But as is so often with Hegel's circular thought, philosophical thinking whose end tends to return us again to the beginning, articulated now more explicitly, perhaps Hegel's nostalgia for the Greeks and his elegy of beauty gone by have something to tell us now of our great need for future beauty? Certainly with the younger Hegel nostalgia for Greek beauty was a dream feeding the hope of a future creation. The dreams of the youth are dimmed, no doubt, in the older Hegel, a cause for scandal among some Left-Hegelians who shift their Hegelian dreaming from aesthetics to politics. Yet here I think it is highly significant that Hegel spent much care in his later years on his *Lectures on Aesthetics*, drawing not only on his philosophical maturity but reminding us again of the continuity of his philosophical concerns from youth onward, with art and beauty and their importance for the whole. Whatever else, Hegel's articulation of past beauty stands as some philosophical justification of an aesthetic exemplar, and exemplars are never completely refuted by the fact that they are not now realized, or perhaps may never be again.

The Ambiguity of Beauty for Hegel and his Era: Enthusiasm and Scepticism

It is an issue well-rehearsed in the thought and general culture of Hegel's time that the modern age has not always provided fertile soil wherein the classical, Greek ideal of beauty might take root. Hegel's own time experienced the ambiguity of beauty, indeed prefigured its eclipse, in its own intense way. This ambiguity is related to the key issues of modernity. For it is related to the sense of fragmentation and division of modern man, for whom work has become an excessively specialized function; for whom religion often has been so inwardized and privatized as to be divorced from the full social life of a substantial community; for whom social life itself has been fractured into the atomized individuals whose ties in the aggregate collective are merely external relations; modern man for whom reason has been turned into a calculative instrument divorced from the deeper spiritual and vital sources of the whole self; modern man whose practical life tends to be so dominated by utilitarian norms that art and beauty become idle luxuries or useless adornments in the merely aesthetic sense. All these features of modernity bespeak a life of disunion and hence a life at odds with the classical ideal of beauty with its strong insistence on the requirements of unity, harmony and wholeness, whether it be in the relationship between reason and the nonrational, between practise and theoretical ideals, between the sacred and the profane, between work and leisure, or in the bond between the individual and his society. This catalogue of disunities, of course, merely mirrors Hegel's own diagnosis of the malaise of modernity. Obviously Hegel was not alone in his diagnosis. Yet in his many writings the different strands of the problem are laid bare with remarkable thoroughness.[4]

What is important first to emphasize here, however, is the extent to which the ideal of beauty was proposed as an essential countercase to modernity's malaise. The ills of the time were granted but without the fall into surrender. Fragmentation constitutes estrangement itself; it is not cause for celebration, as if disunion, as seems to be the case with some contemporaries, were coincident with a certain liberation. The counsel of Horace was taken to heart:

Vos exemplaria Graeca
Nocturna versate manu, versate diurna

The Greek world itself was often identified with this ideal of exemplary beauty, the aesthetic countercase of wholeness to the splintered spirit of modernity. Following the lead of Winckelmann, an idealized Greece was articulated, a Greece youthful and athletic, at once both innocent and spiritual in the realm of the sensuous; as, say, seems to be evidenced in their representations of the nude body, where we find a celebration, without guilt, of something sensuous yet significant. The Greeks were the *aesthetic* people par excellence, a people for whom beauty was the centre and crown of life. Hölderlin in this vein speaks of Greece as *Ein Reich der Kunst*.[5] He gives further testimony to the provocative power of the Greeks in referring to the "devastating glory of the Greeks" — devastating in the way an idealized exemplar shows up what was felt to be the aesthetic poverty of the present.[6] Hegel himself gives expression to a similar ideal in his youthful paean to the Greeks: "In everything great, beautiful, noble, and free they are so far our superiors that we can hardly make them our examples but must rather look up to them as a different species at whose achievements we can only marvel."[7] As Hatfield reminds us in his discussion on Winckelmann and the myth of Greece:

> From Winckelmann to Rilke, from Goethe to George, the majority of the the greatest German writers have been "Hellenists" to some significant degree. It is as if Goethe's successors had taken very seriously his admonition that everyone should be a Greek in his own way. "Jeder sei auf seine Art ein Grieche, aber er sei's."[8]

Hegel's *Lectures on Aesthetics* acknowledge their own debt to the heritage of Winckelmann, and elsewhere his discussion of *Kunstreligion* in the *Phenomenology* must be seen, in some measure, as a continuing reflection of that same tradition.

It must be granted that the spell of Greece, apart from all questions of historical, factual accuracy, was not an impotent, anemic aesthetic ideal. Nostalgia for an idealized exemplar here proved to be a spur to creative undertaking, and the results in German literature (as indeed in English literature with, say, Keats and Shelley) must be deemed impressive. It is not the case, of course, that there existed simply a naive enthusiasm for the ideal, uncurbed by the recalcitrance of present realities. Herder, for instance, is instructive here. While Herder realized the importance of Greek mythology as a perfected work of art, as "the sensuous part of religion," indeed seeing Greek statues as perhaps the most beautiful symbols of fully achieved *Humanität*, still this Greek mythology and the Hellenic *paidea* are now dead. Perhaps in one sense Greek sculpture is beyond history in providing a kind of archetype or norm of human history, an aesthetic concretion of the spirit of *Humanität*. The limit of this aesthetic ideal is, for Herder however, just its suitability for the innocence of youth. Every flower, even the most beautiful, fades. For Herder the Greeks became what they could become, and so should be read by us while young. Herder's historical scepticism, added to his sense of conflict between aesthetic Hellenism and the ethical requirements of Christianity, injected a definite coolness into the ardor of admiration. A complete realization of man required a thoroughgoing reconcilation between the aesthetical and the ethical, a requirement well recognized and strongly articulated also by Schiller.

Other instances in Hegel's time might be cited who voiced some unease with the ideal and the completeness of its contemporary applicability. Heine speaks of an "unhappy hybrid of godhead and stone." Schiller considered it a crucial handicap of contemporary poets that, compared to the Greeks, they suffered from the lack of a living mythology. As a consequence their work is devoid of a necessary center and the resulting aesthetic attitude is impoverished. As should be evident from our previous discussion of art as "aesthetic" and "religious," Hegel would clearly concur, as in fact he does also in the "Earliest System-Programme of German Idealism" and its manifesto call for a new mythology appropriate to a rational age. August Schlegel points to the same problem of the modern lack of belief, and in terms very similar to Hegel's contrast of classical and romantic art he says: "The poetry of the ancients was that of possession, ours is that of longing." Christianity has brought to light something the moderns more fully experience in spirit than did the Greeks, masters of the sensuous, namely, man's relation to the infinite — again a notion that becomes central to Hegel's maturing thought. For Jean Paul, one of Hegel's favorite writers, the Greeks, "this beauty-intoxicated people," *ought not* to be imitated by us. Even the Romans failed and our admiration for their fullness only shows up the poorness of our attainments.

Perhaps the most profound instance of "failure," directly connected to Hegel, is the shattering of Hölderlin in the tension between Greek paganism and Christianity in his tremendous effort to wed together in a perhaps impossible marriage the figures of Christ and Dionysus. Prior to this shattering Hölderlin was already disturbed by the possibility that an undue aestheticism did not hinder the later downfall of Greece, when it lost its sense of the holy, its piety of the whole.[9] And perhaps not unconnected with Hölderlin's shattering, Hegel's own youthful enthusiasm for the Greek aesthetical ideal underwent a tempering with time. Like Hölderlin's own *Erinnerung* of the ancient world, Hegel's admiration sometimes modulates into a kind of melancholy remembering of the stirring possibilities, rather, actualities of a past glory. The melancholy, elegaic note can be heard, for instance, in the well-known words on the passing of Greek *Kunstreligion* in the *Phenomenology*:[10]

> Trust in the eternal laws of the gods had vanished, and the Oracles, which pronounced on particular questions, are dumb. The statues

are now only stones from which the living soul has flown, just as
the hymns are words from which belief has gone. The tables of the
gods provide no spiritual food and drink, and in his games and
festivals man no longer recovers the joyful consciousness of his
unity with the divine. The works of the Muse now lack the power
of the Spirit, for the Spirit has gained its certainty of itself from the
crushing of gods and men. They have become what they are for us
now — beautiful fruit already picked from the tree, which a friendly
Fate has offered us, as a girl might set the fruit before us. It cannot
give us the actual life in which they existed, not the tree that bore
them, not the earth and the elements which constituted their
substance, not the climate which gave them their peculiar character,
nor the cycle of the changing seasons that governed the process of
their growth. So Fate does not restore their world to us along with
the works of antique Art, it gives not the spring and summer of the
ethical life in which they blossomed and ripened, but only the
veiled recollection (*Erinnerung*) of that actual world. Our active
enjoyment of them is therefore not an act of divine worship through
which our consciousness might come to its perfect truth and fulfillment; it is an external activity — the wiping-off of some drops of
rain or specks of dust from these fruits, so to speak . . .

I cite these representative figures of Hegel's era and indicate
something of Hegel's continuity with them to emphasize from the
outset, not just the enthusiasm of the age but more importantly its
profound sophistication in relation to the ideal of beauty. We are not
dealing with the "know nothing" nurturing of a happy illusion. Hegel
and many of the thoughtful minds of his era display a highly
developed self-consciousness, both in relation to the powers of the
beautiful *and* its evident weaknesses. Whenever they do affirm the
beautiful, their affirmation, Hegel's included, is deeply complex,
encompassing as it does some recognition of the negative strands that
must restrain any unbounded, naive enthusiasm.[11] Any serious affirmation of the beautiful must make room for just this proper recognition of such recalcitrant, even ravaging factors. We return more fully
to this issue below in relation to the questions of aesthetic theodicy
and the transfiguration of the ugly. For now we must continue to
develop the ambiguity of the beautiful, since this ambiguity in Hegel's
time moves more insistently towards eclipse in our own.

The lack of a firm, universally compelling religious foundation, the inability to completely surrender to the pagan Greek notion of divinity after almost two millenia of Christianity, the desacralization of nature with the growth of mechanistic science, the advent of historical scepticism regarding the idealized, seamless harmony of the ancients, all of these might easily lead to total disillusion with beauty and the corrosion of all aesthetic ideals. While acutely conscious of these factors, this result did not occur with Hegel and many of his contemporaries. The fragmenting forces of the times might have sealed the death of the ideal. However, with Hegel, as with others, we witness a fighting of the fragmentation, not its celebration or surrender to it. Again it is helpful to remind ourselves of some important representatives of this struggle. Thus when Winckelmann enjoined the imitation of the Greeks, imitation here was not so much intended as the slavish copying of a dead original but rather the creation anew of art in the spirit of the Greeks. Hence imitation of the Greeks in this sense might itself be the hope of an original creation, a hope not entirely unredeemed by the subsequent artistic, indeed philosophical, achievements of German culture. Here we must note that in his *Aesthetics* Hegel himself praises Winckelmann most strongly for opening up something totally new.[12] Notice that Winckelmann is not here assessed by Hegel in terms of the factual truth or historical accuracy of his picture of the ancients. He is rather praised for initiating an aesthetic horizon that is fertile with possibility, an aesthetic perspective that as "opening up" to something new makes space for the future and its creative ventures.

Drawing on the fruitful powers of this perspective, Goethe, Lessing, Schiller all aimed at a new synthesis, each again with some clear consciousness of the tensions between the naturalism of the ancient world, the spiritual dimensions of the Christian era and the *Humanität* of the modern world. Thus also A.W. Schlegel wondered whether, despite the problem of belief in modernity, Greek paganism might be dialectically *aufgehoben*. Reminiscent of Schlegel's universal poetry which includes but transcends the classical, Novalis also hoped for some synthesis of the ancient and the modern, a "Christian Dionysianism" which would be as much a product of the future as of the past. In trying to make good on this hope Hölderlin seems to have been caught in the conflict between Dionysus and Christ. Though he keenly felt the lost unity of modern man, suggesting that perhaps the divine spares modern man because of his weakness, he did expend himself for an all-embracing divine beauty that would unite mankind and nature. Schelling, making up with Hegel and Hölderlin the Tübingen Trinity with their ideal of *hen kai pan* in a new "Church invisible," also felt that philosophy could not turn its back on opposition but must win through to a more absolute, embracing harmony. Opposition may be everywhere manifest; indeed opposition may be necessary to the scheme of things, but opposition is not necessarily final. Beyond the mechanistic science of the modern era and the estrangements it creates between a dead nature and a separated self, "the modern world is ultimately destined to formulate a higher, truly comprehensive unity. Both science and art are moving in that direction, and it is precisely in order that this unity may exist that all oppositions must be made manifest."[13]

What might we say of Hegel himself here, granting his admission, indeed profound analysis of the problematic of modern man? My proposal regarding Hegel here follows the suggestive distinctions Nietzsche later makes between the antiquarian, the monumental and the critical approaches to history.[14] These three can be summarized thus. Monumental history looks to the past to find examples and models not to be found among contemporaries. For it history is punctuated by periodic greatness. The monumental historian is thus no idle tourist rushing through the picture gallery of the past. He rather pauses long at special points to contemplate great things in order to gain sustenance and courage from them. He sees in past greatness the hope of future greatness. History here records the hero not just to record but to inspire to emulation. If heroism were possible once, by contemplating it, it might be possible once again. Antiquarian history, by contrast, expresses not hope for the future but reverence and gratitude for the past. The danger here is that antiquarianism may degenerate into a false worship, a kind of ancestor idolatry: compared to the towering glory of the past, the present is shabby. The result may be a paralysis of the powers of the present. As Nietzsche notes, the antiquarian knows how to preserve life, not how to create it. So indirectly he may undermine the past to which he is devoted, that is he can mummify it. Critical history, in Nietzsche's usage, is willing to turn on the past in the spirit of negation. It would deflate monumental history, showing up the hero as no demi-god, only a flawed mortal with clay feet. Likewise, it would debunk antiquarian reverence, putting a torch to its piety of the past, turning this into a dead spiritless relic in what it thinks is the ashen light of dawn.

How might we apply Nietzsche's threefold distinction to Hegel's aesthetics of the beautiful? While Hegel obviously sympathizes with the powers of criticism to free us from idols, he nevertheless would avoid the danger of unreined criticism, namely that of jubilating in nothing but its own powers of destruction. If criticism is not balanced by something positive, history subsides into a succession of failures: all things that fall deserve to fall and history becomes the history of error. By contrast, the history of beauty, for Hegel, is a history of diverse though linked attainments. Constructive efforts attain their ends in history; time will dissolve them in turn; but the dissolution of the attainment is no absolute repudiation of the previous result. The philosopher turned to history sees the rise and fall, construction and deconstruction in dialectical alternation; but because he sees both, he sees beyond the fall again. For this reason, while one might see some aspects of Hegel's aesthetics of beauty in an antiquarian light, in that we do find in him a kind of piety concerning some attainments of the past, especially the Greeks, there is, I suggest, a large measure of the monumental mode in his approach to the ideal of beauty. The point is already evident in his remarks on Winckelmann above, yet his entire *Aesthetics* might be read as monumental history. Certainly his focus on the hero, the world historical figure in his attitude to history generally reminds us of Nietzsche's notion of the *Übermensch*, placing both beyond the exclusively antiquarian mode. He shares with both Nietzsche and the critical historian the concern to pillory illusory ideals. But more is needed. As we know from his *Encyclopaedia Logic*, Hegel considers the dissolving principle of scepticism to be an essential, though subordinate necessity in the genuine philosophical approach. And as we know from the somewhat melancholy strain in Hegel regarding the pastness of the classical aesthetical ideal, the wounding, corrosive aspect of critical history did clearly strike home with him. Nevertheless, to remain at the level of Nietzsche's critical history would be in Hegel's terms but to reach the stage of negative dialectic, and not to push on to the stage of positive reason, speculative *Vernunft*, with its thrust beyond the dissolving dualisms of negative dialectic towards a synthetic, constructive unity.

The monumental approach to the ideal of beauty here is always marked by such a creative openness to future possibility. Images of already actualized perfection in the history of art, exemplary embodiments of beauty, reveal man's greatness, not just in its pastness but also in its promise, promise once actualized and still serving to inspire the future realization and perfection of human possibility. Once again here with Hegel it can never be a matter of a simple "return to the Greeks," or even of giving ourselves over to the aesthetic with the Dionysiac abandon of a Nietzschean. With Hegel self-consciousness can never go *behind* the sometimes disillusioning results of sceptical criticism; it can only go *beyond* them. Indeed it must go beyond them. The thrust of positive, speculative *Vernunft* in Hegel towards a healing unity that embraces opposition, a *coincidentia oppositorum* that recuperates the spirit after its passage through the harrowing experience of a divisive, sceptical dialectic,[15] is but the rationalized philosophical version of the same exigence for wholeness and unity in every form of experience, including the aesthetic.[16] The ideal of beauty establishes for aesthetic man a genuine *telos* for this basic exigence. If we see the Greeks as providers of exemplary embodiments of such beauty, if we see them as bequeathing to us monumental realizations of this ideal, this need not mean that the Greek achievement necessitates any false closure of beauty's power. We will say more of this below when we attempt to relate beauty to Hegel's recognition of the experience of "infinite grief" in the Christian era, and the secularization of beauty that occurs within the humanistic prose of modernity.

Beauty in Eclipse: Subjectivity in Excess

We have alluded to the seeds of scepticism regarding the ideal of beauty already planted in Hegel's time. Hegel considers it to be one of the hallmarks of the romantic consciousness, essentially possible only after the advent and development of Christianity, that it embarks on an increasing discovery of inward subjectivity and its deepening towards infinity. When we take these two elements together, scepticism about beauty and the infinite abyss of romantic inwardness, we are able to define one of the central difficulties of modern aesthetic subjectivity, if not of modern subjectivity itself. The difficulty has to do with the fact that the infinite inwardness of the subject always seems to outstrip every finite object, every bounded whole. Traditionally beauty was conceived as a harmonious whole, to be taken in, admired by the contemplative survey: the subject found its rest there, since in the harmony of the object some aesthetic equilibrium between the object and the self was established. The restless romantic consciousness in its faustian modernism surpasses and is not satisfied in the peace of such equilibrium. The romantic self does not find the fullness of its own inner requirements reflected and concretized in the limitedness of the external object. It thus tends to float loose of positive anchoring in a rich externality, failing to find itself and its own inner life mirrored in an appropriate "objective correlative," to use the terms of T.S. Eliot. This leads not only to a sense of unease concerning the poverty of externality; it also plants the growing suspicion that inward subjectivity, cut free from any grounding in proper objectivity, is itself doomed to vacuity. Hegel is deeply cognizant of this disjunction between the self and the aesthetic object with the romantic consciousness, and sees in this disjunction the increasing inability of objective beauty to satisfy the full strivings of modern romantic consciousness. An evident representative of this inward turn is Novalis, for instance, when he claims that inward goes the mystic path. In us and nowhere else is eternity with its worlds of the past and the future. For Novalis, in fact, the world itself must be romanticised. The dangers of this inward path are clear, for instance, when Schelling spoke of Novalis as displaying "a frivolity towards things."[17]

The infinite inwardness of human subjectivity is not to be denied for Hegel, yet no merely finite whole seems capable of bringing it to rest. Can beauty then ever maintain its ground in the face of the seemingly inevitable dissolution of objectivity? When romantic consciousness seeks its fullness within itself without proper anchoring in substantial objectivity, one notable result is the Beautiful Soul, *die schöne Seele*. Very clearly Hegel criticized the inner hollowness and outward powerlessness of the Beautiful Soul, both in the *Phenomenology* and in his *Aesthetics*. His contemptuous criticisms of the Beautiful Soul in the aesthetic sphere, of course, also hit the target of exposing the hollowness of all forms of modern subjectivity that remain merely subjective. Nevertheless, in his *Aesthetics* Hegel does distinguish between the *morbid* beautiful soul and the *truly* beautiful soul.[18] The morbid beautiful soul might be seen as the modern consciousness which manifests itself in a restlessness without the possibility of rest, in sheer inner striving without the goal of a gathering, fulfilling *telos*, in a desire so driven to the extreme that desire becomes infected with Kierkegaard's "sickness unto death," namely despair.

In the face of this Hegel still holds out the possibility of a true, genuine beauty. How can this be possible and yet preserve the infinite inwardness of the modern self? It seems it cannot be possible if beauty, in the objective sense, must always be exhausted in finite, limited wholes. True beauty, to satisfy infinite inwardness, must be both objective and yet concretize an infinite richness. Thus true beauty would seem to have to be more than a merely finite whole, but rather a whole that cannot be exhausted in a bounded set of finite predicates. Such a whole would have to be what previously we have called an open whole. And Hegel, we will see, does think there is some resolution to the dilemmas of modern consciousness in beauty as the Ideal, a concrete universal that sensuously embodies infinite *Geist*. In a word, true beauty must stand against the "bad infinity" generated by the infinite restlessness of the romantic consciousness, and so also against the despair about aesthetic wholeness that the "bad infinity" eventually breeds.

It is not to the point here to pose as denouncers of modernity. Its achievements, as are those of modern art, are immense and undeniable. This is a lesson easily learned from Hegel's own positive evaluation of modernity: within its often irrational appearance we can find the constructive workings of reason. Nor after Hegel has beauty been banished without a trace. Yet in the romantic dialectic between aesthetic subjectivity and beautiful objectivity, the moment of aesthetic subjectivity has increasingly tended to predominate, with sometimes disquieting results for beauty. As Jacques Barzun rightly reminds us,[19] romanticism was very much a creative philosophy inspired by great examples from history, not as some of its twentieth century detractors have claimed an impotent nostalgia for a past of perfection that never really existed. Moreover, there is great complexity in the appeals of the romantics to "subjectivity." Their appeals were motivated by more than concern with their own selves: with religion, ethics, politics, society. They did not seek some petty self-realization but struggled, often in the grand manner, their critics might say in too grand a manner, for greatness.

Their strivings here often split two ways: striving to work for man; striving for inner union with the divine. For such reasons the pining inwardness of the Beautiful Soul does not adequately capture the great constructive impulses of romanticism. And it is necessary to insist that these impulses were genuinely constructive in contrast to the essentially levelling effect of the Enlightenment and its primarily critical philosophies. The eighteenth century tended to be a "dissolving" era, while we witness efforts at a real revolution in reconstruction in the early part of the nineteenth century, rather than at its close. However, the creative impulses of romantic consciousness were caught in the dialectical tension between searching subjectivity and grounding objectivity, such that when this tension tilts too much towards subjectivity we discover a movement from the ambiguous affirmation of the beautiful in Hegel's time towards its eclipse in our own. A subjectivity in excess of objectivity tends to win out.[20] And since nothing seems to stand its ground before subjectivity, the modern ego easily becomes infected with the spirit of unbounded suspicion, of "systematic distrust" as Barzun puts it.[21] We witness this impasse of subjectivity very soon after Hegel's death, for instance, with the young Hegelian, Max Stirner, when in elevating his own ego to the absolute, he declares: "All things are as nothing to me."[22]

Yet at the same time, this elevation of the ego to the absolute can suffer a peculiar, paradoxical reversal such that subjectivity itself becomes marked by an ineradicable insecurity. Nothing sustains itself against the strivings of subjectivity, hence nothing reduces the insecurity that drives its incessant strivings. Again as Barzun implies, writing decades ago about a condition we still have not surmounted (as deconstruction makes plain): the insecurity of modern man that nothing allays makes him question whether any mood can sustain itself; if not, "then the ending of *every* lyric in sneers, the petering out of *every* tune in percussion and dissonance, and the decoration of *all* physical beauty with maggots is justified by the twentieth-century world of experience."[23] Even were one to consider this judgment as tending to one-sidedness, it is nevertheless true that out of the insecurity of subjectivity arises the quest for endless novelty and stimulation. The stimulus of the novel, in turn, ministers to a restless consciousness that, in its sense of superiority over the object, very soon becomes bored and jaded. The chase after the shocking and the spuriously original replaces the still contemplation of calm beauty. Again it is instructive to notice how, since Barzun's discussion of a quarter of a century ago, little has changed concerning the aftermath of the romantic dilemma, a dilemma already deeply penetrated by Hegel close on two centuries ago. Prefiguring, say, Foucault's post-Nietzschean announcement of "the death of man" and the various anti-humanisms of the postmoderns, Barzun reminds us that in the aftermath of romanticism we are witness to "the aesthetics of annihilation."[24] We are told that man is played out, obselete (Ginsberg), that harmony is dead (Rosenberg), that randomness and calculated purposelessness are to be the final gestures in the denunciation and dismantling of traditional art.

The violence of the contrast with Hegel is striking. Yet it should not blind us to the fact that Hegel himself, perhaps more deeply than any other thinker in the modern era, understood the dissolving powers of subjectivity, and how even in his own day, while subjectivity was an essential, it had already worked the erosion of other essentials. In advance Hegel has been down many paths, thought by those coming after to be new ground trodden by themselves as pioneers. Thus Hegel's discussion of the so-called Romantic Irony of his own day in connection with Solger and Tieck clearly adverts to the debunking dismantling, deconstructing powers of modern subjectivity. Very interestingly in his *Aesthetics*, Hegel traces some of the deeper roots of Romantic Irony to the formal ego of Fichte, as this is applied to art, say by Friedrich Schlegel.[25] Since the Fichtean ego is, for Hegel, utterly formal and abstract, every positive matter or content is annihilated by absorption in it. Similarly every content has only positive value in virtue of this ego; indeed "whatever is, is only by favor of the I, and what is by my favor I am in turn able to annihilate." The consequence is that, compared to this absoluteness of the abstract ego, "nothing has value in its real and actual nature."[26] The I is able to assert itself as lord and master of everything, whether in morals or law, in matters human and divine, profane or sacred. "Consequently everything genuinely and independently real becomes only a show, not true and genuine on its own account or through itself, but a mere appearance due to the *ego* in whose power and caprice and at whose free disposal it remains. To admit or cancel it depends wholly on the pleasure of the *ego*, already absolute in itself simply as ego."[27] Clearly any absoluteness that Hegel would attribute to art or beauty in their fullness, in both their subjective and objective sides, here begins to retreat into aesthetic subjectivity.

The consequences are, of course, the eventual evaporation of all absoluteness, whether subjective or objective. For since, Hegel continues, there is ultimately no substantial content apart from the ego, the ego in its artistry can be really in earnest about nothing. True earnestness requires immersion of the self in a substantial content. But instead the ironical artist tries to present himself with a "godlike genius," unattached, untouched, looking down in superiority and taking nothing with real seriousness, in fact breaking all bonds in his concentration into himself, in his self-enjoyment. On the one hand this may induce a sense of the vanity of all that is of moral and substantive import in itself, the nothingness of all that is objective and that has essential and actual value.[28] Or, on the other hand, ironical consciousness in its godlike geniality may grow hollow and empty and be seized by a sickly yearning to abandon the unsatisfying isolation of its pure inwardness. Fatigued by its empty, excessive subjectivity, it may begin to exhaust itself in negation.

Clearly Hegel thinks that this attitude is profoundly lacking in that its artistic productions lead ultimately to a self-refuting, self-annihilating result, "irony at its own expense." "The ironical, as the individuality of genius, lies in the self-destruction of what is noble, great and excellent; and so the objective art-formations too will have to display only the principle of absolute subjectivity, by showing forth what has worth and dignity for mankind as null in its self-destruction. This then implies that not only is there to be no seriousness about law, morals and truth, but that there is nothing in what is lofty and best, since, in its appearance to individuals, characters, and actions, it contradicts and destroys itself and so is ironical about itself."[29] It is not hard to find currents very similar in our own time, even down to the lamentation of the artist (as common, it seems, in Hegel's day as in our own) that his godlike superiority is not properly appreciated by the philistine public.

In brief, then, romantic irony, aloof pure subjectivity, smiles with superior condescension on the totality with a kind of aesthetic sneer. It tries to rescue the absoluteness of art by investing that absoluteness in its own ego. In fact, because the inwardness of that ego is empty of substantial grounding in actual objectivity, it helps along the demise of the absolute in the guise of the eclipse of beauty. While debunking the actual, it really is an escapist, nonengagement of the actual. In exploiting the negativity of subjectivity, it never wins through to substantial objectivity and content. Romantic Irony, Hegel is quick to admit, does border on the truly comic. But the genuinely comic does recognize, however implicitly, something of essential and intrinsic value; only thus can it effect a truly merited destruction of false pretension.[30] Here also Hegel acknowledges that Romantic Irony in its powers of dissolution can be very close (as with Solger) to an essential dialectical moment of the Hegelian Idea. Here Hegel explicitly draws our attention to the likeness of Romantic Irony to what he himself terms "infinite absolute negativity." However, Hegel goes on, Solger (and by implication Romantic Irony generally) does not succeed in properly going beyond this negativity. For this negativity is only one element in Hegel's speculative Idea, it is not the whole Idea.[31] In a word, Hegel has been down the path of dissolution but insists on passing through this path in order to go beyond dissolution.

Ancient Beauty and the Modern Expressive Subject:
Hegel in relation to Platonic and Kantian Aesthetics

So far we have looked at some of the complex ambiguities in Hegel, his era and subsequent times. We may now continue to focus on the issue in perhaps more strictly philosophical terms by reference to two fundamental orientations to the question of aesthetic beauty. These two orientations might be summarized under the headings of Platonic and Kantian aesthetics. Platonic aesthetics serves to accentuate the ancient emphasis on the beautiful in its objectivity,[32] its otherness to, yet kinship with, the human psyche. Kantian aesthetics, by contrast, despite its aesthetic formalism in regard to the aesthetic object, puts the eventual stress on aesthetic subjectivity, a stress, of course, entirely compatible with the so-called "Copernican revolution" of the critical philosophy. As with the critical philosophy as a whole, Kantian aesthetics is transcendental in the modern sense in that it discovers the conditions of the possibility of our apprehension of beauty within the powers of the aesthetic subject. Platonic aesthetics is transcendental in the ancient sense in that it attributes a fundamental universality to the idea of beauty, thought of here as having its metaphysical ground in the actuality of being itself. Let us continue briefly with this contrast because, I think, it helps us understand Hegelian aesthetics as attempting to hold together in a unity the strengths of these two orientations, sometimes thought of as incompatible, especially by many post-Kantians.

We begin with the Kantian side of the contrast, since the implications of Kant's aesthetics are directly continuous with themes already discussed. First, the transcendental aspect of Kantian aesthetics is one very important factor in the tendency to neglect the concept of beauty in recent aesthetics.[33] The Kantian emphasis on the self is carried forward in many succeeding thinkers such that the focus of reflections on art is frequently on the creative process of the artist rather than on the beautiful as an object in itself. Of course, much of post-Cartesian philosophy is marked by this emphasis on the subject but though, aesthetically speaking, this emphasis has some roots in the eighteenth century concern with "taste," Kantian thought facilitates a decisive centering on aesthetic subjectivity. Beauty tends to become defined as a special kind of response to the object rather than by the character of the object in itself. This focus on the aesthetic in its specialness is already prefigured in the invention of aesthetics itself as a philosophical science by Baumgarten, a member of the Wolffian school with which Kant himself was very familiar.

One of the consequences of the specialness of the aesthetic is that the nineteenth century romantic often sets out primarily to explore this response itself, a theme already struck by the Beautiful Soul and in the "poetry of poetry" (Schlegel) in Hegel's time, and reiterated in some of the "self-reflexive" art of the twentieth century. The object which evokes this special response proves to be of only indirect concern. It mediately serves the precipitation of the aesthetic attitude. The famous lines of Coleridge, himself deeply schooled in German thought, are representative enough of a post-Kantian extension of the aesthetic in its specialness: "We receive but what we give/And in our life alone doth Nature live." Thus the aesthetic attitude itself resists being exclusively confined to the object in its objectivity. The object may be the occasion of the response; it does not absolutely anchor the response. Again, given this, it should be no surprise that romantic thought should confer great significance on the artist's imagination and powers of expression, and that the psychology of the artist should often merit almost inordinate attention (postmodernism is in reaction to this). This significance was extended even to the audience whom one might normally anticipate to be more passive, that is, more receptive than creative in their contemplation of the aesthetic object. In what amounts to a more expressivist version of eighteenth century "taste," the audience is now enjoined to creatively cultivate the aesthetic attitude. Since it no longer suffices simply to behold the beautiful object, the audience must bring to bear on the object some appropriate aesthetical approach like, for instance, Bullough's "psychical distance."[34] The audience must participate in and retrace, more strongly, it must recreate the creative process of the artist himself. Overall, aesthetic subjectivity comes to enjoy clear priority over the object. Artists, indeed all men, in that all may harbour untapped aesthetic potential, are exhorted to give themselves over to creative self-expression.

What, in very broad outline, is the inheritance of beauty from this legacy of Kantian aesthetics? In the nineteenth century the creative self-expression of the artist was often still tied to ancient ideals of organic unity, noted by Plato and Aristotle, and thought to be one of the distinguishing marks of the beautiful by Plotinus for instance. This ideal served for some time to discipline aesthetic subjectivity: creative self-expression *ought* to produce objects of beauty in this guise. Hence a measure of anchoring of the aesthetic subject in objective unities continued, as in, say, what Abrams speaks of as Coleridge's "aesthetics of organism."[35] An excessive subjectivity, spoken of in the previous section, had not yet, if you like, completely beaten down the object into nothing. Also the specialization and splintering of the self had not always so advanced that it might not draw back from fragmentation. In time, however, and especially in the twentieth century the self, often losing the sense of its own unity and the unity of life surrounding it, now finds itself giving expression to its own alienation and fragmentation. Thus images of beauty seem to desert the contemporary landscape. Indeed the production of such images might even seem mere escapist aesthetics rather than authentic art. Beauty seems a mere anodyne that may dull the painful symptoms but cannot cure the ill.

Indeed, the artist, seizing the possibilities of what he believes to be his marginal status as an "outsider," may consider it appropriate for him to be subversive of what he now holds to be false, reassuring unities. In distinction from the ancient quest for harmonious unity, the absence of beauty now seems to present the opportunity for him to celebrate the strong sense of plurality and dissonance marking the contemporary consciousness. Thus, for instance a developed sense of the *disunity* of life in modernism is articulated in Eliot's *The Waste Land*. In fact this same seizing upon the opportunities of disunity is reflected by such ventures in the intellectual realm as Nietzsche's glorification of manyness and diversity, the pragmatist's ratification of the primacy of pluralism, the piecemeal, anti-systematic character of Wittgensteinian and analytic philosophy, the post-Heideggerian, post-modern radicalization of unmediated difference in such doctrines as deconstruction. In art we might think that, say, Picasso's *Guernica*, genuinely a painting for contemporary times, shows us a kind of symbol and embodiment of how this absence of beauty and the opportunity of disunity, here the absolute disunity of war itself, death itself, might rise to the level of creative art.

Let us now turn to the Platonic side of our considerations. First we are reminded of how recent is the Kantian and post-Kantian emphasis on aesthetic subjectivity. If we think of the Greek tradition as offering the dominant aesthetic tradition up till modern times, if we put aside the somewhat caricatured, too literalistic image of Plato as simply the arch enemy of the poets, if indeed we think of Plato as one of the exemplary carriers of that tradition, what historically we find to the fore is the objectivity of the beautiful. The beautiful (*to kalon*) forms the focus of reflection, but here the beautiful is not some special set of objects or some set of special responses. It does not refer to a peculiar kind of thing, an *objet d'art*, reserved for display in museums. Rather the beautiful can be plurally instantiated in material objects, in human bodies, in actions and customs, in social and political institutions, even in philosophical thought. Thus in the *Symposium* Socrates in his recounting of the speech of Diotima testifies to this plural instantiation of the beautiful, the objectivity of which is guaranteed, of course, by the crowning *noesis* and affirmation of the beautiful itself (*auto to kalon*). A physical object or person, or moral action or institution is not beautiful primarily in virtue of something *we* bring to bear on it; rather it brings to bear on us a certain presence which precipitates our distinctive response. The beautiful hence cannot be called a production of the subjective psyche. Rather the beautiful calls upon receptive powers of the psyche, opening it out to something ingredient in the nature of being itself.[36]

In fact contact with the beautiful, Plato implies, may crystallise in man a certain absolute dimension in that it may release in him his deepest eros. Eros fuels man's surpassing and transcendence, and though this in itself might seem infinitely restless, for Plato it only properly rests on attaining an absolute goal commensurate with the absolute character of its own need. In a way not altogether unlike the romantic self, Plato is not uncognizant of the profound depths of human desire, and how even unbounded desire may arise in the psyche (for Plato, of course, the tyrant is the degenerate expression of such unbounded desire). But unlike some versions of the romantic self, the deepest eros of man's psyche cannot be closed off in a self-sufficient world of inwardness. Nor can Platonic eros be seen to be without *telos*, nor can it be just like Lessing's endless striving where striving itself becomes its own justification. The inherent thrust of eros reveals its correlation with a higher reality, its kinship with the beautiful. It will be important to bear this teleological dimension in mind when we consider further Hegel's approach to the beautiful.

Platonic eros carries man outside himself, beyond himself. In its kinship with the beautiful it ultimately reveals itself as metaphysical desire. Thus even philosophy itself too must deal with the highest beauty as one of its proper objects. The psychological response (in Plato's sense of *psyche*) to beauty cannot be entirely separated from its metaphysical grounding. Consistent with this thrust of eros towards the ultimate, while beauty was seen to be clearly rooted in man's passionate, desiring nature, beauty never sought to merely indulge that nature. An idealizing intention was inescapable. Beauty was ennobling, uplifting, inextricably tied to man's fundamental moral and religious values. Its aim was not to reduce man to the possibilities of his own debasement, though the potential for chaos and violence in the human psyche was not denied (witness again the tyrant). Beauty's purpose was to carry man beyond coarseness, to immortalize the powers of greatness in mortal life, to idealize the human image with the result that beauty might serve to remind man of a higher order of perfection. All of this is very much the opposite of the commodity market of the contemporary art world where temptations to vulgarization are ever present, where the ancient images of perfection risk degradation in the services of commerce — like giving the Mona Lisa a beard in order to sell electric razors.

In brief, then, in Platonic aesthetics beauty has metaphysical meaning, revealing to man something ultimate about being itself. Also as Plato indicates, both in the *Phaedrus* and the *Symposium*,[37] beauty arouses in man a longing, a longing perhaps initially nameless and inchoate, yet one, the implication is impossible to avoid, that we cannot still short of attaining absolute beauty itself. Absolute beauty, of course, most fully brings out the metaphysical dimension of the issue, but it is not, we must insist, that this metaphysical accent robs man of the possibility of genuine participation in the beautiful.[38] On the contrary, because beauty is grounded in the order of being, because it has ontological weight, it can serve to provide a proper ballast for the psyche, giving a *telos* and directional steadiness to the motions of its eros. Here desire cannot be reduced, say, to Humean passion which makes reason its slave, nor to the level of the "pathological" in Kant, the passionate wayward impulses often at odds with moral duty. Nor is Platonic eros the same as Freud's eros, nor yet the hedonistic urge for pleasure subject to the utilitarian's calculations. Given the uplifting, ennobling power of eros, and its teleological thrust to the absolute, it is not accidental that beauty was thought inseparable from the good (*to agathon*) and the total man's implication in its ethical pursuit. As beauty and being cannot be separated, so also beauty and the good were all but identified in the concept of *kalokagathia*. Again, just as the beautiful was not so in virtue of our response alone, so also the good was not good in function of our desire. Rather our desire, or eros, is for the good, and must submit itself to a value it does not itself simply create. The good and the beautiful might emerge for man in his interplay with being, in his relations to the real; neither could be characterized as merely productions or expressions of man alone. Man's own productions, where genuine, are anchored in the order of the actual as such.

To summarize this contrast of Platonic and Kantian aesthetics: The Kantian captures the modern emphasis on the subject, defining the significance of the object in terms of the self's constitutive contribution. The Platonic encapsulates the ancient emphasis on the intrinsic character of the beauty of the thing itself, defining the aesthetic attunement of the psyche in response to this character. Very broadly,

Platonic and Kantian aesthetics correspond roughly to the metaphors used by Abrams to sum up the two fundamental aesthetic positions, corresponding to imitation and creation (see Chapter One): the mirror and the lamp. Platonic aesthetics has a tendency to "mirror aesthetics" — that is, the light man knows is received as a reflection of an other, so his imitation of a model always entails a certain receptivity.[39] Kantian aesthetics tends to be "lamp aesthetics" — that is, the self itself generates the light which illuminates objects, otherwise dark in themselves. Of course, if we make this contrast too stark we fail to do justice to either, since Plato obviously does not reduce the human psyche to some flattened passivity, nor does Kant completely jettison the thing in itself in its otherness.

How are we to place Hegel's notion of beauty in relation to this contrast? Even less so does Hegel acquiesce in its starkness. It is a temptation to oppose these two approaches, or to elevate one in a manner that diminishes the other. Hegel's view of beauty might be seen to consider both approaches as essential to the fullness of the aesthetic situation. In aesthetics, as in other matters, we need not lacerate ourselves with "the quarrel of the ancients and the moderns" but must do justice to both sides.[40] First, Hegel's aesthetics, like the general thrust of his entire teachings, has a clear Janus-like character: it swings on a hinge between the old and the new. He looks back into the history of the west and its metaphysical tradition, intending to gather from that tradition its abiding contribution to the human spirit, not only in aesthetics, but also in religion, in science, in politics and law, in philosophy. At the same time he is firmly placed within the modern consciousness and its contemporary problematic. Tradition and modernity are not finally to be viewed as unmediated opposites. To the contrary, Hegel seeks to uncover the historical genesis of modern self-consciousness within the progressive dialectical unfolding of human possibilities implicit within attitudes older than modernity. Secondly, generally we discover Hegel appropriating Greek thought and carrying forward many of its core concerns into the post-Kantian context. Thirdly, we find this appropriation in Hegel's express desire to deny, or rather rise above, the mutual oppositions of subject and object, self and world, thought and being, oppositions strongly marking modernity since Descartes. The *telos* of his entire thinking is the goal of dialectically overcoming, without reduction, such dualistic antitheses.

This *telos* is specifically articulated in his aesthetics. Here Hegel weaves together the ancient and the modern, the first in his understanding of the metaphysical aspect of beauty, the second in its grasp of the artist's original power and the contribution of this creative power to the proper expression of aesthetic meaning. Beauty and artistic creativity, substantial objectivity and originative subjectivity, both are necessary to the aesthetic situation in its totality. Beauty allows the rooting of art in the nature of the actual; deprived of such rooting Hegel was convinced art would be deprived of its highest significance, indeed its absoluteness. And in looking back into the history of the highest spiritual achievements, Hegel was particularly aware, as we have seen, of the perfection of beauty in the art of classical Greece. In his references to Plato in the *Aesthetics* Hegel explicitly reminds us of the thrust towards universality to be found in Plato's concern with beauty. Moreover, beauty in its universality is not to be divorced from the universality of the good or the true. Hegel here is well aware that the study of such universality can easily slide into an abstract generality, and he himself admonishes us to avoid this result. Plato, he suggests, provides an essential foundation and guide in any inquiry into the universality of the beautiful. Nevertheless, for Hegel, there is an element of abstraction in the Platonic *eidos* which calls out for remedy in terms of the determinations of the concrete and the particular. The fuller demand of the modern philosphical consciousness is for such a concreteness. Notice that despite Hegel's reservations concerning the abstractness of the Platonic *eidos*, we must retain the Platonic stress on metaphysical universality in regard to the beautiful. The genuine philosophical conception of the beautiful must contain within it a reconciliation of two extremes: it must combine the metaphysical universality pursued by Plato with the determinateness of real particularity.[41] We are reminded here of Aristotle's strategy in dealing with the *chorismos* of the Platonic *eidos*: discover the universal not in a beyond but concretely emergent within the determinate particular. Likewise, Hegel's concrete universal need not be seen as a simple repudiation of the Platonic search for the universal, but rather as an attempt at its concrete completion.

At the same time, this reiteration of the concrete universality of beauty implies no erasure of man's originative artistry. Considered from this angle, that is, from the perspective of post-Kantian aesthetics, what is unavoidable for Hegel is that beauty calls forth the urge for articulation and expression. The sense of beauty, our encounter with beauty, must not be lost in mute inwardness but calls for exterior articulation, calls for self-consciousness anchored in fashioned images which, as later the poet Hopkins put it, deal "out that being indoors each one dwells." Only in this way is beauty brought to the level of some explicit, discerning self-consciousness, indeed also brought to public communication, and so allowed to be conserved and consolidated within the full cultural life of a people. For this the fullest, articulate appropriation of beauty, the productive power of the creative self is absolutely essential.

In granting the essential nature of the artist's productive contribution, Hegel was very intent on steering clear of "subjectivism" in the pejorative sense which confines the significance of beauty to its significance only for the self. Coming after Kant, and given his genuine praise of Kant in the *Aesthetics*, we might expect him to acquiesce in the "subjectivist" tone of Kant's treatment of beauty, but this is not the case. Again, not surprising, given his attention to Greek aesthetic ideas, beauty and art cannot be confined either to the emotive or the subjective. Art, precisely because of its link with beauty, is something cognitive, and so helps carry us out of subjectivism in this pejorative sense. While asserting the necessity to conceive of art as "Subject" and not only as "Substance," while granting the artist's original expressiveness, Hegel's interpretation of the full significance of both of these cannot be subjectivistically construed.

This is very clear if we look at his reservations about Kant's aesthetics, which center precisely on this issue of "subjectivism." Kant represents a turning point in modern philosophy, the possibility of a new beginning.[42] He brings out the fundamental dilemmas and contradictions we have to face, as well as, for Hegel, "the self-related rationality or freedom, the self-consciousness that finds and knows itself in itself as infinite." Kant points us towards a solution but in his actual solution he falls back into "the fixed antithesis of subjective thought and objective things." Unity is propounded "merely in the form of subjective ideas of the reason to which no adequate reality could be shown to correspond." Kant brings the reconciled contradictions within our range, but since he only suggests an abstract solution, being brought to a standstill by the fixed antithesis of subjectivity and objectivity, his solution and reconciliation themselves become purely subjective. *The Critique of Judgment* where Kant deals with aesthetic beauty and the teleology of nature is especially instructive here for Hegel.[43] The organic unity and teleological character of beauty, both in art and nature, tend by Kant to be seen only from the point of view of the reflection which subjectively judges of them. The end is left a mere "ought," and when we are compelled to affirm an end, this is only an enunciation of a subjective mode of reflection. Our appreciation of the achieved unity of beauty and its actual reconciling of opposites seems to have been achieved by Kant in great measure, but in fact "this apparently perfect reconciliation is still supposed by Kant to be at the last only subjective in respect of the judgment and the production (of art), and not itself to be absolutely true and actual."[44]

Perhaps here we might also draw attention to the fact that the idea of the "self" in Hegel inevitably gathers to itself more than subjectivistic connotations because (in addition to Greek beauty) he took seriously the Christian notion of the "individual" in its infinite worth and in its historical mediation of the concept of *Geist*, spirit. Seen in this light, the "self" is not some isolated atomic unit that must bridge a yawning chasm between its own separated inwardness and an external world of spiritless objects confronting it. The finite "self" for Hegel is a manifestation of *Geist* and thus inseparable from the whole of actuality considered under the light of *Geist*. *Geist* comes to self-consciousness in the "self," but *Geist* is not identical with the finite self. For Hegel *Geist* has significance for the whole of actuality. Hence once again we find the basis of arguing against the dualistic opposition of inwardness and actuality, self and the real order, the "subjective" and the "objective." In this context, the Hegelian "subject" cannot just have a "subjectivist" significance. Indeed, despite the secularization of the self that seems to be the end result of modernity, despite even the "vanishing" of the self in postmodernism, for Hegel the revelation and expression of self that art effects begins to border on a significance that can only be called religious; and this despite the fact that Hegel was no foe of secularization. As I have argued previously, this significance is implied in the way Hegel speaks of a movement of the human spirit from art to religion in his philosophy of Absolute Spirit.

Beauty and the Overcoming of Metaphysical Dualisms:
Aquinas and Hegel

Let us now develop further the claim that Hegel saw no ultimate incompatibility between beauty as metaphysically significant (the traditional view) and the productive participation of the artist in the articulation of that significance (the modern view). Here we first need to remark how different Hegel's attitude was to the tradition of metaphysics than attitudes that have become common after him. It is a noteworthy feature of contemporary philosophy that its critical attitude to traditional metaphysics often cuts across the divide between Anglo-American analytical philosophy and Continental European thought. Both these two major strains of thought have frequently repudiated metaphysics, sometimes implying that philosophy as traditionally practiced is at an end. Perhaps this view arises most forcefully from what we have called the Nietzschean-Heideggerian heritage. More specifically, the claim is made that since Plato philosphy has been ensnared in a set of fundamental dualisms: body and mind, form and matter, immanence and transcendence, time and eternity, to name but some of the chief. We must step beyond such dualisms and by doing so, it seems, stand outside the discourse of traditional metaphysics. We may not find the same sophistication in historical self-consciousness in Anglo-American analysis as we do in Continental thought. Nevertheless, this same desire to escape dualism, particularly in regard to the mind/body problem, is focused in the many criticisms charged against the Cartesian tradition. Whether stemming from Plato or Descartes, the impression is that traditional philosophy is ineradicably permeated by such fundamental dualisms.

Hegel would have thought it to be an extraordinarily one-sided perspective, however, to read the entire tradition of metaphysics as captive to these dualisms. Dualisms may abound, but on the most fundamental issues, there are many crucial instances incompatible with thinking in terms of simple, stark polarities. The neglected theme of beauty is one crucial case where the metaphysical tradition clearly struggles against merely dualistic thinking. Hegel would not deny that the metaphysical tradition is beset by a whole set of fundamental oppositions, and very obviously his own dialectical mode of philosophical thought exploits the incompleteness of onesided and opposed positions, while at the same time trying to dynamically reconcile their partiality and contradictoriness. Plainly too any sympathy Hegel might have for the metaphysical tradition does not make him a Platonist in the ordinary sense, for in agreement with Aristotle, as we saw, he is critical of the abstract separateness of the Platonic *eidos*. But, of course, a very important consideration regarding beauty is that here, if anywhere, Plato envisages the possibility of at least mitigating, if not bridging, the *chorismos* of concrete reality and intelligible *eidos*, in the way eros as a mediator in the *metaxu* is said by Socrates to bind up the whole. Properly understood, beauty gives the lie to any merely dualistic interpretation of the metaphysical tradition. Those who, like Nietzsche, attack the "logocentrism" of that tradition in the name of art and the aesthetic, simply fail to take into account the significance of beauty for that tradition and its challenge to merely oppositional thought and the simplistic "either/or" of so-called "logocentrism."

Since the received picture of Plato too frequently caricatures his dualism, perhaps a less misleading contrast here might be to compare the views of Aquinas and Hegel on beauty. Thomists are not always sympathetic to Hegel, suspecting him especially of violating the mystery of religion with excessive claims on behalf of philosophical reason, also sometimes charging him with an "immanentism" that, in its disrespect for traditional transcendence, leads either to an unacceptable "gnosticism," or an unacceptable "pantheism." Without downplaying crucial differences regarding religion, and while not forgetting the post-Kantian horizon of Hegel, we ought not to forget that Aquinas and Hegel both stand together in direct relation to a common, very important inspirational source, Aristotle, and so mediately to Greek thought generally. Their affinities are revealed, I suggest, in certain aspects of their non-dualistic yet metaphysical approach to beauty. While the creative contribution of the artist is more to the fore in Hegel, a comparison with Aquinas strengthens all the more the metaphysical aspects of Hegel's aesthetics. Let me also add that the upshot of this discussion here will help us address the basic problem of beauty we have already noted at the opening of this chapter: namely, how can beauty, seemingly a limited, bounded whole, answer to the infinite inwardness of Christian, romantic, modern man? How can beauty allow us to affirm together both subjectivity in its infinite inwardness and objectivity in its substantial actuality — without the dislocation between excessive subjectivity and dead spiritless objectivity? Aquinas and Hegel here will pave the way to further addressing this issue in the next section. But let us now look at some of the relevant details of their views, commencing with a brief review of Aquinas' treatment.

As is well known, Aquinas defines beauty as "that which being seen, pleases" (id quod visum, placet).[45] The emphasis here is on a kind of vision, and also on a pleasure, a delight that is inseparable from that vision. At once we find both a subjective and an objective aspect: objectively something has to be seen; subjectively what is seen affords a delight precisely as seen and in the very act of seeing itself. That is, something comes to visibility in beauty, and the fact that it releases delight in man indicates that man's soul is correspondingly attuned to its reality. Recalling our previous discussion of modern alienation, we note here that beauty is not something entirely strange to man's apprehending powers. Rather, in that it makes possible the experience of delight, the inference is unmistakeable that there is a clear kinship between the objective and the subjective, between beauty and its beholder, a kinship that in scholastic terminology tends to be spoken of as a connaturality.

Much has been written by students of Thomas about the act of vision itself. We might just cite one influential contemporary example. Deeply aware of the main currents of contemporary aesthetics, Jacques Maritain speaks here of a "creative intuition."[46] What generally seems beyond dispute is that the vision of beauty cannot be disembodied in the so-called Platonic manner. The vision of beauty is inseparable from the senses. Beauty discloses its significance through the appearances of the body; correspondingly, only through the attuned senses does man respond and delight in what he comes to see there. Thus the apprehension of beauty is never the act of some completely pure intelligence or detached Cartesian rationality. It must be proportionate to a bodied being. Thus also the self as a whole responds, with the result that its vision is rooted in its entire psychic life, inclusive of the emotional, the spiritual and the rational. Still, the sensuous side of beauty cannot be interpreted in completely materialistic terms. The extremes of sheer materiality and pure reason are inappropriate here.

Why cannot we confine our sights here to an entirely materialistic interpretation regarding the embodied being of beauty and the sensuousness of man's vision? Precisely as calling forth from the full self something deeper than detached intellectuality (*to kalon* is related to "to call," as Maritain relevantly points out), the sensuous nature of man is here suffused by an attentiveness that gathers its force from the informing presence of man's higher powers. Sense and reason, body and intelligence, matter and mind do not here function as separable powers, for the perception of beauty effects a certain fusion of their seeming polarity; beauty effects a suffusing of sense with reason, an enlivening of the body with intelligence, a transforming, transfiguring of matter by the mind. We have it in the words of Aquinas which, of course, simply echo those of Aristotle in *De Anima*: the senses too are a kind of reason (*he d'aisthesis ho logos*).[47] It is in the aesthetic sphere of beauty that this assertion of the closeness, indeed union of *aisthesis* and *logos*, contrary to Nietzsche's counterposing of art and logic, becomes charged with immense significance. The senses here become the significant bodily vessels of concrete reason, living intelligence. Nor need we here think of the senses as just sheerly emotive, a view implied by those hedonistic aesthetic theories which reduce art to the discharge of feeling and emotion. Again the senses here cannot be equated with the domain of the "pathological" in Kant's moral philosophy, that is, manifestations of man's unfree, lower nature, driven by impulse and subject to the iron mechanism of Newtonian nature. We find grounds here for opposing various forms of "noncognitive" aesthetics. Put succinctly, the senses here attain a significant dignity with beauty. For to call the senses a kind of intelligence implies their cognitive power, implies their essential cooperation and essential presence in man's endeavour to self-consciously attain contact with the concretely real.

If the response to beauty is complex, so also is beauty in its objectivity for Aquinas. Again, as is well known, the three characteristics of beauty delineated by Aquinas regarding this objectivity include unity or integrity, consonance, and finally radiance.[48] These characteristics reflect Aquinas's own position within the tradition of classical aesthetics. We need to look at each in turn before then taking up the comparison with Hegel.

Unity or integrity is important because the beautiful object must stand before us, detached from the surrounding flux of inessentials. Thus the beautiful in its unity draws out our attention and concentration. If it were merely merged with its surroundings it would be as nothing for perception; it would not seize hold of attention. Similarly this unity cannot be simple, if for no other reason than that a simple unity, while it might catch our attention, could not concentrate and sustain it. This is obviously necessary if the beautiful is to offer its peculiar pleasure and delight. A simple, uniform unity tends to be dull, not delighting; it palls quickly and soon ceases to please. The unity of the beautiful must be complex in this sense of being capable of feeding a concentrated delight and hence not exhausting it in a quick survey of externals.

Aquinas' second characteristic, consonance, develops further the nature of this sustaining, complex unity. Consonance or harmony cannot be a condition of homogeneous uniformity or simplicity. Some element of heterogeneity, plurality, difference must also be present. That is consonance and harmony only become intelligible given also the presence of their opposites, dissonance and disharmony. Multiplicity and heterogeneity always risk this outcome: where there are many strands, strains may easily arise, and the many may as equally disagree as agree. Consonance (literally meaning "sounding together," almost singing together) helps to signify the conquering the danger of such a divisive state. Beauty as consonance might here be seen as the overcoming of such a state of divisiveness and inaugurating a condition of concord or complex wholeness. A beautiful face, for instance, delights not in the simplicity of uniformity, but because a complex wholeness permeates the entirety of the presence, because the multiplicity of the features are in fact wed to each other in harmony. A slight upset of this mutual accommodation and mutual enhancement of all the parts upsets the balance of the whole and mars the pure integrity of the countenance. Except to the most sensitive, properly attuned observer, this marring effect can sometimes be extremely elusive, like some slightly off-key crow in a choir.

The third characteristic in Aquinas's view of beauty, namely radiance, a characteristic sometimes spoken of in terms of *splendor formae*, brings us back once again to the objective side of the fusion of sense and intellect, above noted from the side of the subject. Radiance is a condition of expression or manifestation. When something radiates, it gives off something of itself. It reveals that its own unity is not, as it were, shrunken into itself, but rather bestows its presence upon the rest of reality around it. Beauty may have unity or integrity, but its unity also exhibits just this kind of bestowing presence. If you like, its nature is not to save itself for itself alone, like some jealous, envious god. Its nature is to communicate itself. The scholastics, in fact, often spoke of the good in just such terms: *omne bonum diffusivum sui.* So also with the beautiful as radiant.[49] We shall see below how this calls to mind Hegel's own repeated acquiescence in the assertion of Plato and Aristotle that God is not envious. In Hegel's philosophy it is a cardinal point that it is God's nature to manifest, disclose, reveal himself. But for the present let us remain with radiance in Aquinas.

Radiance, *splendor formae*: something sheds its light; something lights up something. Here we have a theme recalling the light shed by Plato's Sun, a light whose rays are shed throughout the metaphysical tradition, perhaps even down to some last lingering rays in the Heideggerian *Lichtung*. Here in Aquinas form serves to effect a certain radiance. Form here may be understood as the principle of intelligibility. Nevertheless, any such intelligible principle is not to be comprehended in terms of the normal, caricatured Platonism, often associated with terms like the "intelligible": form as detached, separable, pale and bloodless; form that seems to reside in Hades instead of the supposed Heaven of Plato. If forms may have splendor or radiance, any such separation cannot be the full story concerning their nature. Rather they come to manifestation or disclosure. Thus they cease to be the antithesis of the visible realm; they cease to be principles that are dualistically other to the sensible world. Indeed what is so significant about beauty is precisely that it forces us to acknowledge that the intelligible may shed its light and make its presence significantly felt within the realm of the sensible. Contrary to the often imputed inescapability of metaphysical dualism within the philosophical tradition, beauty reveals to us the sensible radiance of the intelligible.

Again the beauty of the face can serve well to illustrate the point. A beautiful face may show itself as radiant. It is alive with a certain invisible yet quite manifest light. It is a material presence yes, but the materiality of this presence is such that materiality itself is lifted up out of its mere "thereness." Something of spirit comes to shine there and play about the features. Unlike the merely pretty face, there is the dimension of a certain qualitative presence there in the beautiful face. Also unlike the merely pretty face, this quality of presence in the beautiful face and this play of light there may incorporate all the strain, all the opposition, all the wrinkling and weathering of life itself. Its harmony wins over these, as the presence of spirit lifts up and transforms the somewhat battered sensuous externals. Such a radiance of beauty may sometimes be seen in the wise presence of some older faces, a vision of which we sometimes are granted, say, in some of Rembrandt's later self-portraits. The point is, once again, that the radiance of beauty signifies the outward manifestation in a sensible presence of powers of spirit that incorporate and harmonize many strands into a unified consonance, strands that otherwise might be merely negative or even destructive.

If we now turn back to Hegel we can see how he is akin to Aquinas on these four points: the aesthetical response; the nature of unity in the beautiful; the character of consonance; the importance of radiance. First, for Hegel, as for Aquinas, we cannot dualistically separate sense and reason in the aesthetic response. Moreover, the sensuous dimension is inescapably a sensuousness that we cannot materialistically reduce. The beautiful work of art stands before us as embodied, but as such it is addressed to the mind. The sensuous here not only concretely embodies spirit, mind; it poses itself for spirit as a question and a challenge. Sense and spirit coalesce into a living unity such that, as Hegel puts it, the spirit is made sensuous and the sensuous is spiritualized (a formulation echoed when Maritain speaks of such a union as "intelligentiated sense").[50] Thus we discover that the beautiful art work, in the act of making spirit concretely articulate, also spiritually transforms and even transfigures the senses. So also it calls forth man's deepest and highest powers and does not appeal to one side of his being in abstraction from another.

Inevitably, too, because of the involvement of the senses, pleasure and delight mark aesthetic perception. Here, however, pleasure and enjoyment are not bound to practical desire, to usefulness and consumption. Here we experience an enjoyment freed from the utilitarian schema of means and ends. For Hegel the beautiful is not there to be exploited in instrumental fashion. Of course, it may be so exploited, for instance, when beauty is made to serve commercial purposes. But this can mean a kind of violence to beauty considered more properly as a value in itself. It is not the beautiful then that draws our delight in its purity. Rather the product for consumption that beauty is supposed to help sell now forces itself to the center of our attention and displaces aesthetic delight. Within the proper aesthetic context, by contrast, the beautiful is appreciated as an end in itself. Such appreciation stills the urge to exploit the beautiful as simply a means to an extraneous end. Thus the enjoyment of beauty becomes a kind of contemplative pleasure. Indeed, this makes it like to the speculative reason of the Hegelian philosopher for whom the truth, independently of immediate, pragmatic considerations, is worthy of attention as a value in itself. The similarity also with the delighting vision of Aquinas is evident, especially so when we remember that Aquinas himself explicitly couples the vision of beauty with the speculative wisdom of the philosopher.[51]

With respect to the unity of the beautiful, it hardly needs to be repeated how strongly this is emphasized by Hegel. Thus in Hegel, drawing on an old tradition going back to Plato and Aristotle and still alive in the romanticism of the nineteenth century, the beautiful must evince a certain organic wholeness, not be just an adventitious juxtaposition or arrangement of heterogeneous parts. Organic unity is one that rises *immanently* from within the object itself; it is not superimposed *ab extra* in a mechanical manner. Organic unity, we might say, is intimate to the thing itself: it emerges from the appropriateness of the various parts to each other within the inclusive and indivisible embrace of the beautiful thing in its totality. Moreover, such an emergent unity must be complex, not uniform, precisely because it is marked by a high degree of rich, internal differentiation. Hegel strongly insists on this character of the beautiful as an end internally rich of itself, a *Selbstzweck* in the language he uses.[52] In this unity of the beautiful as *Selbstzweck*, we find the presence of a certain perfection: something appears a whole unto itself in a manner that seems impossible to surpass.

To put the matter succinctly, *beauty is a sensuous image of being whole*, the spiritually significant materialization of a possible perfection. And it is not just in Hegel's aesthetics that this concept of being whole is crucially important. Beauty is an intense sensuous manifestation of what it means to be whole. But the requirement of being whole is equally applicable for Hegel to the idea of the true: in Hegel's own famous words, the true is the whole, *Das Wahre ist das Ganze*. This requirement is also applied to the ethical good: against the Kantian dualizing of man into a sharply separated sensuousness and supersensuousness, Hegel calls for the restoration of man's integrity in an ethical reunification of the sensuous and the supersensuous, in a manner not unlike his contemporary Schiller, and one which calls to mind again the Greek ideal of *kalokagathia* in Hegel's emphasis on *Sittlichkeit* as opposed to *Moralität*. So also the requirement of being whole is evident in Hegel's religious views. Here the ultimate form of alienation is the division of man and God which produces the Unhappy Consciousness. This is characterized by a kind of absolute degree of not being whole, by its profound failure to be at one with itself or with God. Here not being whole is coincident with basic religious estrangement. As long as this fundamental discord persists, man is in a state of radical unhappiness, radical unfulfillment. All these factors, taken together, indicate that aesthetic beauty in Hegel, with regard to this issue of unity or wholeness, intertwines unavoidably with these other cognate concepts of the true, the good and the holy.

Turning now to the third point, what might be identified as the Hegelian version of Aquinas' *consonantia*? For Hegel, man's alienation or estrangement, taken in the widest sense possible, arises from division, from contradiction, from discord. The many different forms of alienation are various concrete specifications of this fundamental divisiveness. The important point here, however, is that division, disagreement, dissonance for Hegel all inevitably generate counterthrusts to alienation. They immanently generate their own impetus towards a resolution or reconciliation. Aesthetically, the creative making of works of beauty concretizes this immanent impetus to effect such a healing reconciliation. However, no reconciliation can be genuine if it merely works by repression. Aesthetic beauty thus cannot ultimately satisfy if it is merely built upon a suppression or a denial of the discord. Rather aesthetic beauty must, as it were, follow through the directionality of the strain of discord, searching out within that strain itself the goal of harmony. For Hegel, discord and dissonance are ineradicably real, but they are not ultimate or absolute.

It is possible that the oppositions that do tear man apart may also be surpassed and a new, more rich unity be brought into being in a way reminiscent of Nietzsche's claim: what does not destroy me makes me strong.

For Hegel the beautiful art work may be such a *coincidentia oppositorum* in this sense: it is not just a mere laying side by side of the opposites, their juxtaposition which in no way transforms their opposition; rather it requires the confrontation and interplay of the opposites such that they interpenetrate and coalesce into a new unity — such would be a living as opposed to an abstract reconciliation. In many places Hegel points to this by indicating that the art work is a dialectical unity of many basic oppositions: freedom and necessity; sensuousness and spirit; unity and variety; openness and wholeness; the particular and the universal. Let us remind ourselves what such a dialectical unity is. A dialectical unity is one which embraces within itself elements that, outside the unity, strain, even war against each other; yet within the dialectical unity, these elements in tension are not deprived of their vital dynamism but in their living energy are gathered into a more encompassing embrace. Their inclusion within that embrace affects their previously antagonistic interplay with the result that their erstwhile tension now ceases to degenerate into merely destructive dissonance. Their dialectical interplay generates there a kind of dynamic consonance.

This dimension of the dynamic brings us directly to the fourth point of comparison between Aquinas and Hegel, namely with respect to the radiance of beauty. Perhaps it is with respect to this point that the comparison of the two is most important, for here, I suggest, we begin most fully to discern the metaphysical significance of beauty. What might correspond in Hegel's aesthetics to Aquinas' radiance? Above we already noted that this idea of "radiance" implies an element of "self-bestowing," of "self-diffusion," of "self-communication." Now these elements tie in very closely with Hegel's characterization of the beautiful in these terms: beauty, says Hegel, is the Ideal or the sensuous shining of the Idea.[53] Of course, the meaning of Hegel's Idea is many faceted. To avoid spreading our discussion too widely it suffices to say here that the Idea has both logical and ontological significance for Hegel, in addition to many theological echoes that arise from some of the resonances of its Neoplatonic connotations. Religiously speaking, the Ideal manifests that divine in sensuous shape. Obviously, then, the Idea is not identical with some subjectivistic "ideas" we just happen to have in our minds, like the subjective ideas of the classical empiricism of Locke and Hume. Apart from the many controversial issues surrounding Hegel's Idea, the most important point for our purposes is that Hegel's characterization of the beautiful lights up the significance of *Schein*, shining. There is an ambiguity in *Schein*, of course, as we see, for instance, in Hegel's discussion of *Schein* in the *Science of Logic*. *Schein* can have some of the negative connotations connected with the notion of semblance or illusory being: *Schein* in this sense is something that is merely a "show," something that is merely apparent and not in full possession of substantial reality. Such a negative connotation is exploited by those who tend to dismiss beauty as only a "mere" show, a mere sensuous image which remains at the level of surface externality without penetrating to the level of the truly essential.

An element of this negative view is operative, for instance, in Plato's disparagement in the *Republic* of art as "mere" imitation, "mere" *mimesis*. It is relevant to point out here too that Nietzsche seems to credit himself (and Heidegger's examination of Nietzsche seems to concur on this point) with being the first to really reverse this Platonic disparagement of *Schein* and explode its negativity in a new doctrine of the senses. Nietzsche gives himself credit a little too quickly. For if we drew attention only to some of the negative connotations contained in the ambiguous notion of *Schein* we would do a serious injustice to Hegel's aesthetic views. For the shining of the Idea in the Ideal has this very important, positive implication: namely, that something basic and ultimate *comes to appearance*, is disclosed or made apparent in the *Schein* or "shining." It is not in Nietzsche but in Hegel's *Aesthetics*, indeed in Hegel's *Logic* that we find the basis of a so-called "new" interpretation of the senses. Thus, to cite a crucial instance, it is in the *Logic* (this is a tough paradox for Nietzsche to swallow, given his hostility to "logocentrism") that Hegel points the way to the possibility of a *positive concept of appearance* when discussing *Erscheinung*. *Erscheinung* is not the opposite of *Wesen*, essence, but rather the making appear, the making concretely present of the essential.[54] Here we see how totally inappropriate it is to charge Hegel with the "sin" of so-called metaphysical dualism. For here we find the resources to justify the view that there is a profound movement away from dualistic opposition in Hegel, a movement with significant repercussion in Hegel's aesthetic treatment of the positive appearance that characterizes the beautiful.

Above we noted Hegel's approval of Plato and Aristotle in holding that God is not envious: Hegel's God is an appearing God, a divinity that is self-disclosive. An analogous consideration might be here applied to the appearance of the beautiful; for Hegel beauty is the self-disclosure of the Idea, the Idea made sensuously manifest. *Schein*, "shining" has the dynamical dimension in this respect: what seems statically closed in on itself turns out to be otherwise — it emerges into appearance. Thus the positive connotations of "appearance" are unavoidable in our consideration of the beautiful. To return again to the example of the beauty of the human face: this beauty is simply unintelligible without reference to the positive character of its appearance. We cannot here do away with the character of appearance and be left with some pure residue of reality without appearance. The face is rather a sensuous presence that unfolds a reality into appearance, the reality of the "self-communicating" person. It brings the two together, appearance and reality, so that something real and true may appear, may show itself. Beauty must be held to be of fundamental importance because it crucially reveals this positive import of appearance. Beauty brings to the fore authentic, genuine appearance, in Hegel's case, the authentic, sensuous appearance of spirit or *Geist*.[55]

Beauty as Concrete Universal and as Transcendental Concept: The Aesthetic Dilemma of Modernity Revisited

We can now restate the fundamental problem of beauty that we discussed in the opening sections of this chapter, for we are now in a more advantageous position to deal with it. As we recall, we previously noted that after Christianity and Romanticism a fundamental aesthetic question of modernity concerned the disproportion between beauty in its objectivity and the deepening of modernist subjectivity. Aesthetic subjectivity tends to be in excess of objective beauty. Romantic subjectivity serves to unloose something of the unlimited inwardness of the self and its infinite unrest. Beauty, at least in its classical shape, presents us with a bounded harmonious whole, hence limited whole. Hence it seems unable to match the unrest of subjectivity and so to bring its striving, its seeking to the level of contemplative seeing. Must beauty in its substantial objectivity then always fall so short of the infinite inwardness of modernistic subjectivity? This, I venture, is one of the basic dilemmas of aesthetic modernity. If we simply choose beauty in its objectivity, must we then be false to modern inwardness? If we choose modern inwardness, what prevents the eclipse of beauty and the eventual hollowing out of inwardness itself?

Can our discussion of Hegel and Aquinas to this point be of any help?[56] In the first section of this chapter I also noted that beauty can only withstand the dissolution of its wholeness by modern subjectivity if that wholeness cannot be confined to the merely finite level. To bring active subjectivity to contemplative seeing and undo its disproportion with finite objectivity, beauty must be a whole not exhausted by a limited set of finite predicates. That is, it must be an objective whole that yet concretizes an infinite significance, so standing before aesthetic subjectivity as a nonalienating other, and thus making available a fundamental aesthetic attunement[57] between self and other. Now the fact is that Hegel does conceive the beautiful as a concretion of infinite *Geist*. How are we to make sense of this? My suggestion here is that our discussion of the shining of the Idea in the beautiful points in the direction of some solution. For the character of this shining is that it is for Hegel a sensuous embodiment of infinite *Geist* which provides a genuine reconciliation of subjectivity and objectivity: *both* may be seen to disclose the infinite. Beauty is a whole that sensuously concretizes the infinite; as whole it ministers to man's need for substantial objectivity; as infinite, it responds and answers to man's own infinite restlessness. As a further suggestion in the direction of some solution, I now propose that the aesthetic shining of the Idea for Hegel can be helpfully illuminated if we compare beauty as a *concrete universal* (in Hegel's terms) with beauty as a *transcendental* concept (in Thomistic terms). Let us now develop the relevance of this proposal.

Hegel's aesthetics, of course, is situated in the context of post-Kantian thought, and because of this the notion of the "transcendental" is unavoidably bound up with the question of subjectivity. The "transcendental" in Kantian usage refers us not to knowledge of objects but to the conditions within the knowing subject which make possible our knowledge of objects. By contrast, the older Aristotelian-Thomist usage of the term "transcendental" refers us not to the knowing subject but to certain universal "features" of being itself, namely, being as true, being as good, and more controversially, being as beautiful. Hegel himself was critical of Kant's critical philosophy for according too one-sided a dominance to subjectivity, with the result that we find ourselves again trapped in a new dualism between the subject and the object, between thought and being. These new dualisms were, for Hegel, signs of the failure of the Kantian project to effect a genuine reconciliation of the knower and the known. Hegel, however, does not abandon the Kantian usage but, I suggest, in his efforts to reintegrate thought and being, logic and ontology, he seeks to make the newer meaning of the "transcendental" compatible with the more ancient.[58] An aesthetic expression of this concern might be seen, for instance, in the way Hegel in his *Aesthetics* claims to be primarily concerned with the beauty of fine art rather than the beauty of nature. This might be seen to reflect the turn from the Aristotelian-Thomist view of the "transcendental" (beauty as a universal characteristic of being, here of nature in its objectivity) towards the Kantian "transcendental" (beauty made possible as a meaningful appearance to man *after* the productive contribution of the aesthetic self). It would be a serious mistake, however, to think that Hegel sets to one side the beauty of nature. This is a mistaken impression gained by some of Hegel's readers who fail to proceed beyond the general introduction to his aesthetics. When we do proceed beyond this point, the fact is that there is an extensive discussion of Beauty in general in Hegel's *Aesthetics*, and particularly of the beautiful in nature, all of which indicate a strong insistence on Hegel's part that this theme of natural beauty is not to be neglected. Beauty in its universality demands as much.

The fact remains, however, that Hegel does give greater attention, indeed his main attention, to the beauty of art. Does this entail the exclusion of the metaphysics of aesthetic beauty, in that this latter matter demands clear reference to the objective side of the issue, as is plain from our discussion of the Greeks and Aquinas? Our answer must be that such an exclusion cannot be warranted for Hegel. Granting the philosophical cogency of the Kantian transcendental turn, granting Hegel's primary focus on the beauty correlative to art, the metaphysical dimension emerges strengthened in Hegel rather than diminished. Certainly, in line with previous discussion, beauty is not to be subjectivised in the Kantian fashion; rather its metaphysical meaning is to be seen more explicitly, seen more self-consciously in relation to man as self, as *Geist*. Beauty is for man; for man essentially participates in the fuller, explicit articulation of the beautiful. Aesthetic man, for whom beauty is and through whom silent beauty emerges into articulation, cannot be reduced to the level of some privatised psyche, but can be properly understood in relation to infinite *Geist* and its manifold manifestations throughout the whole of what is.

In this context we must understand Hegel's claim that the beauty of art stands higher than the beauty of nature. Though it is often seen in this light, such claims need not be seen as expressing an arrogant anthropocentrism. Man appears as the most highly developed, most well-formed of nature's creations. Indeed, if we recall Hegel's discussion of the beauty of the human face and generally of the human figure, it is evident that for Hegel nature attains in the case of man a kind of aesthetic acme. This might be misconstrued as arrogant anthropocentrism, of course. It is more helpful, however, to understand man's grandeur here as nobly crowning the aesthetic powers of nature, not basely lording it over nature in unwarranted conceit. Concentrating in himself the powers of nature, man nevertheless takes the further step in actively bringing these powers to articulate self-consciousness.

We might here think of the importance of genius (genius, of course, is also very important in Kant's *Critique of Judgment* on just this issue)[59] as providing some link between nature and articulation: the genius partakes of both, yet he effects a transition in his singular self from the elemental energy of one to the formed expression and self-conscious workmanship of the other. Out of this transition from nature to articulation the beauty of *Geist* in being itself, whether in nature or man, is awakened to itself. Without man the beauty of nature remains silent, just there. The Kantian sense of the transcendental is essential to the active articulation of the beautiful in the fullest sense. But what is revealed in the work of art can reveal the metaphysical dimension of beauty even more fully than natural beauty. A simple objectivism might seek to defend this dimension by confining the issue to nature. But for Hegel beauty that has worked through the productive power of the artist emerges in the more fully articulated form: in a form that is less capricious, in a form that has been filtered through the artist's self-consciousness, in a richer, idealized shape. And this idealization may be for Hegel a more genuine revelation of the real. No doubt there can be "idealizations" which amount to falsifications of the real, as when the "idea" involved is an empty idea, a merely abstract concept. But what the genuine work of art articulates is a concrete universal. Hence its beauty is not a falsifying idealization of the real but a true realization of the ideal, an overcoming of the disjunction of the ideal and the real. To say with Hegel that beauty is the Ideal is precisely to say that beauty presents the conjunction of ideality and actuality in a concrete image of the Idea.

The point is related to the common notion, reiterated in Kant's *Critique of Judgment*, that art produces a *second nature* over and above the first nature of externality. This notion is developed in Hegel's insistence that free spirit is spirit that has been "twice-born," a rebirth that seems to have an existential significance for Hegel himself and many of his disciples.[60] The aesthetic version of the point is couched in explicitly religious language in Hegel's *Aesthetics*. There Hegel says that art is higher than nature because art is more adequate to the representation of *Geist* and divine ideals. Art tries to articulate *Geist* in a more permanent expression than is possible with immediate nature whose existence is vanishing, transient and mutable. Mere permanence, however, does not constitute anything higher for art. Rather in Hegel's view it is the fact that in the art work there is an accentuation of the significant presence of *Geist*: the art work has received what Hegel calls "the baptism of the spiritual."[61] Here Hegel takes issue with the attitude that (here again he does not refrain from religious language) nature is God's work while art is only a human production. In this antithesis between nature as a divine creation and art works as the finite product of merely human activity, Hegel detects a fundamental misconception concerning the nature of the divine. The implication of this attitude is that the divine does not work in man or through man but is limited only to nature external to man. The true conception of art abandons this mistaken antithesis. In fact, for Hegel we need to take a view almost the opposite, namely that, as Hegel puts it, "God is more honored by what spirit does or makes than by the productions or formations of nature."[62] In man divinity is made manifest, for Hegel, indeed is operative in a form that is appropriate to the true conception of God. Since for Hegel the true conception recognizes that God is *Geist*, it is only with man as himself *Geist* that the divine discloses itself in a form approaching any adequacy. Once again, we must insist that Hegel is not intent on reversing a first dualism of nature and man which privileges nature and downgrades man. There is little point in setting up a second dualism which privileges man by downgrading nature. It is rather that for Hegel the divine is operative in *both* nature and man, though not with the same articulate fullness in both. In Hegel's own words: "Now in art-production God is just as operative as he is in the phenomena of nature; but the Divine, as it closes itself in the work of art, has been generated out of the spirit, and thus has won a suitable thoroughfare for its existence, whereas just being there in the unconscious sensuousness of nature is not a mode of appearance appropriate to the Divine."[63]

If we examine beauty as a concrete image of the Idea and take account of Hegel's notion of the concrete universal, we might find some grounds in Hegel's thought for rejoining the Kantian sense of the "transcendental" with the Aristotelian-Thomist usage. Here we must look again at the "radiance" of beauty, beauty as the sensuous "shining" of the Idea. Now the concept of "shining," or "radiance" has the very important meaning of not being susceptible of confinement to the level of the unity of a simple thing. Thus the presence of beauty is not just "thingly." Or better, a beautiful thing reveals a presence that seems elusive and impossible of easy fixation, like light dancing on the eternally moving waters of the ocean. We must note this because it brings out in Hegel the fact that with beauty the presence of *Geist* in sensuous shape cannot represent any simple "objectification" or "reification" of *Geist*. A presence more ultimate than that of the finite object comes to appearance in and through the finite beautiful thing itself; in this appearance the finite thing discloses this more ultimate presence. Hegel himself speaks in many places of the finite and the infinite, always insisting on never absolutely separating the two. Carrying through this insistence on non-separation, perhaps we can make some sense of the presence of the beautiful as one very significant, sensuous embodiment of the infinite power of *Geist*. Just as the shining of light illumines things while not being itself just a thing, so the shining of the Idea reveals the beauty of things by bringing to appearance more than their mere "reified" thinghood. In its beauty, that is, the finite thing points beyond its own finiteness; but this "beyond" is right here, it is not an empty *Jenseits*; for with the finite beautiful thing this "something more" is no empty absence but made concretely present.

We can restate the point by correlating this "non-reified" aspect of beauty with the question whether beauty is a "transcendental" in Aquinas' sense. Truth, unity, good, being are said to be transcendentals, explicitly identified as such by Aquinas. Some controversy surrounds beauty, however. Some say it is to be assimilated to the case of the good; others speak of beauty as a "quasi-transcendental." Maritain, a most able defender and perhaps the most bold explorer of Thomist aesthetics, accords beauty a genuine transcendental status. What exactly is at stake with respect to this status? In the traditional meaning the transcendentals were said to denote universal characteristics of being, pervasive in being and proper to being as such, and ultimately making possible our intelligible discourse about being. As universals, however, they are not just any "ordinary" universals: general characterizations which supply common features of a plurality of instances of things of a certain kind. "Humanity" is an "ordinary" universal in this sense; that is, it refers us to a kind of being, man, and specifies general characteristics common to all instances of this one kind of being. Transcendentals, on the other hand, are said to be universal in an even more universal sense; they are "super-universal," as it were. That is, they are universal not just in virtue of being applicable to one kind of being but in virtue of being applicable to all and every instance or manifestation of being. Thus they are said to characterize being itself as its most fundamental universality.

It is not necessary here to go into further detail concerning the precise status of beauty as a possible transcendental in Aquinas. Enough has been said to suggest the main point here. Even if some Thomists do deny beauty full transcendental status, our study of Hegel's aesthetics does not bar us from agreeing with Maritain when he speaks of beauty as bordering on such a type of metaphysical universality. For such metaphysical universality is not only more than our normal generalizing universals; it is also more than "reified" thinghood. This reveals itself in the recalcitrance beauty displays to being encapsulated in abstract generalizing concepts. Beauty can never be captured fully by such concepts, for it is not a simple general feature; it is always a certain qualitative presence. Hence those aesthetic theories that deny the adequacy of the analytic intellect to beauty are here correct. Hegel agrees with this denial in that beauty cannot be encompassed by what he calls *Verstand*. At the same time, this qualitative presence of beauty that is not susceptible to generaliza-tion in abstract concepts is more than the mere present thinghood of a "reified" particular. Beauty may be singular but its significance is not that of a sheer inarticulate "this" — precisely because the singular embodiment of beauty reveals something of the transcendental nature of beauty, reveals indeed something concerning the whole of being, of being *qua* being in the Aristotelian terms. Put somewhat differently, the Platonists are wrong, if by Platonism we understand the attempt to assimilate beauty to an abstract idea. Similarly the positivists are wrong, if we understand them to restrict beauty and its value to our emotive response to a particular thing, as, say, in A.J. Ayer's analysis of the aesthetic. Beauty is both concrete and universal in a way that neither of these extremes grasp, a way which the Aristotelian-Thomist notion of transcendental universality does help to specify.

In Hegelian terms, the concrete universal has something of the same universality for it too is neither the separated Platonic *eidos* nor the pointillistic particular of the nominalist or the positivist. As a concrete universal beauty is not reducible either to a detached intel-lectual grasp of an abtract universal, nor to an emotive response to a sheer particular. Kant claims that "the beautiful is what gives pleasure universally without a concept." We might mistakenly under-stand this to mean that beauty is just pleasure in the emotivist sense, that it is without any reference to concepts at all. Thus it is easy to move from Kant's statement to an emotivist theory of the aesthetic, like the positivist Ayer. Commenting on Kant's statement, Maritain rightly says that this view is vitiated by the neglect of the relation of beauty to the intellect, a neglect not found in Aquinas, according to Maritain.[64] A similar point must be made with respect to Hegel. Hegel does not neglect the relation of beauty and mind, particularly in its highest form of reason or *Vernunft*. Hegel agrees with Kant's freeing of beauty from abstract concepts but not with the freeing of beauty from the concept considered as a concrete universal. Hegel's defense of the necessary link of beauty with the immediacy of man's passionate nature (passion is essential for Hegel in *every* great work of man), Hegel's defense of art's infinity — both of these are related to the recalcitrance of beauty to abstract concepts. But what Hegel means by a concrete concept is very different from Kant's concept, which ultimately, as Hegel's criticism of Kant implies, turns into a subjectivistic construction of *Verstand*, not the true concept of *Vernunft*.

Hegel's agreement with the view that beauty cannot be grasped by an abstract concept, and yet his "cognitivism" in aesthetics, can only be understood against the background of both beauty and the true concept as concrete universals. Thus the Idea in Hegel might be said to function similarly to the transcendentals in Aristotle and Aquinas, but within the post-Kantian context. The Hegelian Idea, articulating itself into the series of fundamental categories unfolded in the *Logic*, is not an abstract idea in our own private consciousness nor in any otherwordly Platonic heaven. Rather it refers us to the intelligibles that ontologically ground the metaphysical structures of actuality and that logically ground the intelligibility of man's rational discourse about the real. As the sensuous shining of the Idea, as the Ideal, beauty for Hegel is "transcendental" in the two usages we have discussed. It is transcendental in the ancient sense in grounding the aesthetic in a metaphysical context. As such it answers to the need for the grounding of the aesthetic in the actualities of objectivity, and not just in some vague indeterminate way with some abstract, indefinite universality. Beauty must be concretized in individual wholes, but since such wholes "shine" with the Idea in its infinity, they cannot be reduced to limited particulars.

Here by what might have seemed like a detour we have come back again to the aesthetic dilemma of modernity. For since such wholes cannot be pinned down to limited particularity but are concretely universal, subjectivity in its infinite inwardness need not experience the temptation to transgress their presence into the empty space beyond, into an empty beyond. Thus such wholes appeal to the "transcendental" in the more modern usage: beauty in its concrete universality calls forth the spiritual need in the self to participate in the articulating of the beautiful, to concretize, to conserve and to communicate the Ideal in great works of art. What here of the peculiar universal delight we attain with beauty as the Ideal — universal delight as opposed to a merely inward "emotive" satisfaction, or to a "pathological" passion in its isolated particularity? If we couple this universal delight with the Ideal as disclosing the Idea in a concrete universal, I believe it is difficult to avoid the conclusion that the beautiful testifies to what we might perhaps call a metaphysical affirmation of the actual. This brings us to the question whether and in what way beauty in Hegel is tied up with an aesthetic theodicy.

Aesthetic Theodicy and the Transfiguration of the Ugly

Hegel explicitly presents his philosophy of history as a theodicy: philosophical reason makes intelligible the presence of the divine working in history. The issue of theodicy is not without important aesthetic ramifications. First, the project of any theodicy is defined by an effort to reconcile the affirmation of God's goodness and power with man's encounter with evil in the world. Is God's goodness powerless to defeat that evil? Or is God's power lacking in good will to overcome the evil? In one case we have the appearance of an impotent goodness; in the other the appearance of an indifferent, perhaps even hostile power. In both cases we encounter a recalcitrance to affirming the value of what is. Considerations parallel to the ethical also apply to the aesthetical. In this case the difficulty parallel to evil consists in the question of the ugly. When we experience the ugly, we sometimes recoil before a deformed, disordered, disharmonious reality. The ugly may indeed give rise to a revulsion to the real, indeed a deep disgust with being itself. A significant contemporary example of this might be the kind of experience imaginatively described by Sartre in *Nausea*, carried forward in reflective form in *Being and Nothingness*: being in its unjustified, unjustifiable brute thereness. Sartre's ontology might thus be seen to originate in the aesthetic experience of the metaphysical ugliness of being.

Our question is: how do we affirm the beauty of being if our experience of what is is shot through with the recalcitrance of the ugly? Do we just affirm the value of beauty and yield the concession that it is impotent before the ugly? Or affirming beauty, do we assert that its power is just indifferent to the ugly? In the first case we seem to end with something like the impotent, morbid beauty of the Beautiful Soul, wistfully yearning for a universal affirmation that ought to be but never actually is. In the second case, we seem to find ourselves with a kind of militant aestheticism that aggressively asserts the power of beauty over against the ugly, but does so by restricting its realm to a specialized, hence less than universal significance. In both cases, in fact, we seem to end up with something very similar, namely, a beauty that now impotently, now militantly, sets itself off from the ugly, in antithesis to the ugly. But since we encounter the ugly in our experience of what is, any affirmation of such beauty would seem inevitably to be forced to narrow its range and so become incapable of extending its affirmation to the whole. Just as evil presents a fundamental resistance to the ethical affirmation of the goodness of being, so the ugly offers a counterpart resistance to affirming beauty as a concrete universal or transcendental category. Thus any Hegelian claim to concrete universality regarding beauty seems to be contradicted by the inescapable presence of the ugly.

There is this further connection of theodicy and aesthetics, in that one of the recurrent and highly influential answers to the problem of evil has an inescapable aesthetic ring to it. One kind of theodicy gives God an alibi, as it were, by attributing the origin of evil to man's free-will, as we find especially in the Augustinian account. Another kind of theodicy (sometimes called the virtue defense in distinction from the free-will defense) may emphasize the fact that opposition, suffering, evil are necessary contrasts in man's struggle to be virtuous and so to actualize his essence. The world is not a hedonistic paradise but in the poet Keats' words, "a vale of soul-making."[65] Without its contrast opposite, evil, we just would not know or realize the good. Obviously Hegel's interpretation of the original fall as *necessary* to the process of man's self-conscious, knowing realization is not at odds with this view. Struggle with opposition is absolutely necessary for Hegel in all forms of experience, and not just in the process of man's ethical realization. Otherwise, as in the prelapsarian paradise of Eden before evil, man would remain in immediate, innocent, unknowing unity with being. Man is called to a mediated wholeness of being, one impossible without the struggle with opposition and the labor of the self in process of becoming — Hegel's variation on Keats' "soul-making." If the free-will theodicy focuses on the origin of evil, if you like, on its archaeology, this second, virtue theodicy focuses on the end or purpose of evil, its teleology. The aesthetic and the teleological, however, are interconnected. In Kant's *Critique of Judgment*, for instance, aesthetic teleology comes out in beauty as a possible symbol of the morally good, uniting the sensuous and the supersensible, giving us some relation to the ideal of completeness. Hegel's aesthetic teleology extends beyond man's moral perfection, though perhaps it is highly significant that Kant also tries to couple beauty and the teleology of nature in the *Third Critique*. We find here a series of efforts to envisage wholeness with the result that the dualism between man and nature, beauty and the whole is not a stark polarity.

This effort to envisage wholeness is most pronounced in the third type of theodicy. For in this third type of theodicy, sometimes just called the "aesthetic theodicy," the teleological justification of evil becomes most strongly emphasized. In this theodicy evil is seen as a necessary part of the whole, such that within the whole it ultimately contributes to the harmony of the whole. This idea of the harmony of the whole has an august ancestry, and its link with aesthetic beauty is here clearly evident. In this vein, for instance, the Pythagorean mystic vision of the music of the spheres and of the kinship of mathematical *logos* with the universal *harmonia* yields a cosmology as deeply aesthetical as it is logical in its basic character. Similarly, we find this aesthetical character in Plato's cosmogony in the *Timaeus*:[66] the Demiurgos is like an eternal artist who, to generate the best world possible, produces in accordance with the eternal, which, of course, for Plato is marked by self-sufficient wholeness and serene harmony. The world is said to be a cosmos, which for the Greeks signified a well-governed unity — the aesthetic note is unavoidable — an adornment, a thing of harmonious beauty.

The creator God of the Judaeo-Christian tradition, too, is said to possess the true vision of the whole, like a cosmic artistic creator, integrating providentially the discordant noise of history in an eschatological harmony. Aquinas resorts to this aesthetic theodicy in exploiting the metaphor of the painting to make sense of evil: just as in the total painting, shadows and darkness are necessary to the balance and illumination of the entirety, so evil produces the contrast necessary to the beautiful order of the whole.[67] We cannot adequately view the world as a divine art work, for as finite we are confined to a limited part and cannot clearly follow through limited discords to their divine *dénouement* and resolution. This convergence of the ethical and the aesthetical should not, of course, totally surprise us. The Greek notion of *kalokagathia* already alerts us to their inseparability in traditional thought; and in Aquinas, the convertability of being and the good, indeed the characterization of beauty as itself a kind of good, brings out further this link. In our own day, Whitehead continues this tradition. Not surprisingly, the parallels between Whitehead and Hegel are being increasingly explored by contemporary scholars. Not surprisingly also, Whitehead drew great inspiration for his own metaphysical thought from the Romantic poet Wordsworth, himself a poetic heir to the French Revolution (at least before his later creative decline) and the cultural heritage of Hegel's era. Not unexpectedly again, Whitehead, somewhat like Aquinas, points to the identification of the ultimate good with the aesthetic beauty of the whole.[68] If we can talk about the "value" of the world at all, it is in terms that recall the value of a work of art.

Since the beauty of art for Hegel is never a mere facsimile imitation of externality, it expresses an essential choice. All art selects what it considers essential for presentation, hence all art is the expression of value, indeed, if only implicitly, an affirmation of a basic evaluation of existence. A basic orientation towards the whole, man's pervasive sense of being comes into play here. For Hegel the basic values of different historical epochs, the overall orientation to being as a whole, whether this be affirmative or not, is tied up with that epoch's sense of the divine. For Hegel art too (and here its absolute dimension for him is revealed again) reveals such basic orientations and affirmations. As we see from Hegel's discussion of Symbolical, Classical and Romantic art, the ideal of beauty each of these expresses serves to articulate the total attunement or affirmation of a people or of an era or of a civilization to being as a whole. Beauty, or indeed the lack of beauty exhibits this fundamental orientation in sensuous form, even where that basic orientation stands against the affirmation of beauty or even denies there is any whole at all, as happens in some strands of modernity. This is the fundamental level at which we are to situate the affirmation of the beautiful, such that we see its close link with the notion of aesthetic theodicy. Hegel stands in the tradition of aesthetic theodicy when, for instance, he stresses that the true is the whole. The true here, of course, cannot be confined just to the correctness of propositional truth. Ultimately it refers us to, as it were, the metaphysical soundness of the actual, as in the term "a true friend" — that is, one who withstands, stands up before the fragmenting forces also at work within the actual. Beauty as we saw offers for Hegel the sensuous embodiment of wholeness, an embodiment that is significant because it is a concretion of absolute *Geist*. Just as we might say that the beautiful is the whole, so we might also say that the beautiful is the true, just in the above sense that ties us to the metaphysical soundness of the actual. Hegel is repeatedly disparaging of any form of philosophical thought which brings no more than metaphysical charges against the actual itself. The task of philosophy, in aesthetics as elsewhere, is not to rail against the actual but to struggle to bring to light its initially hidden rationality. Just so the affirmtion of beauty need not be an escape from the ugly, nor even be its contemptuous negation, but may be man's wrestling with its initially negative face for the purposes of its transformation.[69]

By those who bring metaphysical charges against the actual I mean, of course, those whom later Nietzsche would address as nihilists. The differences of Hegel and Nietzsche are more frequently noted (by Deleuze, to name but one current instance),[70] but here we see something of their sameness. For both insist on rising above nihilism, Nietzsche through an atheism that has insistent aesthetic overtones, Hegel through a theodicy which has similar aesthetic features. We need to bear in mind here that in the tradition of aesthetic theodicy Hegel stresses very strongly that no justification of the actual must blind itself to the discordant notes and negative features of the actual. He affirms rather their necessity (as indeed Aquinas also seems to do). In Hegel's aesthetics we find a repeated refusal to deny opposition. Genuine affirmation must be won out of the very affirmation of opposition, the affirmation of its inescapable necessity.

Like Goethe, Hegel is set against the spirit of denial. Yet beauty for him is not some coy "sweetness and light," a merely domesticated Apollonianism, the ideal of Winckelmann gone to aesthetic softness. There is, of course, the stress on the tranquility and serenity so essential to Winckelmann. Yet Hegel's aesthetic views extol no quietist passivity. He was acutely sensitive to the tragic, destructive conflicts in Greek culture, particularly revealed in its drama. As a student of Aristotle's theory of tragedy, he was well aware that though tragic destruction yields pity for nobility caught in inescapable conflict, yet there is no beauty without terror. So also he reminds us of the "infinite grief" that comes to human history with Christian and Romantic art, gathered into the embrace of that most devastating of experiences, the experience of the "death of God." This experience might here be seen, again clearly in advance of Nietzsche, as that confrontation with actuality, now seeming to be drained of its ultimate value, actuality devoid of the absolute, and so the ground of the beauty of its being vanished. Just as he says that philosophy begins in the experience of division, so also, I suggest, he would concur with Rilke: the beginning of beauty can be in the terrible. Every merely escapist aesthetics of beauty must be derided; beauty rather must seek to accept and include within itself the divisive, destructive forces of complex conflicts.

One of the overall aims of Hegel's philosophy is to help further man's genuine being at home in the world. Beauty contributes essentially to this being at home, but its contribution cannot be genuine if it affirms a fake reassurance, a facade harmony which prettifies existence, hence falsifies it. At first glance Hegel's doctrine of beauty as the Ideal might seem to lend itself to this interpretation. We can avoid this conclusion, however, if we dwell on beauty as involving an active process whereby it effects a genuine idealization. In this way the actively embracing, including character of beauty can be manifest. Thus if we return to the experience of the ugly, we can ask what the beauty of art effects here? Part of our answer must include the following. Even in the most painful and merciless presentation of the ugly, art effects a transposition of the ugly into a new context. In presenting the ugly art already affirms the ugly, yet also sets it forth for contemplation within a new framework. That is, it frees the ugly from the immediate revulsion we might feel, thus mediating a release of our perceptions which allow us to see the ugly both as it really is and yet to see it differently. The beauty of art in this sense might be seen as the aesthetic *Aufhebung* of the ugly: that is, the recognition and acknowledgment of the ugly; the transcendence and supersession of the ugly in its unmediated and meaningless being; the preservation of the ugly in a new more inclusive context where we affirm it differently, that is, released from the sense of recoil and revulsion with which we first greet the ugly in its immediacy and mere thereness. When Hegel speaks of art as higher than nature something of this is at stake: art divines and mediates an affirmative significance, a beauty that the immediate surfaces of given life do not straightaway yield. The struggle of the artist is to release and articulate the spiritual significance thus revealed. The ugly, here the negative in aesthetic guise, must not remain outside art but must be incorporated within the Ideal itself as a necessary moment that compels the spiritual honesty of the artist.[71]

Clearly also Hegel's *Aesthetics* show him to be cognizant of the fact that, in contradistinction to Greek art which sometimes tended to put to one side, even repress certain experiences of the ugly, the experience of the ugly grows wider, more universal in the modern era and its art. This, however, is a challenge to the ideal of beauty, not necessarily a sign of its impotency or redundancy. With the widening of the experience of the ugly, the embracing powers of beauty in the modern age demand a universality genuinely extended to all this is. This reminds us, of course, of Hegel's view of the historical extension of freedom itself from the Greek world where only some are free to the modern world where, after Christianity, *all* are accorded at least the right to be free. Such ethical and political freedom is aesthetically reflected in Hegel's own view of modern art as having no special subject matter. Even the most base themes of prosaic life now can legitimately be taken up. The conservative may see this as perhaps an aesthetic dissolution but for Hegel it represents the possible widening of art's embrace. Here Hegel was well aware of the aesthetic significance of Terence–like tolerance: *humani nihil a me alienum puto.*[72] In this tolerance the modern era serves to raise the stakes concerning art's universality. Within this tolerant universality and its sometimes promiscuous, chaotic pluralism, Hegel recognizes the difficulty for the artist of perceiving and articulating any emergent wholes. Yet to do this still remains the aesthetic goal for Hegel, a goal approximated by one of the most universal of artists, one who even in his modernity is tolerant, indeed affirmative of all that is, and who in his art presents this complex affirmation, namely Shakespeare.[73]

The question of what art does to the base issues of prosaic life, the way its idealizing power may open up the spiritual significance of the ugly, releasing even the ugly into a new context of beauty, these bring out what we can call the theme of transfiguration in Hegel's aesthetic theodicy. No doubt Hegel did not think that the aesthetic alone, considered as some specialized, priviliged form of consciousness, could constitute a full theodicy. Nevertheless, the relation of art and the absolute, and the idealizing power of beauty both contribute essentially and profoundly to a transfigured sense of all that is. Hegel speaks of philosophy itself in just these terms: philosophy is not a consolation; it is more, it reconciles, it transfigures reality.[74] So also with art. The concept of positive appearance, previously noted in connection with the doctrine of the Ideal, gives substance to this theme of transfiguration. Once again we may note illuminating affinities with Nietzsche's aesthetics. Hegel's concept of the Ideal and the notion of positive appearance it yields (*Erscheinung* as the transfiguration of *Schein*, the transformation of illusory being into the shining of the essential) recalls Heidegger's claim that Nietzsche tries to give us an inverted Platonism and a new interpretation of the senses. Heidegger quotes Nietzsche: "I wish an even greater spiritualization and augmentation of the senses."[75] What Heidegger neglects is that this is old Hegelian wine in new Nietzschean bottles. The doctrine of positive appearance is Hegel already inverting Platonism, inverting the excessively dualized Platonism, that is. In words almost exactly echoed by Nietzsche, it is Hegel who first speaks of the beauty of art as the spiritualization of the senses. Indeed a version of the view is also to be found in Marx's concept of labor as the formation of the senses: Marx carries the concept of labor outside the work of art, but also carries forward the theme of transfiguration, only now interpreted in terms of revolutionary politics.

Nietzsche too realizes the fundamental problem of the ugly. Ugliness, he says, seems to be the contradiction of beauty, the negation of art, what art excludes.[76] Yet if we listen to some of the things Nietzsche says about art, it is impossible to suppress the suspicion that we have heard a similar motif already in Hegel. For like Hegel, Nietzsche calls attention to the transfiguring, perfecting power of art. Like Hegel, we find him talking of the power of beauty to embrace conflict, even violent opposition: "Beauty therefore is, to the artist, something which is above all order of rank, because in beauty contrasts are overcome, the highest sign of power thus manifesting itself in the conquest of opposites; and achieved without a feeling of tension: violence being no longer necessary, everything submitting and obeying so easily, and doing so with good grace; this is what delights the powerful will of the artist."[77] Likewise too, beauty for Nietzsche entails an "aesthetic yea" ("This is beautiful" is an affirmation) reminiscent of the metaphysical affirmation at the heart of Hegel's aesthetic theodicy. Hegel's own discussion of Greek tragedy is echoed in Nietzsche's belief in the tragic artist's refusal to shun the terrible and questionable things in life — his strength consists, like that of Hegel's thinker, in consenting to stare the negative in the face.

Hegel's own distinguishing between the morbid impotence of the Beautiful Soul and the more substantial, genuine, robust beauty resurfaces in Nietzsche's distinction between the decadent and tragic artist. "A similar case would be that of the artists of decadence, who at bottom maintain a nihilistic attitude to life, and take refuge in the beauty of forms (the "love of beautiful" may thus be something very different: it may be the expression of impotence in this respect.) The most convincing artists are those who make harmony ring out of every discord . . . . The depth of the tragic artist consists in the fact that his aesthetic instinct surveys the most remote results, that he does not halt short-sightedly at the thing that is nearest, that he says Yea to the whole cosmic economy, and that he justifies the terrible, the evil, the questionable; that he more than justifies it."[78] All of this compares with Hegel's affirmation of opposition, the necessity of the negative, yet out of negation arising the "yes" to what is, a "yes" which serves as an apotheosis of being itself. Indeed Nietzsche's description of the tragic artist reminds us somewhat of Hegel's conception of the philosopher: one who knows, without flinching, about the "slaughterbench" of history, the unintelligibility of good without evil, the necessity of the fall, the struggle to embrace the ugly within beauty, even indeed the "death of God."

There are, of course, deep differences with Hegel, not to be minimized. Hegel, for instance does not villify "*logos*" as "logocentrism," nor couple the "logical" with the "ugly" in opposition to the aesthetic, as Nietzsche does.[79] Ultimately too there is much less of the note of individualistic subjectivity in Hegel. Moreover, Hegel's aesthetic theodicy, in its pursuit of the theme of transfiguration, does not divorce beauty from truth and the good. Nietzsche tends to so divorce truth and beauty; especially in the *Birth of Tragedy* beauty sometimes seems a consolation for what Nietzsche seems to see as the horror of metaphysical truth. Where Nietzsche, as Heidegger points out in his study, sees a discordance of truth and art, Hegel sees their continuity, their concord. Thus for Hegel art can never be merely aesthetic, but beauty itself must be grounded in the ultimate truth of what is, in art's bond with the absolute. Dealing with the same problem of Hegel and his era, namely the lack of a central, organizing mythology, and the secularization of nature and society by the forces of mechanistic science and modern economics, dealing also with Hegel's problem of the romantic consciousness, dealing with these problems with a similar reverence for the exemplars and inspirational sources of the Greek acme and the balanced wholeness of the Goethean ideal, Nietzsche's aesthetics might be seen as an heroic effort to resacralize a world devoid of the divine, so to rescue it from its valueless thereness, its indifferent nihilist being. Hegel's aesthetic theodicy might be seen to share this intention but, by contrast, it implies that actuality can be rescued from valueless thereness, only if beauty is grounded in the ultimate truth of what is, only if art's bond with the absolute is properly safeguarded. Short of this, one suspects for Hegel that Nietzsche's ideal of the tragic artist runs the risk of collapsing again into the decadent artistic type he so strenuously wished to transcend, and that beauty's transfiguring power would eventually wither away.

The Future of Beauty

I have dwelt on Nietzsche and Hegel in the preceding pages because this brings us again closer to what seems to be the current status of the beautiful. Many contemporaries see in Nietzsche the antithesis of Hegel, and many of these also seem to feel that the ideal of beauty itself is bankrupt. My point is this: if Nietzsche is our contemporary, so also is Hegel, and indeed, as I believe, in ways more helpful than Nietzsche, helpful indeed in dealing with some of the very difficulties that Nietzsche himself explored. Hence it might be appropriate at the close of this study to venture some final reflections on Hegel and the future of beauty, taking into account the complexities in Hegel's teachings concerning art and the absolute. Of course, in Hegel it goes without saying that his attitude towards the future always evinces a certain ambiguity.[80] Far from being the unhesitating prophet he is often, a la Popper, thought to be, his philosophy tends to be cautious, if not downright hostile to any efforts at prediction. The dialectical character of Hegel's philosophy is turned to comprehend the process of becoming in what has become, in the *Erinnerung* that comprehends the rationality in the becoming of what now is, not in clairvoyance with respect to what is yet to become. The same task of *Erinnerung* marks Hegel's aesthetics. Yet, as previously noted, for Hegel philosophical *Erinnerung* is not identical with Nietzsche's antiquarian history, the working over of the old just for the sake of the old; it has some likeness to monumental history which tries to comprehend what may be hatching in the present and for which the history of past greatness provides some inspiring precedents. That is, while eschewing uncritical clairvoyance, the Hegelian remembrance of the past and grasp of the present clearly cannot be absolutely divorced from the directionality of history towards the future. And indeed Hegel's aesthetics, particularly in its penetration of the strengths and flaws of romantic consciousness is plainly clairvoyant in some sense of the gathering eclipse of beauty that, in some respects, has only deepened since.

Hegel diagnosed many of the contemporary forces creating challenges for, when not antagonistic to, art and beauty, all of them tied to key aspects of our theme, art and the absolute: the creative freedom accorded to the modern artist seemingly unanchored from the discipline and order of classical *mimesis*; the precariousness of art in a predominantly scientific age and the difficulty of renewing the relation of image and concept, poetic sources and philosophical reflection, thus helping art recuperate after the loss of its earlier naivete and philosophy recover a way back to concreteness out of its maze of abstractions; the fragmenting forces of modernity, the social and economic alienation that is heightened for the artist by the lack of a unifying religious mythology and the consequent hemorrhaging of the spiritual power of the aesthetic; modern man's continuing need for a significant end, some articulate unifying *telos* in the flow of time itself, and art's contribution to this; the debunking spirit of modernity, its celebration of the negating powers of contradiction, aired through Romantic Irony and given recent shape in the philosophy of deconstruction. All of these themes have been the focus of the different previous chapters. They come to some focus in the eclipse of beauty, the gathering signs of which a troubled Hegel noted.

For Hegel art and the aesthetic do not represent any panacea. Nor can they, even when in wholesome, healthy condition, answer to all the dimensions of the modern problematic. Yet the orientation to the actual that they articulate and realize is absolutely essential in any effort to address that problematic in its fullness. As we have argued throughout, with respect to some of the chief elements of that problematic, Hegel's aesthetics is astonishingly timely. Hegel appreciated the passing of classical beauty, yet also for him there is no absolute death of beauty. No eclipse is absolute. In the elegiac, sometimes nostalgic note we find in Hegel's celebration of classical beauty, we may detect some germ of hope. Though Hegel describes a surpassing, he does not prescribe the grave. Since the future is not closed, there is no bar to the possible recuperation of beauty in its inspiring power. It is hard to think that Hegel would have expended such prodigious energy on his aesthetics if the net gain of the entire enterprise were to just inter art and beauty, as Croce and others imply. Nietzsche describes a romantic in these terms: one whose "great dissatisfaction with himself makes him productive — who looks away from himself and his fellows, and sometimes, therefore, looks backwards." Hegel's own dissatisfaction with the fragmenting forces of his era and his backward philosophical look perhaps make him romantic in this sense. If the backward look is to avoid antiquarian barrenness, the beauty it seeks to recover must be on the *other* side of contemporary fragmentation. The backward look may become creative in a new way. Since it is a literal impossibility to return to the past, the only way to "recover" its power is by creating in the present and into the future. Hegel does not foreclose this possibility.

Perhaps here Hegel's notion of *Aufhebung* reminds us a little of the Heideggerian retrieval of the tradition: not simply to discard what seems just dead and gone, but to renew a dialogue with the greatest human possibilities, and so to confer an added density of meaning on the present. Heidegger implies that his own turning back to dialogue with the tradition may make possible a leap forward. With Hegel's *Aufhebung*, we retrace a process of becoming to comprehend it; yet this comprehension is not just a return to a beginning; more fully it is the discernment, even in the beginning, of the movement of becoming towards a *telos*. Generally, the Heideggerian retrieval seems to imply that the origin is most primordially rich, while the development out of and after the origin tends to fall away from this original richness. With the Hegelian notion of *Aufhebung*, the beginning is not what is absolutely rich, but rather its implicit richness is only realized and redeemed in the explicitly and fully articulated *telos*. Hence in Hegel we never find counsel of a return to the primitive, as some Nietzschean views seem to imply. Rather we need to press through towards the *telos* — which in this case means, not to retreat behind modernity to classical beauty but to pass beyond both the passing of the classical and the decomposing forces of modernity.

Obviously, too, because of this pressing through to a *telos*, any Hegelian hope for the future must differ from the Heideggerian-Nietzschean view. The teleological dimension of Hegel's thought inevitably means that Hegel's ideal of aesthetic beauty will always have a tendency (to use Nietzschean terms) for the "Apollonian" to dominate. The Nietzschean emphasis on the Dionysian, of course, is of a piece with a return to origins that tries to get behind the occluding accretions of later developments. Plainly too this is continuous with a certain celebration of the primitive in modern culture. Indeed we might venture to describe the development from pre-Hegelian to post-Hegelian aesthetics in these terms. We have passed from the "noble simplicity and tranquil grandeur" of Winckelmann's ideal, through the passionate *Sturm und Drang* of the troubled Romantics, through Hegel's efforts to recover unity and discover the voice of the divine in the whirlwind, to Nietzsche and his successors where the storm blows and the whirlwind turns but no divine sound is uttered — nothing, it seems, but man alone raising his forced voice above the clamor of chaos, while, now grim, now exultant, he lashes himself to the mast of meaninglessness. Apollo seems to have become a drowned god.

As Nietzsche speaks of the matter, Apollo represents the *principium individuationis*. And undoubtedly contemporary problems are sometimes compounded by the accentuated stress on the individual self, whether in Christianity, in romantic art, or in post-Christian, post-romantic culture. For Hegel, however, we cannot step behind self-consciousness — selfness is inerasable. For Hegel there is no step behind modern self-consciousness. Any modern return to origins in this sense is itself the result of modern self-consciousness (its awareness of the problematics of modernity) and so is not really the return to the primitive it intends and claims to be. It is also false to think of Hegel as not cognizant of the power of the Dionysian. Nietzsche was far from being the first Germanic Dionysian. The question really is how we discipline and shape the undoubted dynamism of the Dionysian, what kind of aesthetic education (in Schiller's terms) we give it, what *Bildung* it must undergo to properly realize its otherwise undifferentiated and formless power. For Hegel (as ultimately for Nietzsche too), art cannot be art without the Apollonian. Nor can there be an art now which avoids completely the infinite inwardness of the self. But Dionysus, if allowed to be the whole, ultimately destroys wholeness. We must struggle to affirm wholeness, ever in tension with the equally necessary recognition of fragmentation.

While being an Apollonian, Hegel is a complex, guarded one, one for whom a "sweetness and light" Apollonianism is impossible. As should be evident, it is less a Nietzschean Dionysian primitivism than the infinite negativity of Christian, post-Christian subjectivity that poses for Hegel the greatest challenge to the beautiful formed wholeness of the Apollonian ideal — for this infinite negativity easily overflows finite boundaries and limits, even into torment and delirium. Still Hegel opposes himself to an infinite, formless ferment, looking to a wholeness that will gather into itself the infinite power of *Geist*. To avoid the extremes of formless infinity and dead, finite form, to balance and unify infinite *Geist* and concrete wholeness may be extraordinarily difficult and rare. For this Hegel looks to the articulated end rather than to the primitive beginning. The question again is whether a new wholeness, recalling classical harmony, is possible *after* the emergence of this infinite inwardness of subjectivity, the "infinite grief" of the Christian experience, and the desacralization of the world effected by modern secularity. Nothing in our discussion of Hegel makes this an impossibility. The transfiguring power of beauty reveals its importance again here. This power is not exhausted by the Greek ideal and its achievement. The Greek ideal may be exemplary but it is not insurpassably absolute. After the "infinite grief" of Christianity and its secularized version, namely the nihilism of more recent times, we still need to put beauty where the ugly is, and transfigure the prose of the secular world, perhaps find a new piety of the secular in the way, say, at the beginning of the modern era Dutch painting seems to have done for Hegel.[81]

Is the above possibility of a new wholeness likely? Throughout his life Hegel's hope for a new wholeness alternated between being buoyed up and being deflated. Yet the hope was never entirely extinguished. This might seem rather minimal, but given some subsequent repudiations of the hope itself, it is far from negligible. Hegel is open to the future as the ground of the renewed disclosure of the essential; some later thinkers will repudiate the notion of the essential altogether. One such essential for Hegel was the ideal of beauty; some later thinkers will jettison the ideal entirely. Hegel's thought involves a diagnosis of the crisis of the whole, and a constructive effort to ground a new whole. After Hegel the crisis of the whole becomes such that the very notion of wholeness suffers onslaughts of unremitting criticism. So much so that Hegel's constructive labor seems almost *archaic* to the contemporary view — itself a monument in the way the Greeks often seemed to Hegel and his contemporaries. The question for us is whether these monuments can still offer back life to the living. Hegel himself seems to have suffered many burials and yet so surprises us with an equal number of "revivals" that we suspect that Hegel, like the art Croce thinks he buried, is not interred beyond recall.

Even Hegel's song of elegy for classical beauty is not only a hymn of mourning but is also a hymn of hidden hope. What was great shows what was possible for man, what was actually great; and something akin, once realized as a possibility, can never again be just an empty possibility, feeding on a vain hope. There is melancholy in Hegel's celebration of classical beauty, but melancholy is only the other, open side of a secret longing. Obviously Hegel, as an historical realist, chastized in himself any such romantic nostalgia. But the desire for the ideal and its actual embodiment remains real. Without this Hegel's philosophy loses an essential part of its *raison d'être*. Once asked about a perhaps analogous question of the possibility of future life, namely regarding the hope of immortality, Hegel is reputedly to have just silently pointed towards the Bible.[82] This might seem straightaway to offer the simple affirmative answer: yes, there is a future. However, in the Bible, we also read:

Go thy way, eat thy bread with joy, and drink thy wine with a merry heart, for God now accepteth thy works . . . Whatsoever thy hand findeth to do, do it with thy might; for there is no work, nor device, nor knowledge, nor wisdom, in the grave whither thou goest. (*Ecclesiastes* 9:7,10)

Hegel says nothing, and his silent pointing is profoundly ambiguous. Even his wife seems not to have known his attitude to immortality, shorn of all ambiguity.[83] Is there a future for beauty and if so, what might be its shape? Perhaps it is not fortuituous that the just cited passage (from a work better known for its cry of "vanity of vanities") might be turned to our theme and seen to say: apart altogether from a future life, seize the day and work to transfigure life now! We come back to the transfiguring work of beauty. How might beauty so work to transfigure life? Again Hegel remains wisely silent. This ambiguity is perhaps infuriating to some, but it can be seen as consistently dialectical.[84] Is this a silence which says "no," the silence of closure before past, achieved glory? Or is it a different silence, the silence of openness before the promise of future possibility? We would like to think, given our study here, that Hegel's song for the past, revealing his obvious love of art and aesthetic beauty, makes his silence an opening of the second kind.

Notes

Introduction

1. In recent decades Jack Kaminsky's *Hegel on Art* (Albany: SUNY Press, 1962) is one of the few book-length studies in English of Hegel's aesthetics — one seriously flawed by its divorce of art from Hegel's system as a whole. It would appear that we have to go as far back as J.S. Kedney's *Hegel's Aesthetics* (Chicago: Griggs and Co., 1892) for a previous book-length exposition. For work outside of the Anglo-American context, see the comprehensive *Bibliographie zur Ästhetik Hegels 1830–1965* compiled by W. Henckmann, in *Hegel-Studien*, 5, 1969. See also the bibliography compiled by Joseph Flay in *Art and Logic in Hegel's Philosophy*, W.E. Steinkraus and K. Schmitz (eds.), (New Jersey: Humanities Press, 1980), pp. 239–249. Stephen Bunjay's *Beauty and Truth: A Study of Hegel's Aesthetics* (Oxford: Oxford University Press, 1984) appeared while the present work was sufficiently advanced in press as to make it impossible for me to adequately assess its contribution. I anticipate publishing a review of Bunjay's book in a future volume of the *Journal of the History of Philosophy*.

2. See, for instance, John Toews, *Hegelianism: The Path Towards Dialectical Humanism, 1805–1841* (New York: Cambridge University Press, 1980), p. 86, where he says: "The inner consolidation of Hegelianism into an academic school centered in Berlin was intimately connected to the external consolidation of the ties among Hegelianism, the Prussian Kultusministerium, and the Berlin literary and cultural elites ... Moreover, the influence of Hegelianism in Berlin was not confined to the university. The sympathy and support of patrons of literature and the arts like the Varnhagens, the Veits, and the Mendelssohns and influential cultural critics and journalists like Forster and Moritz Saphir (1795–1858) made Hegelianism an extremely

important, if not completely dominating, presence in the Berlin literary world and general culture scene." On the cultural context of Hegel's Berlin see Otto Pöggeler and A. Gethman-Siefert (eds.), *Kunsterfahrung und Kulturpolitik im Berlin Hegels, Hegel-Studien 22* (Bonn: Bouvier Verlag Herbert Grundmann, 1983).

3. See Merold Westphal, "The New Flight of the *Owl* at the End of the Hegel Revival: An Official Welcome to the New *Owl* from the President of the Hegel Society of America," in *The Owl of Minerva*, Vol. 15, No. 1, Fall, 1983, pp. 5–11, where he claims that the task of Hegel scholarship is not just to win a place in the sun for Hegel, but to move beyond any isolationist posture and treat of Hegel's importance in the contemporary philosophical conversation.

4. The details of this interplay (with the addition of political issues) in the development of Hegel is set forth in H.S. Harris, *Hegel's Development: Towards the Sunlight, 1770–1801* (Oxford: Clarendon Press, 1972).

5. G.W.F. Hegel, *Vorlesungen über die Ästhetik* I, in *Werke*, ed. E. Moldenhauer and K.M. Michel (Frankfurt: Suhrkamp Verlag, 1969–1971), Bd. 13, pp. 20–21; English translation by T.M. Knox, *Hegel's Aesthetics* (Oxford: Clarendon Press, 1975), Vol. I, p. 7. In future citations I will refer to these as VA and HA, respectively.

6. This, of course, is a recurring, one might almost say undying, controversy in Hegel's aesthetics. For a good recent discussion see Curtis Carter's, "A Re-examination of the 'Death of Art' interpretation of Hegel's Aesthetics," Ch. V of *Art and Logic in Hegel's Philosophy*. See my remarks in a Review of this volume in *The Owl of Minerva*, Vol. 12, No. 4, June 1981, pp. 7–9.

7. Religion in Hegel's philosophy has received much better treatment than art. See, for instance, E. Fackenheim, *The Religious Dimensions in Hegel's Thought* (Bloomington: Indiana University Press, 1967); Quentin Lauer, S.J., *Hegel's Concept of God* (Albany: SUNY Press, 1982); Bernard Reardon, *Hegel's Philosophy of Religion* (New York: Harper and Row, 1977); Darrell Christensen (ed.), *Hegel and the Philosophy of Religion* (The Hague: Nijhoff, 1970); Raymond Williamson, *Introduction to Hegel's Philosophy of Religion* (Albany: SUNY Press, 1984); James Yerkes, *The Christology of Hegel* (Albany: SUNY Press, 1982). Also William Desmond, "Hegel, Philosophy and Worship," *CITHARA*, 19:1, 1979, pp. 3–20; "Hegel and the Problem of Religious Representation," *Philosophical Studies* (Ireland), Vol. XXX, 1984, pp. 9–22.

8. Vincent Descombes in *Modern French Philosophy* (New York: Cambridge University Press, 1980), pp. 150–151, speaks of Derrida's thought as

requiring a double reading, a double science. Relevantly, Hegel who often is thought to function as an antitype to this kind of reading (Descombes very well brings out the role of Hegel in recent French philosophy as the antagonist who, it seems, can never be quite put down completely) lends himself (as a dialectical thinker) to a double reading, a reading however which need not produce the same result as decomposing destruction. Our "double" reading of Hegel's aesthetics rather attempts to be recuperative of the immanent, intricate complexity of his thought, doing justice to its embracing, many-sided character. This, of course, means that Hegel's thought is marked by internal tensions and the strain of ambiguity. A "double" reading is required by dialectical thought in this sense: we must do justice to the different poles in tension, the opposites and contraries gathered within the embrace of dialectical thinking. That is, if dialectic seeks a *coincidentia oppositorum*, then we can read this coincidence of opposites with the intention of making intelligible sense of the opposites themselves, as well as making sense of their movement towards coincidence. Put succinctly, it is nondialectical to have a single reading that reduces this coincidence to a univocal identity. The inherent complexity of Hegel's dialectical texts is thereby simplified and distorted. Nor is this "doubleness" a duplicity in the sense of an evasive deception — this would be to reduce a dialectical reading to unwarranted equivocal terms. I treat of this more fully in Ch. V below. I might note the same problem applies to the "doubleness" of Hegel's dialectical approach to religious *Vorstellung* (being both affirmative and critical), as I argue elsewhere (see "Hegel and the Problem of Religious Representation," cited note 7).

9. Like the undying issue of the "death" of art, Hegel's so called "swallowing up" of art and religion is a simplistic misrepresentation that continues to be repeated. It is a caricature which, because of repetition, seems to have taken on the status of an eternally frozen picture of Hegel and so bars our way to a less simplistic Hegel. To illustrate the continued presence of this view let me but cite a very recent example, Charles Hartshorne, *Insights and Oversights of Great Thinkers: An Evaluation of Western Philosophy* (Albany: SUNY Press, 1983), pp. 209–210: "Because Hegel does not see the true relations of universal and particular, he cannot properly relate philosophy and religion or philosophy and art. (On this point, Croce in *What is Living and What is Dead in Hegel* is helpful.) Hegel writes almost as though philosophy digests and swallows up religion, science and art . . . He does suggest a hegemony of philosophy that is unjustified. Times have changed. Today the problem is to give philosophy prestige at all. To that extent a philosopher must be partly on Hegel's side . . ." Hartshorne goes on, nevertheless, to try to save what is genuine in the system. Of course, if you emphasize the kinship of art and philosophy (as I do in Ch. II), the question

of the prestige of philosophy in a scientific age becomes somewhat different. I do not deny that Hegel gives a kind of "hegemony" to philosophy, but I do deny that the primacy of philosophy (a complexly qualified primacy) is adequately rendered in the language of "swallowing" or its variants.

10. Paul Ricoeur, *The Conflict of Interpretations*, trans. Kathleen McLaughlin (Evanston: Northwestern University Press, 1974), p. 62. Interestingly, here (pp. 62–78) Ricoeur approaches the problem of double meaning but tilts his view towards "the equivocalness of being" rather than a dialectical view.

11. The overall thrust of Hegelian thought to reconcile the ancient and modern is well recognized, but see especially Stanley Rosen, *G.W.F. Hegel: An Introduction to the Science of Wisdom* (New Haven: Yale, 1974).

12. Hartshorne's remarks, cited above, imply some such rebuke. The rebuke is far more shrill in recent French philosophy, as Decombes, *op. cit*, makes clear. The rebuke takes on tones of Nietzschean denunciation in Gilles Deleuze, *Nietzsche and Philosophy*, trans. H. Tomlinson (New York: Columbia University Press, 1983). Any such rebuke should be set in the context of Hegel's assertion that conceptual comprehension (*Begreifen*) is not a grasping comprehension (*Ergreifen*). *Phänomenologie des Geistes*, ed. J. Hoffmeister (Hamburg: Felix Meiner, 1952), p. 545; *Phenomenology of Mind*, trans. A.V. Miller (New York: Oxford University Press, 1977), p. 475.

13. In advance of Hegel, Kant in the *Critique of Judgment* (par. 49) speaks of aesthetical ideas as straining after a maximum of completeness, like the ideas of reason. Kant, of course, does not fall foul of the accusation of "totalitarian closure." Might we not see Hegel as developing the Kantian insight concerning aesthetical ideas, instead of, as the charge implies, reversing it. Some, no doubt, will argue that Hegel's development tends to pervert Kant's insight, but this is not necessary. For a preference for Kantian over Hegelian aesthetics see Rüdiger Bubner's essay "Hegel's Aesthetics: Yesterday and Today," Ch. II of *Art and Logic in Hegel's Philosophy*. Also "Über einige Bedingungen gegenwärtiger "Ästhetik"" in *Neue Hefte für Philosophie*, Vol. 5 (Gottingen: 1973).

14. See, for instance, William Empson, *Seven Types of Ambiguity* (Harmondsworth: Penguin Books, 1962). Of course the ambiguities in Hegel split between Left, Right and Centre among his followers after his death. See, Toews, *Hegelianism* on the many strands plucked by his followers from Hegel's ambiguous legacy.

Chapter One

1. See, for instance, M.H. Abrams, *The Mirror and the Lamp* (New York: Oxford University Press, 1953). The two metaphors of Abrams' title, as his classic study makes clear, correspond roughly to imitation and creation in our discussion here. Thus he says (p. viii): "The title of the book identifies two common and antithetical metaphors of mind, one comparing the mind to a reflector of external objects, the other to a radiant projector which makes a contribution to the objects it perceives. The first of these was characteristic of much of the thinking from Plato to the eighteenth century; the second typifies the prevailing romantic conception of the poetic mind." As our discussion throughout this study will hopefully make clear, this is an "antithesis" that Hegelian aesthetics indicates is less than ultimate, as is the related antithesis of ancient and modern. A recent criticism of the tradition of philosophy as captive to the model of the mirror is Richard Rorty's *Philosophy and the Mirror of Nature* (Princeton: Princeton University Press, 1979). Hegel is not captive to this model, though it is ironical that he is often thought to sum up and epitomize the said "tradition" of philosophy, often by disciples of Heidegger. Rorty himself is not unsympathetic to Hegel, though his Hegel is a truncated Hegel, that is, Hegelianism without the absolute.

2. For a discussion of some of the excesses of creationist language (in relation especially to Nietzsche and Sartre), see Mary Midgely, *Heart and Mind* (New York: St. Martin's Press, 1981), Ch. 3, "Creation and Originality."

3. *Enzyklopädie der philosophischen Wissenschaften, Werke*, Bd. 10, par. 558; English trans., *Hegel's Philosophy of Mind: Being Part Three of the Encyclopaedia of the Philosophical Sciences*, trans. William Wallace (Oxford: Oxford University Press, 1971), p. 294.

4. Plato, *Apology* 22 b–c.

5. Charles Karelis focusses on this contrast of Hegel and Plato in his interpretative essay in *Hegel's Introduction to Aesthetics*, trans. T.M. Knox (Oxford: Clarendon Press, 1979), pp. xxix–xxii.

6. This issue of reference is still a very much debated question in contemporary theory, with many thinkers tending to be critical of external reference. See, for instance, Charles Altieri, *Act and Quality: A Theory of Literary Meaning and Humanistic Understanding* (Amherst: University of Massachusetts Press, 1981), Ch. 8. Interestingly, Altieri ends with a humanistic Hegelianism (pp. 318 ff.), Hegel once again without the absolute. Altieri's

"expressivist" Hegelianism strips Hegel of all the metaphysical claims that might make the contemporary reader "uncomfortable" (p. 319). From the standpoint of the present study of art and the absolute, it is just such metaphysical claims that make Hegel's aesthetics both interesting and challenging.

7. Of course, though much of contemporary theory tends to be anti-mimetic, not all of it is. For a defense of the mimetic dimension of literature, in all its cultural ramifications, see Gerald Graff, *Literature Against Itself: Literary Ideas in Modern Society* (Chicago: Chicago University Press, 1979), *passim*, but see pp. 6 ff.

8. *VA*, I, pp. 64–70; *HA*, I, pp. 41–46.

9. Ibid., p. 65; p. 42.

10. Ibid.

11. Ibid., p. 66; p. 43.

12. Plato, *Republic*, 601–602.

13. *VA*, I, pp. 69–70; *HA*, I, pp. 45–46.

14. *Phänomenologie*, pp. 19–20; *Phenomenology*, p. 10.

15. *VA*, I, pp. 50–51; *HA*, I, pp. 31–32.

16. Ibid., pp. 194–95; pp. 146–47. See *Encyklopädie*, paragraphs 411 and 558.

17. Ibid. pp. 60–61; pp. 38–39.

18. See *Encyklopädie*, paragraph 450.

19. See Ibid., paragraph 556.

20. See *VA*, I, pp. 104; *HA*, I, pp. 73 ff.

21. Ibid., p. 111; p. 79.

22. B. Croce, *Aesthetics as Science of Expression and General Linguistic*, trans. Douglas Ainslie, 2nd ed. (London: Macmillan, 1922), pp. 302–3.

23. See, for instance, Walter Kaufmann's remark in *Hegel: Reinterpretation, Texts and Commentary* (New York: Doubleday, 1965), p. 158: "Hegel does not, like most philosophers, search for an image to illustrate his ideas: his difficulty often lies in getting across insight and image at once — or, in other words, in communicating his own vision."

Chapter Two

1. Friedrich Nietzsche, *On The Genealogy of Morals*, trans. W. Kaufmann and R.J. Hollingdale (New York: Vintage Books, 1969), III, 25. The issue is implicit in Goethe's famous words (*Faust*, I, 2038-9): "Grey is all theory and green only life's golden tree."

2. On this point and the importance of Hegel's friendship with Hölderlin, see for instance, Johannes Hoffmeister, *Hölderlin und Hegel* (Tübingen: J.C.B. Mohr, 1931); Dieter Henrich, "Hegel und Hölderlin," in *Hegel im Kontext* (Frankfurt: Suhrkamp Verlag, 1971), pp. 9-40; also Henry Harris, *Hegel's Development: Towards the Sunlight*, pp. 57 ff. On Novalis' poetry as prefiguring Hegel's philosophy, see Theodor Haering, *Hegel: Sein Wollen und sein Werk* (Leipzig: B. G. Teubner, 1929), vol. I.

3. Thus the term *aufheben*, with the meaning of cancelling, surpassing and yet preserving, appears in an aesthetic context in Schiller, carrying there the resonance which Hegel was to exploit later more systematically. See Friedrich Schiller, *On the Aesthetic Education of Man: In a Series of Letters*, trans. with intro. by Reginald Snell (New York: Frederick Unger Publishing Co., 1965), Letter 18, pp. 88-89. See also Hegel's letter to Schelling where he calls Schiller's *Aesthetic Education* a "masterpiece." *Briefe von und an Hegel*, ed. J. Hoffmeister and R. Flechsig (Hamburg: Felix Meiner Verlag, 1952-1960), I, p. 24. Even among Hegelians we find a tendency towards this polarity of art and the concept. For example in the previously cited volume *Art and Logic in Hegel's Philosophy*, no contributor makes a serious effort to *bring together* these two sides of Hegel's thought, the implication seeming to be that they are essentially discontinuous topics. See my review of this volume in *The Owl of Minerva*, vol. 12, no. 4, June 1981, pp. 7-9.

4. For very insightful discussion of this issue see Carl G. Vaught, *The Quest for Wholeness* (Albany: SUNY, 1982), Ch. 4. Vaught is critical of Hegel for neglecting the implications of these underpinnings and takes issue with Hegel on the tendency to closure which he claims springs from this neglect. On this issue and the possibility of an "open" reading of Hegel, see my review of Vaught in *Philosophical Studies* (Ireland), vol. XXIX, pp. 322-26. We might remark here that there is an analogous version of this difficulty in contemporary linguistic philosophy. See Richard Rorty, *Philosophy and the Mirror of Nature*, p. 12, where he speaks of pictures and propositions (what I am calling the aesthetical and the logical): "It is pictures rather than propositions, metaphors rather than statements, which determine most of our philosophical convictions." The problem is also very much alive in contem-

porary European thought. For instance, Paul Ricoeur in "Metaphor and Philosophical Discourse," Ch. 8 of *The Rule of Metaphor*, trans. R. Czerny, (Toronto: University of Toronto Press, 1977) seems to argue for some discontinuity, though also "interanimation" between the poetic and the philosophical, the metaphorical and the speculative; while Jacques Derrida in "White Mythology: Metaphor in the Text of Philosophy," trans. F.C.T. Moore, *New Literary History*, VI, i, Autumn 1974, pp. 5–74, implies that metaphysical, philosophical language is really metaphor which tries to efface, never completely successfully, its own metaphorical nature. The Hegelian realm of Absolute Spirit, where we discover a *dialectical interplay* of art, religion and philosophy indicates, I argue, a desire to preserve *both* the discontinuity and interrelatedness, or the difference *and* identity of art and philosophy — identity and continuity in terms of the *content* of *Geist*; difference and discontinuity in terms of the respective form in which art and philosophy articulate *Geist*.

5. See, for instance, Charles Taylor, *Hegel* (New York: Cambridge University Press, 1975), p. 471, where he says that religion and philosophy "characterize the absolute in declarative sentences which are intended as correct descriptions," while art "does not 'say' anything in a straightforward sense at all." This is a somewhat simplified contrast. For can we say that Hegel's philosophy is ever a set of straightforward descriptive propositions? Does dialectical thinking ever describe anything straightforwardly? Is not this to treat dialectical thinking as literalistic description and thus to make nonsense of what Hegel thinks about finite propositions, and particularly what he says about the speculative sentence. One wonders whether Taylor is working with some version of the "two uses" theory of language. See some remarks on the prose/poetry distinction in the review of *Art and Logic*, cited note 3. See also Quentin Lauer, "Hegel as Poet," Presidential address to the Hegel Society of America, Clemson University, October 1982. This address was published as Chapter 1, *History and System: Hegel's Philosophy of History*, Robert L. Perkins, ed. (Albany: SUNY Press, 1984).

6. Walter Kaufmann, *Hegel: Reinterpretation, Texts and Commentary*, sec. 28. See also Mark C. Taylor, *Journeys to Selfhood: Hegel and Kierkegaard* (Berkeley: University of California Press, 1980) who very well develops the importance for Hegel of Schiller's ideal of aesthetic education. On this ideal see Chapter 3, and the comparison of the *Phenomenology* with the *Bildungsroman*, p. 77. Others, as Taylor there indicates (note 20), have recognized this important similarity, including Lukács and Josiah Royce. A similar point is made in M.H. Abrams, *Natural Supernaturalism: Tradition and Revolution in Romantic Literature* (New York: Norton, 1971) where the growth of philo-

sophical consciousness in Hegel's *Phenomenology* is compared to the growth of the poet's mind in Wordsworth's *Prelude* (pp. 225 ff., especially pp. 236–37).

7. G.W.F. Hegel, *Phänomenologie des Geistes*, p. 563; *Phenomenology of Spirit*, pp. 492.

8. G.W.F. Hegel, *The Difference between Fichte's and Schelling's System of Philosophy*, trans. H.S. Harris and W. Cerf (Albany: SUNY Press, 1977), pp. 88–89. We might also mention here another early statement in which Hegel says that "the philosopher must possess just as much aesthetic sense as the poet. Men without aesthetic sense is what philosophers of our time are. The philosophy of spirit is an aesthetic philosophy." "Earliest System-Programme of German Idealism," *Werke* (Frankfurt: Suhrkamp Verlag, 1969–1971), Bd. 1, p. 235; trans. in H.S. Harris, *Hegel's Development*, p. 511. For discussion of this controversial text see Harris pp. 249–57. Also Mark Taylor, op. cit., p. 73, and Quentin Lauer, art. cit.

9. Trans. Walter Kaufmann, *Hegel: Text and Commentary* (New York: Doubleday, 1966), pp. 113–18.

10. Gabriel Marcel, *Man Against Mass Society*, trans. G.S. Fraser (South Bend, Indiana: Gateway Editions, N.D.), p. 2.

11. See the review article of George di Giovanni, "Burbidge and Hegel on the Logic," *The Owl of Minerva*, vol. 14, No. 1, September 1982. There he says (p.4) that the real problem is whether "the immediate existential presence of the mind to its world (let's call it intuition) can be sufficiently articulated in thought or not . . . " This is what I am calling the problem of concreteness. See also his comments (p. 5) on the transition from logic to nature as "artistic," "metaphorical." di Giovanni's comments are on John Burbidge's *On Hegel's Logic: Fragments of a Commentary* (Atlantic Highlands: Humanities Press, 1981).

12. *Phänomenologie*, p. 30; *Phenomenology*, p. 19. On the early appearance of this issue see Harris, *Hegel's Development*, pp. 37 ff.

13. See G.W.F. Hegel; *VA*, I, pp. 100 ff; *HA*, I, pp. 70 ff.

14. *VA*, I, pp. 91–92; *HA*, I. pp. 63. Here we might note Abrams' remark, *Natural Supernaturalism*, pp. 192–3: "At no other place and time have literature and technical philosophy been so closely interinvolved as in Germany in the period beginning with Kant. The major German poets and novelists (as well as Coleridge, and later Carlyle, in England) avidly assimilated the writings of the philosophers; many of them wrote philosophical essays; and all incorporated current philosophical concepts and procedures into the subject

matter and structure of their principal works of imagination. And on their part philosophers remained closely in touch with literature; Schelling and Hegel themselves wrote poetry, and both these thinkers gave literature and the arts a prominent — Schelling, in his central period, the cardinal — place in their metaphysical systems." For a study of the parallels of Schelling and Wordsworth, see E.D. Hirsch, *Wordsworth and Schelling: A Typological Study of Romanticism* (New Haven: Yale, 1960); for a study of the affinities of Hegel and Blake, see David Punter, *Blake, Hegel and Dialectic* (Amsterdam: Rodopi, 1982).

Though religion was to come further to the fore, art never lost something of this Schellingian ultimacy for Hegel. Indeed when Hegel calls for a new *mythology of reason* (in the "Earliest System-Programme;" see note 8 above), a certain union of art and religion lies implicit in the notion of such a mythology. Given the interrelation of aesthetics and metaphysics, Jack Kaminsky's desire to free Hegel's aesthetics from its metaphysical underpinnings is highly questionable in his *Hegel on Art: An Interpretation of Hegel's Aesthetics*. The present emphasis on concreteness runs counter to the "minimalist" interpretation of Klaus Hartmann, "Hegel: A Non-Metaphysical View," in A. MacIntyre ed., *Hegel: A Collection of Critical Essays* (New York: Doubleday, 1972). In Hegel's aesthetics we deal with one form of experience which demands "maximal" interpretation. On Hegel's Logic as a system of categories see Alan White's excellent, *Absolute Knowledge: Hegel and the Problem of Metaphysics* (Athens, Ohio: Ohio University Press, 1983).

15. On the universality of *poiesis* see Plato's *Symposium*, 205b–c.

16. See Chapter One.

17. On art and concrete universality, see *VA*, I, pp. 76–7; *HA*, I, pp. 51–2. On the spiritualization of the sensuous, see p. 61; p. 39. This spiritualization of the sensuous is Hegel's way of uniting the *Formtrieb* and *Stofftrieb* of Schiller, or what Nietzsche later spoke of as the Apollonian and Dionysian principles in the art work.

18. On the problem of the concrete universal in aesthetics, see for instance, W.K. Wimsatt Jr. and Monroe C. Beardsley, *The Verbal Icon: Studies in the Meaning of Poetry* (New York: Noonday Press, 1958), p. 77. Also Patrick Hutchings, "The Poetic Particular: A Note towards the Criticism of Professor W.K. Wimsatt's The Concrete Universal," in *Proceedings of the Fifth International Congress of Aesthetics: Amsterdam, 1964* (The Hague and Paris: Mouton, 1968), pp. 690–92. See Brian Martine's fine discussion in *Individuals and Individuality* (Albany: State University of New York Press, 1984). The view he develops is in response to Hegel and in part is grounded in reflection on the art work.

19. "The individual is the determinate universal"; see *Werke*, Bd. 6, p. 298.

20. On art as an end see *VA*, pp. 44 and 64 ff.; *HA*, I, pp. 25 and 41 ff. On art and perfection see Chapter Four.

21. J.N. Findlay, *Hegel: A Reexamination* (New York: Humanities Press, 1958), p. 74. See also Charles Taylor, *Hegel*, Ch. XI, especially pp. 225–27 on the peculiarity of the Hegelian concept; Quentin Lauer, S.J., *Hegel's Concept of God*, Chapter 2.

22. See R.G. Collingwood, *The Principles of Art* (Oxford: Clarendon Press, 1938), p. 37.

23. On *Verstand* and *Vernunft* see my "Hegel, Philosophy and Worship," *CITHARA*, 19:1, 1979, pp. 11–17.

24. "*Das Wahre ist das Ganze*," *Phänomenologie*, p. 21; *Phenomenology*, p. 11. On this crucial issue of wholeness, see Walter Kaufmann, *Discovering the Mind: Goethe, Kant, and Hegel* (New York: McGraw-Hill, 1980), pp. 226 ff., where Hegel's quest for completeness is said to be "grotesque." Kaufmann is not right to oppose Goethe and Kant, the poetic-thinker and the rationalist-thinker, with respect to Hegel's insistence on wholeness or completion. Rightly Kaufmann finds *both* the poetic and the rational in Hegel, but he is wrong to consign the notion of completeness only to the rational, scientific, Kantian side. To the contrary, the perfection of the art work gives us a poetic wholeness which the philosophic concept attempts to match. Hence it is most important to articulate what poetic completeness might mean in order to understand what Hegel might mean in seeking wholeness for the philosophical concept. Kaufmann implies that "completeness" entails the reduction of the panorama of history, but, as I will try to indicate in Chapter Four, the sense of an ending in art throws important light on this issue of the "end" of history.

25. *Enzyklopädie der philosophischen Wissenschaften*, *Werke* Bd 10, paragraph 15; see also *Phänomenologie* 20, 559; *Phenomenology* 10, 448.

26. On *Erinnerung*, see *Phänomenologie*, pp. 563–64; *Phenomenology*, p. 492. See Donald Verene's excellent *Hegel's Recollection: A Study of Images in the Phenomenology of Spirit* (Albany: State University of New York Press, 1985). Verene very well brings out the provocative cast of Hegel's imagistic mind and (something too often forgotten) Hegel's sense of humor.

27. The implication of growth is contained in the very word "concrete" (*concrescere*), so not inappropriately Hegel illustrates the concrete concept with the image of the plant; *Enzyklopädie*, paragraph 161, Zus.

28. *Phänomenologie*, p. 10; *Phenomenology*, p. 2.

29. *Phänomenologie*, p. 67; *Phenomenology*, p. 49.

30. On the dramatic possibilities of logic, see Louis William Flaccus, *Artists and Thinkers* (Freeport, NY: Books for Libraries Press, Inc., 1967), pp. 135 ff. On the *Phenomenology* as possessing an histrionic dimension, see Jacob Loewenberg, "The Exoteric Approach to Hegel's *Phenomenology*," *Mind*, 43 (1934), p. 440. See also Abrams' remark (op. cit., p. 236) on the *Phenomenology*: "Hegel's book, taken as a literary form, is thus one of the earliest, yet at the same time the most intricate and extreme, of modern involuted works of the imagination. It is a self-contained, self-sustained, and self-implicative puzzle book, which is enigmatic in the whole and deliberately equivocal in all its parts and passing allusions." My only disagreement with this is the possibility of equivocation in the use of word "equivocal." Hegel's strategy is properly dialectical. What this means in relation to equivocation, see below Chapter Five. Hegel's dialectical strategy in the *Phenomenology* is informed by clear consciousness of his overall purpose. On this see Joseph Flay's excellent *Hegel's Quest for Certainty* (Albany: State University of New York Press, 1984).

Chapter Three

1. I use the phrase "*exclusively aesthetic*" here because, as will be clear in the body of the argument, there is no intent to deny the aesthetic dimension of art. The question is whether, granting this dimension, it is susceptible of a religious interpretation. For terminological convenience I will speak below of the aesthetic conception as contrased with the religious conception, once again bearing in mind that the issue is not one of repudiating the aesthetic but of whether the religious completes the aesthetic — a possibility rendered problematic by the exclusively aesthetic conception. On the difficulty of the religious conception see Charles Karelis' remark that this conception "may seem fantastic" in his interpretative essay to *Hegel's Introduction to Aesthetics*, p. xxviii. See also Karsten Harries, "Hegel on the Future of Art," *Review of Metaphysics*, 27 (1973–74), pp. 677–96.

2. On this, for example, see A. Boyce Gibson, *Muse and Thinker* (Harmondsworth: Penguin, 1972), Ch. II; see also Eric Gill, *Art* (London: The Bodley Head, 1934), Chapters II and III where he discusses the lack of rigid division of labor prior to the fifteenth century, and the fact that art was not a strongly separated, specialized activity, set apart from day to day life, including its religious dimension.

3. See below, section IV, for discussion of this attempt to make art into a religion in the nineteenth century. The concept of the poet as *vates* was, of course, present in Hegel's friend Hölderlin who in many ways epitomized the tension of the religious and the poetic, prefigured their split that was to become more problematical with the subsequent increasing secularization of life, and responded to the hemorrhaging of the religious spirit within the poetic impulse. See Johannes Hoffmeister, *Hölderlin und Hegel* (Tübingen: I.C.B. Mohr, 1931); Dieter Henrich, "Hegel und Hölderlin," in *Hegel im Kontext* (Frankfurt; Suhrkamp Verlag, 1971), pp. 9–40; also H.S. Harris, *Hegel's Development: Towards the Sunlight.*

4. On post-Kantian subjectivism, intimately bound up with expressivist currents in aesthetics, see, for example, Hans-Georg Gadamer, *Truth and Method*, translation edited by Garrett Barden and John Cumming (New York: Seabury Press, 1975), pp. 39 ff. The pervasive presence of the expressivist ideal and its importance for all the areas of human meaning is well treated in Charles Taylor, *Hegel*, passim, but especially Chapters I and XX.

5. G.W.F. Hegel, *Phänomenologie*, p. 20; *Phenomenology*, p. 10.

6. Hegel, of course, was thoroughly conversant with this aspect of art, especially as emphasized by Schiller.

7. For one of the most important instances of this aesthetic of expression, see R.G. Collingwood, *The Principles of Art* (Oxford: Clarendon Press, 1938).

8. In *Beyond Good and Evil*, section 225, Nietzsche states, for instance: "In man, *creature* and *creator* are united; in man there is matter, fragment, excess, clay, mud and madness; but in man there is also creator, sculptor, the hardness of the hammer, the divine spectator and the seventh day — do you understand this antithesis?"

9. There is a clear analogy here between the cases of art and religion. On the strictly religious version of the issue, see Walter Jaeschke, "Speculative and Anthropological Criticism of Religion: A Theological Orientation to Hegel and Feuerbach," *Journal of the American Academy of Religion*, XLVIII/3, pp. 345–64. The defense of Hegel's movement from the anthropological to the speculative interpretation of religion here mirrors the shift from art as aesthetic to art as religious in the present chapter. On the religious issue *per se* see my paper "Hegel and the Problem of Religious Representation," *Philosophical Studies* (Ireland), vol. XXX, pp. 9–22.

10. This is the strategy of Paul Weiss in *Religion and Art* (Milwaukee: Milwaukee University Press, 1963). The argument of the present chapter is

closer to, for example, Paul Tillich's approach to the religious meaning of modern art when he says: "It is not an exaggeration to ascribe more of the quality of sacredness to a still-life by Cézanne or a tree by Van Gogh than to a picture of Jesus by Uhde." *The Religious Situation*, trans. H.R. Niebuhr (New York: Meridian Books, 1956), p. 89.

11. This tends to be the common interpretation of how philosophy relates to art and religion in Hegel. That is, the emphasis falls on the *difference* in the form of *Geist*, not on the continuity of *Geist* itself as the active content working variously in all three forms.

12. It is true that their separation was already in process since the Renaissance, as already noted. Indeed we might note how the eighteenth century emphasis on "taste" as a special aesthetic capacity (taken up philosophically in Kant's *Critique of Judgment*), reflects this separation, even to the extent of aesthetics itself becoming a distinct science with Baumgarten. A good deal of this emphasis is retained in Hegel's *Lectures on Aesthetics*, but Hegel always retained key elements of the older outlook. This is not surprising given his early desire, with Hölderlin, to bring about a "new mythology of reason," a desire impossible without the sacral power of art. "Earliest System Programme of German Idealism," *Werke* Bd. 1, p. 235; trans. in H.S. Harris, op cit., p. 511; for discussion of this controversial text see Harris, pp. 249–255. It is not fortuitous in this context that in the twentieth century, Heidegger's interlocutor (in his dialogue of thinker and poet) is so often Hölderlin, given that this dialogue has much to do with the kinship of poetry and the holy in an age which experiences the eclipse of divinity.

13. On the divine *afflatus*, see G.W.F. Hegel, *Enzyklopädie der philosophischen Wissenschaften*, *Werke*, Bd. 10, paragraph 560; on the "pathos" of the artist as coming from the gods, see for instance, VA, II, p. 52; HA, I, p. 458.

14. See particularly *Das geistige Kunstswerk, Phänomenologie des Geistes*, pp. 506 ff.; *Phenomenology*, pp. 439 ff. See Howard Kainz, "Hegel's Theory of Aesthetics in the *Phenomenology*," *Idealistic Studies*, 1972 (2), 81–94.

15. VA, I, pp. 456 ff.; 466 ff.; HA, I, pp. 354 ff.; pp. 362 ff.

16. On the religious limitations of the anthropomorphic art of classical Greece see, VA, II, pp. 23–24; HA, I, pp. 435–36.

17. On *Erinnerung* see *Phänomenologie*, pp. 563–64; *Phenomenology*, p. 492; VA, II, pp. 128 ff.; HA, I, pp. 518 ff.

18. Mention of Augustine is not irrelevant to romantic art in that for Augustine it is not the external world of things but the inward self that is

the proper, most rich way to God. Not surprisingly Augustine has been spoken of as an important ancestor of existentialism, which in turn has been called a late product of the romantic spirit. On this see William Desmond, "Augustine's *Confessions*: On Desire, Conversion and Reflection," *Irish Theological Quarterly*, 47:1 (1980:1), pp. 224–33.

19. On this see Mark Taylor, *Journeys to Selfhood: Hegel and Kierkegaard*, *passim*.

20. *VA*, II, pp. 132–33; *HA*, I, pp. 521–22.

21. *Ibid.*, p. 113; p. 80.

22. As one indication of this we might perhaps think of how the poet's words come to say *more*, suggest *more* than he self-consciously intends; how the power of language, *logos*, takes on an inexhaustible life of its own, never entirely within his possession.

23. As we explored in Chapter One; see also Karelis, pp. xxix–xxxii.

24. On this inward turn with Romantic art, see Eric Heller, *The Artist's Journey into the Interior* (New York: Random House, 1959), particularly Ch. V on Hegel. On this interiorizing movement within religious representation see "Hegel and the Problem of Religious Representation."

25. Jacques Maritain, *Art and Scholasticism and the Frontiers of Poetry*, trans. J.W. Evans (South Bend: Notre Dame University Press, 1974), p. 60.

26. See Jacques Barzun, *Classic, Romantic and Modern* (Garden City, New York: Doubleday, 1961), Ch. X.

27. On the god and the artist see *Enzyklopädie*, paragraph 560.

28. The idea of "inspiration" (as in Plato's divine madness, or Nietzsche's Dionysian intoxication) is extremely important, of course, for the religious interpretation of art. The question is not one of denying the experience but of whether our interpretation of it entails the complete abnegation of finite selfhood. See, for instance, Owen Barfield, *Poetic Diction* (London: Faber and Faber, 1928), pp. 109, 169–70, 189–90; also G. Van der Leeuw, *Sacred and Profane Beauty: The Holy in Art*, trans. D.E. Green (New York: Holt, Rinehart and Winston, 1963), pp. 148–51. On this contrast of passivity and self-activity, we might think of the contrast between some Medieval artists who did not sign their work and some contemporary artists, whose signature on a table napkin is sold. We do not buy pictures of apples and pears, say, but a *Cézanne*, a *Matisse* — we buy the artist in his self-expression, the artist's *name*.

29. On Left and Right Hegelians see K. Löwith, *From Hegel to Nietzsche*, trans. D.E. Green (New York: Doubleday and Co., 1967), Ch. II especially; Lawrence S. Stepelevich (ed.), *The Young Hegelians: An Anthology* (New York and Cambridge: Cambridge University Press, 1983); David McClellan, *The Young Hegelians and Karl Marx* (London: Macmillan, 1969). Also John Toews, *Hegelianism*.

30. It is not only religious critics, like Kierkegaard, who tend to fault Hegel on his purported attenuation of finiteness. Twentieth century philosophy, in the main, sees itself as unHegelian on this issue, whether in Continental thought with its emphasis on finiteness, particularly with Heidegger and subsequent developments shaped by his influence; or in the Anglo-American analytic tradition, with its antisystematic stress, its rejection of idealism, and its often modest conception of the capacity of philosophy.

31. *Enzyklopädie*, paragraph 573. For a recent defense of Hegel against the charge of pantheism, see Quentin Lauer, S.J., *Hegel's Concept of God*, pp. 274 ff.; also pp. 250 ff. The unity of the divine and the human can be viewed, of course, from very different angles ranging from the mystical to the reductionistic. In the *Aesthetics* Hegel speaks of Christianity and its art-form, romantic art, as completing the *anthropological* principle, the revelation of God in human form. This completion need not imply a humanistic reduction, or anthropological reduction of God, but rather the revelation of the full religious significance of the anthropological, the human. On the religious completion of the anthropological by Christianity in the *Aesthetics* see n. 17 above. Löwith, op cit., pp. 36–39 does not do proper justice to this in relation to art in Hegel, through he is superbly sensitive to Hegel's ambiguous complexity in relation to religion.

32. Kierkegaard sometimes speaks of Hegelianism as an aesthetic system implying here a certain limitation. There is a revealing contrast here between Kierkegaard and Hegel. For Kierkegaard the aesthetical, when viewed from the absolute seriousness of religion, is not ultimately serious, being a kind of game, a playing with life's possibilities, not an ultimate coming to terms with actuality. For Hegel, given the relation of art and religion, there is a deeper seriousness to the aesthetical, even on its own terms: it is a coming to terms with the actual, with all the seriousness, pathos and depth of its concern with the absolute.

33. Max Stirner's essay "Art and Religion" (Stepelevich, op. cit., pp. 327–34) is a revealingly clear example of the "aesthetic" as opposed to the "religious" conception of art. See also Löwith, op. cit., pp. 294 ff. on Ruge and the "politicization of aesthetic education."

34. On this see, for instance, Piotr Hoffman, *The Anatomy of Idealism: Passivity and Activity in Kant, Hegel and Marx* (The Hague: Nijhoff, 1982), pp. 98–99, 104–105; also my review of this, *Philosophical Studies* (Ireland), vol. XXX, pp. 335–38. See also Istvan Meszaros, *Marx's Theory of Alienation* (London: Merlin Press, 1970), Ch. VIII. Meszaros well emphasizes the intertwining of humanistic, aesthetic and economic strands (e.g., p. 190). Henri Lefebvre, *Dialectical Materialism*, trans. John Sturrock (London: Jonathan Cape, 1968) grants the importance of Hegel's aesthetics for the problem of fragmentation of modern man (p. 47), but levels the standard charge of conceptual reductionism (p. 48). Labor takes on a "creative" or "poetic meaning" (p. 129) in the production of "the total man" for Lefebvre (see pp. 148–67, especially pp. 164–65). For a recent concise discussion see Terry Eagleton, *Marxism and Literary Criticism* (Berkeley and Los Angeles: California University Press, 1976).

35. See *The Essential Frankfurt School Reader*, A. Arato and E. Beghardt (eds.) (New York: Urizen Books, 1978), Part II, "Esthetic Theory and Cultural Criticism," especially Benjamin's "The Author as Producer," pp. 254–69; and Adorno's "On the Fetish Character in Music and the Regression in Listening," pp. 270–99. Marcuse has developed the importance of the aesthetic in *Eros and Civilization* (Boston: Beacon Press, 1955), Ch. 9; *One Dimensional Man* (Boston: Beacon Press, 1964), pp. 238 ff.; *An Essay on Liberation* (Boston: Beacon Press, 1969), passim, particularly Ch. 2. George Lichtheim's *Lukács* (London: Collins, 1970) is excellent on what he calls "Lukács' attempt to fuse Hegelian aesthetics with Marxian sociology" (p. 123). See also, Martin Donougho, "The Cunning of Odysseus: A Theme in Hegel, Lukács, and Adorno," *Philosophy and Social Criticism* (1981), pp. 13–43. Donougho is very clear on the sacred dimension of art for Hegel, but tilts more humanistically than the present interpretation.

36. J.P. Sartre, *What is Literature?* trans. B. Frechtman (New York: Philosophical Library, 1949). Some recent studies emphasizing aesthetics and politics include R. Aronson, *Jean-Paul Sartre – Philosophy in the World* (London: New Left Books, 1980); Pietro Chiodi, *Sartre and Marxism*, trans. K. Soper, (Atlantic Highlands, N.J.: Humanities Press, 1976), brings out the Hegelianism in Marxism and Existentialism, even when these *oppose* Hegel (pp. 124–44; Dominick La Capra, *A Preface to Sartre* (Ithaca: Cornell University Press, 1978), gives a "deconstructive" view of Sartre and literature. See the interview with Sartre, "The Purpose of Writing," in *Between Existentialism and Marxism*, trans. John Mathews (New York: Pantheon Book, 1974), pp. 9–32.

37. Camus also places the artist, conceived of as a creator, at the center of a world which has discarded Hegel's Absolute, and any nostalgia for such an Absolute. Like Nietzsche's Dionysian man, the artist becomes a guardian against nihilism, a rebel struggling for man's meaning against an absurd world. Even a dash of Marxist proletarianism is introduced into this aesthetical ideal, for as Hochberg put it (in "Albert Camus and the Ethics of Absurdity," *Ethics*, 75, no. 2 (January 1965), pp. 87–102): since we must have plumbers as well as painters, Camus' solution lies in turning the plumber into an artist. Hochberg recognizes the Hegelian element in Camus, though it is Hegelianism without the Absolute. Though Camus seems to find something absolute in art, and though this seems akin to Hegel, the precise nature of this absoluteness is not Hegelian. For it is one which rejects the relation of art and religion, indeed defines art in its *opposition* to religion, not in their dialectical kinship.

38. Charles Taylor, op. cit., p. 546. The entirety of Ch. XX, "Hegel Today" is directly relevant here, though Taylor is perhaps too acquiescent in post-Hegelian expressivism, reading this in too post-Hegelian a fashion.

39. Martin Heidegger, *Nietzsche, Volume I: The Will to Power as Art*, trans. David F. Krell (New York: Harper and Row, 1979), pp. 88–90.

40. On the spiritual malaise of the eighteenth and nineteenth century in relation to Hegel and Kierkegaard see Mark Taylor, *Journeys to Selfhood*, Ch. 2.

41. On the pervasiveness of this among contemporary movements in art and literature in France, see Herbert Lottman, *The Left Bank* (Boston: Houghton Mifflin, 1982). For very extensive documentation see J. Ruhle, *Literature and Revolution: A Critical Study of the Writer and Communism in the Twentieth Century*, trans. J. Steinberg, (New York: Praeger, 1969). See also R. Aron, *The Opium of the Intellectuals*, trans. T. Kilmartin (New York: Norton, 1962), pp. 42 ff., "The Prestige of Revolution," where he points out the dream of a common mission between the artistic *avant-garde* and the political *avant-garde* (p. 43). Also Ch. IX: "The Intellectuals in Search of a Religion."

42. Harris, op. cit., treats extensively of the interwining of religion and politics in the young Hegel. James Yerkes, *The Christology of Hegel* is also illuminating. See my review of Yerkes in *Bulletin of the Hegel Society of Great Britain*, no. 8, 1983, pp. 25–27. We might also note the interplay of the aesthetical and the political during Hegel's own time, for instance, in the manner Wordsworth was intoxicated (for a time at least) by the French Revolution. We might also think of the political concerns of Byron and

Shelley. Shelley brings the two together when he calls poets "the unacknowl-edged legislators" of the universe in his *Defense of Poetry*. Though Shelley is sometimes thought of as a "blithe spirit," an ineffectual angel, he had a very sharp eye for social and political reality. On the relation of art and politics in Hegel, see John McCumber, "Hegel's Anarchistic Utopia: The Politics of his Aesthetics," *Southern Journal of Philosophy*, XXII, no. 2, 203–10.

Chapter Four

1. See, for example: B.T. Wilkens, *Hegel's Philosophy of History* (Ithaca & London: Cornell University Press, 1974); W.H. Walsh, *An Introduction to the Philosophy of History* (London: Hutchinson University Library, 1951).

2. For commentators who put emphasis on the political character of the Hegelian completion see particularly A. Kojève, *Introduction to the Read-ing of Hegel: Lectures on the Phenomenology of Spirit*, trans. James H. Nichols, Jr. and Allen Bloom (New York: Basic Books, 1969); on the completion of world history see Stanley Rosen, *G.W.F. Hegel: An Introduction to the Science of Wisdom*. Ch. 2; on the relation of metaphysics and politics see Raymond Plant, *Hegel* (Bloomington: Indiana University Press, 1973). For a recent defense of Kojève, see Barry Cooper, *The End of History: An Essay on Modern Hegelianism* (Toronto: University of Toronto Press, 1984).

3. For a discussion of this in relation to historicism, see William Des-mond, "Hegel, History and Philosophical Contemporaneity," *Filosofia Oggi*, IV: 2 (1981), pp. 221–26.

4. G.W.F. Hegel. *Enzyklopädie der philosophischen Wissenschaften*, para-graph 562: " . . . *Die Geschichte der Religionem mit der Weltgeschichte zusam-menfallt.*"

5. For some remarks on the relation of history and art history in rela-tion to Hegel's notion of the individual see George Dennis O'Brien, *Hegel on Reason and History* (Chicago and London: University of Chicago Press, 1975), especially pp. 165 ff. O'Brien's remarks are not irrelevant to our present concern. However, my focus is not on art history as illustrating crucial aspects of the general nature of history, but on the way the art work illuminates the possibility of the completion of a process of historical becoming.

6. Something of this will emerge in this chapter. Here Hegel's religious rendition of the aesthetic reminds us of Hölderlin's sacred poetry which bespeaks the holy and so sacralizes and fulfills time itself. On Christianity

and "The End of Days" see James Yerkes, *The Christology of Hegel*, pp. 161 ff. On the apocalyptic and eschatological aspects of modern literature, see Frank Kermode, *The Sense of an Ending: Studies in the Theory of Fiction* (New York: Oxford University Press, 1966).

7. See Merold Westphal, *History and Truth in Hegel's Phenomenology* (New Jersey: Humanities Press, 1979). For wide ranging discussion of the many sides of Hegel's philosophy of history, see *History and System: Hegel's Philosophy of History*, ed. R.L. Perkins (Albany: State University of New York Press, 1984). This volume contains the papers read at the 1982 sessions of the Hegel Society of America. Some of the material in the present chapter was first read as a paper at that meeting and appears in this volume. Curtis Carter, commenting on that paper, makes a number of points that introduce a certain analytic precision into the discussion. While limited space precludes the making of all possible distinctions, let me but say that my view tends to have a more dialectical understanding of art, where artist, act and object cannot be ultimately abstracted from each other in the fullness of the aesthetic situation. Moreover, clearly I do not deny that art may be turned to instrumentalist purposes, nor does Hegel; but the whole point is that such an instrumentalization of art, for Hegel, turns art away from its true vocation. Again, it is not a question of extracting a message from art or using it as an end, but of philosophically acknowledging the emergence and articulation of a rich significant wholeness with great art, one which expresses, for Hegel, the spiritual wealth of a people. Moreover, Carter seems to have failed to notice that I explicitly refer to Hegel's notion of the art work as *Selbstzweck*; in Hegel's hands this is not unrelated to the Aristotelian notion of *telos*. The Aristotelian inspiration of Hegel is well known, but what is interesting is that Hegel tries to do justice to crucial aspects of the Aristotelian perspective within a post-Kantian context (again Carter fails to note my explicit reference to Kant's aesthetics also). Hegel's efforts to span the divide between the ancient and the modern is a pervasive theme in the present study, but especially in Chapter Six. Many of Carter's particular points, I believe, are met more fully within this larger perspective. Carter entirely neglects the religious dimension of the issue, and the manner in which this ties art to absoluteness in Hegel's aesthetics.

8. *Poetics*, 1451, 5–6.

9. On dialectic in imaginative form, see, for instance, David Punter, *Blake, Hegel and Dialectic*. See also Gary Shapiro's excellent "Hegel on the Meanings of Poetry," *Art and Logic in Hegel's Philosophy*, especially p. 43.

10. *VA*, I, pp. 14; *HA*, I, p. 2.

11. If asked how this wholistic view of art squares with the fragmentary character of so much modern art, I agree that modern art does often put the emphasis on struggle and opposition, sometimes to the point of almost completely submerging the principle of wholeness traditionally constituent of art. But I am inclined to add with Hegel that struggle and opposition are moments within the total impulse of art which do not exhaust that impulse. If indeed any art work or movement of art were exclusively under the dominating influence of opposition and struggle there would finally be no art *work* at all. There would be war, not work, war moreover which left no traces of its battles, having collapsed completely in its own destructions. Even the most jarring of contemporary art remains a work only because the necessity of some perhaps tortured wholeness is not entirely absent. This fragmentariness of contemporary art indeed has been cited by some as evidence of Hegel's clairvoyant powers in relation to the so-called "death of art." Yet, the longer historical dialectic may perhaps hint at a different conclusion. Though the movement of opposition and antithesis has had a long innings in modernism, the principle of wholeness was never entirely destroyed, and some might wonder if the necessity of wholeness has perhaps begun to reassert its sway. In any case, I put forward these remarks as suggestions for reflection, not as assertions with the character of solid certainty. I take the issue up again more fully in Chapters Five and Six.

12. *VA*, I, p. 61; *HA*, I, p. 39.

13. See *VA*, I, p. 39; *HA*, I, pp. 21–22 where Hegel remarks on the emptiness of the Platonic Idea. We might add, however, that Plato himself does not completely exclude some access to eternity. If time is a moving image of eternity, as the famous words of the *Timaeus* (37D) have it, we have some access to the original, however partial, in this image. This is entailed by the very nature of an image.

14. *VA*, I, pp. 22–23; *HA*, I, p. 9.

15. See, for example *Enzyklopädie*, paragraph 558, where Hegel speaks of the human form as the highest and truest external matter in which the spiritual purpose of art is given corporeity and visible expression.

16. On the end character of art see *VA*, I, pp. 44 and 65 ff; *HA*, I, pp. 25 and 41 ff. The end character of the art work is related to its internal teleology, its internal necessity. Thus Hegel speaks of the art work as *Selbstzweck*. On this see Charles Taylor, *Hegel*, Ch. XVII.

17. This will be taken up again below.

18. See my remarks in *The Owl of Minerva*, 12, 4 (1981), pp. 7–9.

19. A very good example of this matter of the "eternalization of the temporal" is presented by Keats' "Ode on a Grecian Urn."

20. VA, II, pp. 225–29; I, 222–24; HA, I, pp. 597–600; 168–9.

21. On this see Stanley Rosen, G.W.F. Hegel, pp. 123–40.

22. Hegel does compare reading the newspaper to a modern secular form of prayer, though, as is clear from the tone of his references to the "prose of the modern world" in his Aesthetics, Hegel is hardly a simple glorifier of the mundane.

23. Art and Logic in Hegel's Philosophy, p. 12.

24. See VA, I, pp. 152 ff.; HA, I, pp. 112 ff., where Hegel speaks of the art work as a free infinity. Also Taylor, Hegel, p. 473.

25. On Vernunft as like the highest contemplative enjoyment of ancient theoria see my "Hegel, Philosophy and Worship."

26. For instance Hegel's discussion of Greek art in the Aesthetics is very much a history of Greek mythology. Also his discussion of Christian art strongly stresses the sense of concrete historical individuality, especially in modern romantic art.

27. On this dialectic see my article, cited note 3 above. Interesting to note here, Hegel had the nickname of "the old man," "der Alte," a nickname not altogether just since Hegel's sense of history is not antiquarian. Compare with the apotheosis of "the child" by Nietzsche in Thus Spoke Zarathustra. See my "The Child in Nietzsche's Menagerie," SEMINAR, V, 1981, pp. 40–44.

28. As John Toews in Hegelianism amply documents, this would appear to be the dialectic through which the Hegelian heritage began to decompose.

29. Hegel's Philosophy of Right, trans. T.M. Knox (Oxford: Oxford University Press, 1967), pp. 10–12.

30. See note 14.

31. As Descombes makes clear in Modern French Philosophy, the issue is still alive even in the Nietzschean currents that dominate after the Marxist rendition of the end of history in political terms. This current Nietzschean version of the end of history with its emphasis on "play" has a strong aesthetic dimension, and indeed reminds us of the resort to play by Schiller in his concept of aesthetic reconciliation. It is interesting to note how one of Hegel's successors, David Frederich Strauss, claimed that Hegel's philosophy "is the return of all things." The truth in this view is related to the circular

and sublating character of Hegel's thought. We need not see Nietzsche's proclamation of Eternal Recurrence as the absolutely original utterance Nietzsche sometimes seems to imply it is. The idea is very ancient, as Hegel was well aware in his own appropriation of images of circularity. Nietzsche wants Greece without Christianity, Dionysus versus the Crucified, as he put it; Hegel wants *both* Greece and Christianity, as some of our previous remarks indicate. On Strauss, see Toews, *Hegelianism*, p. 170.

Chapter Five

1. See, for instance, Gerald Graff, *Literature Against Itself*, pp. 3 ff. "The Triumph of the Vanguard." Also Renato Poggioli, *The Theory of the Avant-Garde*, trans. G. Fitzgerald (New York: Harper and Row, 1971); Hilton Kramer, *The Age of the Avant-Garde* (New York: Farrar, Straus and Giroux, 1974).

2. T.S. Eliot, *Selected Prose*, ed. F. Kermode (New York: Harcourt Brace Jovanovich, 1975), p. 177.

3. G.W.F. Hegel, *Die Vernunft in der Geschichte*, ed. J. Hoffmeister (Hamburg: Felix Meiner, 1953), pp. 79–80; *The Philosophy of History*, trans. J. Sibree (New York: Dover, 1956), p. 21. Against the charge of easy metaphysical complacency, it is impossible not to grant the deeply tragic pathos in words of Hegel such as these: " . . . when we see the evil, the vice, the ruin that has befallen the most flourishing kingdoms which the mind of man ever created, we can scarce avoid being filled with sorrow at the universal taint of corruption . . . Without rhetorical exaggeration, a simply truthful combination of the miseries that have overwhelmed the noblest of nations and politics, and the finest exemplars of private virtue — forms a picture of most fearful aspect, and excites emotions of the profoundest and most hopeless sadness, counterbalanced by no consolatory result. We endure in beholding it a mental torture, allowing no defense or escape." *ibid.*

4. This theme is, of course, central to the *Phenomenology*. I have dealt with it elsewhere in "Hegel, Philosophy and Worship." In his philosophy of religion Hegel speaks of the death of God as "a monstrous, frightening image, which brings before the imagination the deepest abyss of estrangement." G.W.F. Hegel, *The Christian Religion*, ed. and trans. Peter Hodgson (Missoula, Montana: Scholars Press, 1979), pp. 201–2; *Vorlesungen über die Philosophie der Religion*, ed. G. Lasson (Hamburg: Meiner, 1925), vol. 2, pt. 2, pp. 157–58.

5. Vincent Descombes in *Modern French Philosophy* recounts the movement from humanistic Left-Hegelianism to anti-humanistic anti-Hegelianism

as, say, in Gilles Deleuze. For an exception in American criticism see Charles Altieri, *Act and Quality* (pp. 318 ff.) who defends teleology and a secularized, humanistic Hegelianism in relation to literature.

6. See J. Derrida, "Le puits et la pyramide: Introduction à la semiologie de Hegel" in *Hegel et la pensée moderne*, J. d'Hondt, ed. (Paris: P.U.F., 1970), pp. 27–83. Also *Glas* (Paris: Galilee, 1974), where Derrida studies Hegel and Genet. Also "From Restricted to General Economy: A Hegelianism without Reserve" in *Writing and Difference*, trans. A. Bass (Chicago: University of Chicago Press, 1978), pp. 251–77. On Derrida's complex attitude to Hegel see, for instance, the remark in *Of Grammatology*, trans. G. Spivak (Baltimore: Johns Hopkins University Press, 1976), p. 26: "Hegel is also the first thinker of irreducible difference." A selected translation of *Glas*, dealing with *Kunstreligion* in the *Phenomenology* is to be found in *CLIO*, vol. 11, no. 4, 1982, pp. 339–59. Martin Donougho, in "The Semiotics of Hegel," ibid, pp. 415 ff., rightly presents the doubleness in Derrida's deconstruction as an act of "homage cum iconoclasm" (p. 418), performed not only on Hegel but on other representative figures of the metaphysical tradition.

Let me here say that I am not claiming that Hegelian dialetic is philosophically unproblematic with respect to *all* forms of difference or otherness. In another work I hope to develop a view which deals with some of the difficulties regarding otherness bequeathed to us by dialectical thinking. What I am saying here is that dialectic yields something far richer than its antagonists often allow. In the end many supposedly "post-Hegelians" overcome Hegel simply by bypassing him. If we need a defense of an otherness that cannot be subsumed into dialectic, we must pass through dialectic, not simply bypass it. In the present work I am trying to bring a generous hermeneutic to the reading of Hegel. Elsewhere, as I said, I hope to deal more systematically with the difficulties of dialectic and otherness.

7. Merold Westphal in "Dialectic and Intersubjectivity," *The Owl of Minerva*, vol. 16, no. 1, Fall 1984, pp. 39–54 examines some of the affinities of Hegel and contemporary holisms, but he correctly points out that these holisms tend to be only negatively dialectical (p. 45) and so incomplete from a full Hegelian viewpoint. Interestingly, George di Giovanni's (ibid., pp. 80–83) likening of the negative dialectic of Adorno to the young Hegelians, particularly Bruno Bauer, calls to mind resemblances between the "critique" of Left-Hegelianism and contemporary deconstruction.

8. See Michel Foucault, *The Order of Things* (New York: Random House, 1970), pp. 385–86. "Rather than the death of God — or rather, in the wake of that death and in profound correlation with it — what Nietzsche's thought heralds is the end of his murderer: it is the explosion of man's face in laughter, and the return of masks . . . "

9. This is the impression created by some of the contributors to the symposium "Professing Literature" in *The Times Literary Supplement*, December 10, 1982, pp. 1355–63. See also the remark of Geoffrey Hartman in *Deconstruction and Criticism* (New York: Seabury Press, 1979), p. ix: "The separation of philosophy from literary study has not worked to the benefit of either."

10. See Martin Heidegger, *Nietzsche, Volume I: The Will to Power as Art*, trans. David F. Krell (New York: Harper and Row, 1979).

11. See Harold Bloom's article "The Breaking of Form" in *Deconstruction and Criticism*, Ch. I.

12. Here there is a curious agreement with Whitehead when he says that all philosophy is but a footnote to Plato. Whitehead meant this as a compliment to Plato. When the Nietzscheans, Heideggerians and deconstructionists see metaphysics as the historical working out of Platonism, they imply some rebuke. Lest some traditional literary critics be surprised at the introduction of metaphysics, see for instance J. Hillis Miller's "The Critic as Host," in *Deconstruction and Criticism*, where metaphysics and "obvious meaning" come under fire.

13. Friedrich Nietzsche, *On the Genealogy of Morals*, III, 25.

14. On Platonism and nihilism, see Heidegger's *Nietzsche*, vol. I. especially pp. 151–61.

15. On purposeless becoming, see for example *The Will to Power*, trans. W. Kaufmann and R.J. Hollingdale (New York: Vintage Books, 1968), pp. 377–78; on form as fiction, *ibid*, p. 282. This emphasis on purposeless becoming, the innocence of becoming, leads, of course, to a strong insistence on the importance of play. See my "The Child in Nietzsche's Menagerie."

16. For just one representative statement, see *The Will to Power*, p. 277: "Logic is bound to the condition: assume there are identical cases."

17. Thus Heidegger in *Einführung in die Metaphysik* (Tubingen: M. Niemeyer, 1953), p. 28, speaks of his own task as attempting to bring "Nietzsche's accomplishment to a full unfolding." On Nietzsche's influence on Heidegger, see Krell's remarks in his analysis of the Nietzsche volume, pp. 245 ff.

18. This notion of the "unthought" is to be found, for instance, in Heidegger's discussion of Hegel in *Identity and Difference*, trans. Joan Stambaugh (New York: Harper and Row, 1974). In this volume we also have Heidegger's discussion of the principle of identity.

19. On this and its reverberation throughout the nineteenth century, see Karl Löwith, *From Hegel to Nietzsche*. The links as well as the differences between Heidegger and Hegel are discussed in H.G. Gadamer, *Hegel's Dialectic*, trans. P.C. Smith (New Haven: Yale, 1976), Ch. 5. For a discussion that is sensitive to the "open" side of Hegel, one that also sees the affinities between the Heideggerian *Überwindung* and the Hegelian *Aufhebung*, see David C. Hoy, "The Owl and the Poet: Heidegger's Critique of Hegel," *Boundary* vol. IV, no. 2, Winter 1976, pp. 393–410. Hoy is sensitive to the connection of art works and origins in Heidegger. Though Hegel, as we have seen in a previous chapter, does not neglect origins he also strongly insists on the thrust to teleology, indeed the attainment of an end in great art.

20. Theodore Geraets, "The Impossibility of Philosophy ... and its Realization," *The Owl of Minerva* 16, 1 (Fall, 1984), pp. 31–38, interprets the Hegelian *Idee* as self-articulation, and asks whether thinking as such self-articulation precludes the possibility of closure. He concludes that the free intelligence of philosophy for Hegel "cannot be found in a closed system, but only in sharing the essentially open, eternally producing activity, generation and fruition of eternal self-articulation, i.e., of the idea, being in-and-for itself — as absolute spirit." (p. 38) Below we examine dialectic as an open process of self-articulation which, nevertheless, appropriates itself in its self-articulation.

21. Jacques Derrida, *L'Ecriture et la différence* (Paris: Editions de Seuil, 1967), pp. 426–28. Also Paul de Man's remarks on figuration in *Deconstruction and Criticism*, p. 61.

22. For a very clear statement of the issues of deconstruction in terms of the intertwining of the univocal and the equivocal, see Miller's contribution to *Deconstruction and Criticism*.

23. See de Man's reading of Shelley's *The Triumph of Life* in terms of a "chain of metaphorical transformations," *Deconstruction and Criticism*, p. 58. If one were to judge by this volume, *The Triumph of Life* would appear to be *the* text, it gets so much attention. Miller, art. cit., pp. 229 ff., speaks about the "prisonhouse of language" from which we can effect "no escape" by means of a "simple referential grammar."

24. The question of whether dialectic can be understood ontologically is controversial among Hegel's commentators. Hegel himself does speak of dialectic as a principle exemplified in the actual itself. See, for instance, *Enzyklopädie der philosophischen Wissenschaften*, paragraph 48. For recent discussion of dialectic see Michael Rosen, *Hegel's Dialectic and its Criticism* (New York: Cambridge University Press, 1982). Rosen's book gives us a

vigorous analysis of dialectic, so much so that one is then astonished at the abrupt, blithe dismissiveness of his conclusion regarding Hegel's overall thought as a species of "sheer Neo-Platonic fantasy" (p. 179). Without blinking Rosen goes on to admit that this dismissal cannot be demonstrated. This sheer dismissal reminds one of the Left-Hegelian taboo on the thinker having anything to do with the so-called "mystical," "mystifying" Hegel.

25. See *Will to Power*, p. 550. In this passage Nietzsche's description of the world as eternally moving between contradiction and concord has an extraordinarily Hegelian ring to it. The difference comes out elsewhere (e.g., p. 379) when Nietzsche says: " . . . the world is not an organism at all, but chaos."

26. Unlike Hegel, Nietzsche implies that language *cannot* do justice to Becoming (*Will to Power*, p. 380). Hegel implies that justice can be done if language itself becomes dialectical.

27. For some discussion of *Verstand* in relation to experience and *Vernunft*, see my "Hegel, Philosophy and Worship," pp. 11–17.

28. On the "internal opposition of thought to itself," see *Enzyklopädie*, paragraph 26; on dialectic generally see John Findlay, *Hegel: A Reexamination*, Ch. III.

29. *Enzyklopädie*, paragraph 24, zus.

30. G.W.F. Hegel, *Phänomenologie des Geistes*, pp. 29–30; *Phenomenology of Spirit*, p. 19.

31. *Hegel's Science of Logic*, trans. A.V. Miller (New York: Humanities Press, 1969), p. 32.

32. See *Phänomenologie*, pp. 48 ff.; *Phenomenology*, pp. 35 ff.

33. *Enzyklopädie*, paragraph 82.

34. In a very "Nietzschean" passage in the *Phenomenology* (pp. 27–28), Hegel speaks of truth as a peculiar Bacchanalian revel which combines drunken intoxication with complete calm, that is, as a kind of unity of Dionysus and Apollo.

35. "Trace of an absence" is the kind of language Derrida employs. See Bloom's remark about modern poetry and what he calls "an achieved dearth of meaning," *Deconstruction and Criticism*, p. 12. I realize, of course, that the category of "presence" raises many hares for Heideggerians and post-Heideggerians. "Metaphysics of presence" tends to be a somewhat pejorative, tainted term. One is tempted to reply: "presence" is extraordinarily complex,

indeed in some cases it may be inexhaustible. "Absence" falls prey to all the criticisms that Stillingfleet and Berkeley brought against Locke's material substrate as an "I know not what"; or to Hegel's criticisms of Kant's unknowable *Ding-an-sich.*

36. See Eric Heller, *The Artist's Journey into the Interior* , p. 82. Harold Bloom notes a connection between Paul de Man and Romantic Irony, indeed cites Schlegel as de Man's "truest precursor," *Deconstruction and Criticism,* p. 16. We will discuss the attitude to Romantic Irony displayed by Hegel in his *Aesthetics* more fully in Chapter Six.

37. We have already noted the Nietzschean heritage, but one might also note Derrida's own concern with Husserl's project, and then in turn the connection betwen Husserl and Descartes. Miller (see note 13 above) speaks about oscillating between logocentrism and nihilism. The dizziness of Miller's oscillation is enlivened by a cheerful nihilism à la Nietzsche. The nihilism of some deconstructionists, however, may veer from thoughtful cheerfulness to a kind of thoughtless complacency. See, for instance, the remark of the editors of *The Question of Textuality: Strategies of Reading in Contemporary American Criticism,* William V. Spanos, Paul A. Bove and Daniel O'Hara (eds.) (Bloomington: Indiana University Press, 1982), p. 8: "We can connect nothing with nothing, one might say." They speak of having to pass through Nietzsche, but such remarks make one wonder whether instead they are passing out into vacancy.

38. We might note that though Nietzsche is now seen by some thinkers as anti-dialectical (especially Gilles Deleuze in *Nietzsche and Philosophy*), Peter Heller quite clearly sees Nietzsche's dialectical characteristics in *Dialectics and Nihilism* (Amherst: University of Massachusetts Press, 1966). Heller voices his concern for reintegration against what he views as modern decline (p. viii). In connection with Nietzsche he clearly sees that we are witness to the "emergence of a Hegel without Hegel's absolute, or rather to a more than Hegelian addiction to dialectic which was deprived of all faith in an enduring and harmonious condition of being." (p. 80)

39. *VA,* I, pp. 92 ff; *HA,* I, pp. 63 ff.

40. Denis Donoghue, "Deconstructing Deconstruction," *New York Review of Books,* vol. 27, no. 10 (June 12, 1980), pp. 37–41.

41. On this see, for instance, Graff, op. cit.

Chapter Six

1. Kant, of course, recognizes the irreducibility of beauty to ordinary hedonistic, "pathological" terms, and in the *Critique of Judgment* strongly points out the peculiar universality in beauty. He also strains severely against the limits of aesthetic formalism in his discussion of the aesthetical idea and his notion of the sublime.

2. This Pythagorean notion is related to the issue of aesthetic theodicy, taken up below. On contemporary philosophy and "the noise of the world" see, for instance, Vincent Descombes, "An Essay in Philosophical Observation," in *Philosophy in France Today*, Alan E. Montefiori (ed.), (New York: Cambridge University Press, 1983), especially pp. 75 ff. See also the essay by Claude Lefort, particularly his remark (p. 90), which is very appropriate to the present chapter: "Far from endorsing the criticism of certain contemporaries who condemn, under the name of Romanticism, the double phantasy of *revelation* and *creation*, it seemed to me that the nineteenth century witnessed the formation of an enigma which confronts us still and which lies at the heart of our modernity, detaching us from the classical tradition." Relevantly, Merleau-Ponty's *The Prose of the World* (a notion very present in Hegel's *Aesthetics*) is cited by Lefort in this connection.

3. See E.M. Butler, *The Tyranny of Greece Over Germany* (Boston: Beacon Press, 1958). Also Henry Hatfield, *Aesthetic Paganism in German Literature* (Cambridge, Mass: Harvard University Press, 1964).

4. Recent studies emphasizing either the harmony of the classical ideal or the fragmentation of modernity include, Bernard Cullen, *Hegel's Social and Political Thought: An Introduction* (New York: St. Martin's Press, 1979); Philip J. Kain, *Schiller, Hegel and Marx: State, Society, and the Aesthetic Ideal of Ancient Greece* (Kingston & Montreal: McGill-Queen's University Press, 1982); John Toews, *Hegelianism*.

5. Hölderlin, *Sämtliche Werke*, ed. Friedrich Beissner (Stuttgart, 1946–1961) II, p. 167. See Hatfield, op. cit., p. 150.

6. See Butler, op. cit., p. ix.

7. G.W.F. Hegel, *On Christianity: Early Theological Writings*, trans. T.M. Knox (Philadelphia: University of Pennsylvania Press, 1971), p. 153; *Hegels theologische Jugendschriften*. ed. H. Nohl (Frankfurt am Maine: Minerva, 1966), p. 221. See also Kain, op. cit., Ch. II; Cullen, op. cit., espec. pp. 7 ff. We might also note the fact that Hegel composed and addressed to Hölderlin

a poem entitled *Eleusis*, which as Harris in *Hegel's Development* says is "Hegel's testimony that the Greek spirit has not after all 'flown'" (p. xxv). For discussion see Harris, pp. 244–48. Also A. Olson, "Renunciation and Metaphysics: An Examination of Dialectic in Hölderlin and Hegel during their Frankfurt Period," *Man and World*, 15 (1982), pp. 127–28. An English translation of "Eleusis" is to be found in G. Mueller, *Hegel: The Man, his Vision and Work* (New York: Pageant Press, 1968), pp. 60–62.

8. Hatfield, op. cit., pp. 4–5.

9. On Herder see Hatfield, Ch. IV. Hatfield's work also contains ample discussion of Hölderlin, Ch. IX; on Schiller, Ch. VIII; on Schlegel, pp. 181 ff.; on Jean Paul, pp. 192–93. On Heine, see Butler, op. cit., Ch. VII.

10. *Phänomenologie, pp. 523–524; Phenomenology*, p. 455. This passage has been the subject of comment, by Gadamer and Ricouer for instance. Here we just cite the melancholy side of the passage. Everything is not entirely lost for Hegel, however, as the rest of the passage seems to imply. The possibilities of recuperation in Hegel's aesthetics will be dealt with more fully throughout this chapter. Here we just note the ambiguous and somewhat guarded attitude of Hegel to ancient art, even in the act of realistically acknowledging its demise, indeed in his finding a rationale in its necessary downfall. *Erinnerung* need not be a merely external mode of memory, but may be a deeper interiorized appropriation of its spiritual meaning.

11. Hatfield (p. 53) cites Herder's statement of forthright scepticism: "Set up Greek statues so that every dog pisses on them and still you won't give the slave who passes them every day, the ass who drags his burden, any sense that they are there, or that they should come to resemble them." See also Santayana's ironical evaluation of Winckelmann's ideal in *Three Philosophical Poets* (Cambridge, MA: Harvard University Press, 1910), p. 175.

12. *VA*, I, pp. 89 ff.; *HA*, I, pp. 61 ff.

13. F. Schelling, *On University Studies*, ed. and trans. E. Wilkinson and L.A. Willoughboy (Athens, Ohio: Ohio University Press, 1966), p. 69. See also David Punter, *Blake, Hegel and Dialectic* (Amsterdam: Rudopi, 1982), pp. 59–71.

14. F. Nietzsche, *The Use and Abuse of History*, trans. A. Collins (Indianapolis: Bobbs-Merrill, 1949). When we consider Hegel's *Reason in History*, trans. R. Hartman (Indianapolis: Bobbs Merrill, 1953), we find some interesting affinities with Nietzsche, for instance, their focus on the hero, the world historical individual. Such figures are living, or once living exemplars of human powers at their most extended and significant. In their time they

may be catalysts or instruments of *Geist* in history. After their time, they may be not only reminders of past greatness, but their memory may be a model of present and future inspiration — monumental individuals in Nietzsche's terms. Hegel himself, of course, is very aware of critical history, the "higher criticism" of his own time. Nor is he flattering towards it (see Toews, *Hegelianism,* for discussion of Hegel's relation to Schleiermacher and the Historical School, pp. 60 ff.). Hegel, of course, is aware of the uniqueness of each age, and the often shallow nature of appeals to the examples of the Greeks and Romans, say, during the French Revolution (*Reason in History,* p. 8). We are reminded of Hegel's remarks in his philosophy of religion about historical theologians who are like bankers always handling somebody else's money, or like blind men handling the frame of a painting but unable to see its beauty.

15. This is not just rhetoric, as the even more sharp language in the *Phenomenology* concerning the highway of despair, and the Golgotha of spirit reveals.

16. On this exigence for wholeness see, for instance, H.G. Gadamer, *Reason in the Age of Science,* trans. F.G. Lawrence, (Cambridge, Mass: MIT Press, 1981), Ch. I. Also the essays "Hegel's Philosophy and its Aftereffect until Today" and "The Heritage of Hegel."

17. On this in relation to the Romantic attitude to death, see Jacques Choron, *Death and Western Thought* (New York: Collier, 1963), pp. 156–61. See also Albert Hofstadter, "Art: Death and Transfiguration. A Study of Hegel's Theory of Romanticism," *Review of National Literatures,* 1 (1970), pp. 149–64.

18. *VA,* I, p. 96; *HA,* I, p. 67.

19. Jacques Barzun, *Classic, Romantic and Modern* (New York: Anchor Doubleday, 1961), p. 14.

20. Something of this disproportion between subjectivity and objectivity is implied for instance by Eliot's notion that modern consciousness, compared to the more unified religious culture of the middle ages is marked by a certain "dissociation of sensibility." Disintegration in artistic consciousness here may be just a sensible mirror of the disintegration in the whole of modernity, spoken of earlier in the context of Hegel's understanding of the fragmentation of his own times. See R.S. Lucas, "A Problem in Hegel's Aesthetics," *Renaissance and Modern Studies,* 4 (1960), pp. 82–118. Also L. Santoro, "Hegel's Aesthetics and the 'End of Art'" *Philosophical Studies* (Ireland), XXX, pp. 62–72.

21. Barzun, op. cit., p. 117.

22. See *The Young Hegelians*, Lawrence Stepelevich ed., p. 335.

23. Barzun, op. cit., p. 121.

24. Ibid., p. 143.

25. VA, I, pp. 93 ff.; HA, I, pp. 64 ff.

26. Ibid., p. 93; 64.

27. Ibid., p. 94; 65.

28. Ibid., p. 96; 66.

29. Ibid., p. 97; 67.

30. Ibid.

31. Ibid., pp. 98–99; 68–69.

32. I am putting to one side here the controversial, knotted issue of Plato's criticism of the poets in the *Republic*. We might note, however, that this criticism is consistent with the Platonic emphasis that beauty cannot be merely aesthetic in the sense of *l'art pour l'art*; the totality of ethical life is implicated with beauty. Even in Plato's criticism of inadequate images of the divine, he testifies to his sense of the profound power of the image to shape and move man with respect to the ultimate things.

33. Note, for instance, how R.G. Collingwood in *The Principles of Art*, perhaps one of the most sensitive and provocative works of aesthetics in twentieth century English philosophy, excludes beauty in the Greek sense from consideration, focusing instead on art as expression and imagination (pp. 37–41). Note also how this aesthetic view is grounded in a Kantian-style epistemology. On this see, William Desmond, "Collingwood, Imagination and Epistemology," *Philosophical Studies* (Ireland), vol. XXIV, pp. 82–103.

34. Edward Bullough, " 'Psychical distance' as a factor in Art and as an Aesthetic Principle," *British Journal of Psychology*, V, 2 (1912), pp. 87–118.

35. M.H. Abrams, *The Mirror and the Lamp*, pp. 218 ff.

36. *Symposium*, 209e6–212a10.

37. Compare the ascent to beauty in the *Symposium* with *Phaedrus* 249d5 ff.

38. Think here of the notion of "begetting on the beautiful" in Socrates' speech in the *Symposium* 206c1 ff.

39. A contemporary attack on this aspect of Platonism is to be found in Rorty's *Philosophy and the Mirror of Nature*. Such an attack is connected with the anti-representational motif of some modern art, the criticism of referential language in literature, and various attacks on "representational thought" and the correspondence theory of truth by pragmatists, Heideggerians, and Wittgensteinian analysts, to name but some examples.

40. See J. Ritter, *Hegel and the French Revolution*, trans. Richard D. Winfield (Cambridge, MA, and London: MIT Press, 1982), p. 62.

41. *VA*, I, pp. 39–40; *HA*, I, pp. 21–22.

42. *VA*, I, pp. 83–84; *HA*, I, p. 56.

43. *VA*, I, p. 85; *HA*, I, p. 57.

44. *VA*, I, pp. 88–89; *HA*, I, p. 60.

45. *Summa Theol.* Ia, q. 5, art. 4, ad 1.

46. Jacques Maritain, *Creative Intuition in Art and Poetry* (New York: Pantheon Books, 1953). See also *Art and Scholasticism and the Frontiers of Poetry*, trans. Joseph W. Evans (South Bend: Notre Dame University Press, 1974), Ch. V.

47. *Summa Theol.* Ia, q. 5, art 4, ad 1; also I–II, q. 27, art 1, ad 3.

48. *Summa Theol.* Ia, q. 39, art 8. See James Joyce's discussion of these three characteristics in *A Portrait of the Artist as a Young Man*, Ch. 5.

49. On beauty and the good, see *Summa Theol.* Ia, q. 5, art 4, ad 1; I–II, q. 27, art 1, ad 3. Also Maritain, *Art and Scholasticism*, pp. 167–70.

50. On the spiritualization of the senses see *VA*, I, p. 61; *HA*, I, p. 39. Maritain refers to "intelligentiated sense" in *Art and Scholasticism*, p. 164.

51. The kinship of art and philosophy is made most explicit for Hegel by his assigning of both together, along with religion, to the realm of Absolute Spirit. On art and the speculative intellect, see *Summa Theol.* I–II, q. 57, art 4; on the analogy with wisdom, Maritain, *Art and Scholasticism*, pp. 33–34.

52. Hegel speaks of the art work in terms of an internal teleology, internal necessity, what he terms *Selbstzweck*. On this see, Charles Taylor, *Hegel* Ch. XVII.

53. On the Idea and the Ideal see *VA*, I, pp. 104 ff.; also p. 17: " . . . das Schone hat sein leben in dem *Scheine*." Hegel here is aware of the ambiguity in *Schein*, which he treats more fully in his *Science of Logic*, trans. A.V. Miller, 394 ff.

54. *Science of Logic*, pp. 499 ff.

55. On the spiritual significance of the face, see, for instance, Hegel's remarks on Rauch's bust of Goethe, VA, II, pp. 84–85; also pp. 383 ff.; HA, I, p. 484; II, pp. 727 ff.

56. We might here note how Erwin Panofsky in *Gothic Architecture and Scholasticism* (New York: Meridian Books, 1958) speaks of the Medieval *manifestatio* and *concordantia* as involving an "acceptance and ultimate reconciliation of contradictory possibilities" (see p. 64). Panofsky even mentions the Hegelian triad (p. 86); in places he all but speaks of a cathedral as being the dialectical *Aufhebung* of other building (pp. 78–79). Just as Panofsky speaks of the cathedral as a kind of "visual logic" (p. 58), Hegel's discussion of architecture points to a similar, as it were, dialectical synthesis in stone.

57. Such a phrase has contemporary overtones in Heidegger, though it draws upon all the connotations of musical harmony which, as we know, one will find as far back as the Pythagorean *harmonia*.

58. Hegel's debt to Aristotle is well recognized, of course, by many Hegel scholars, but the recognition is found, perhaps a little surprisingly, elsewhere too. Thus Von Wright reminds us that Hegel is a great renewer of the Aristotelian tradition, defending "teleological intelligibles" over against any "Galilean" reduction, particularly in relation to human action. This teleological emphasis on the unity of the whole is, of course, of direct relevance to the concept of beauty. See Richard Bernstein, "Why Hegel Now?" *Review of Metaphysics*, XXXI, 1 September, 1977, especially pp. 42–43. Also Henry Paolucci, "The Poetics of Aristotle and Hegel," *Review of National Literatures*, 1 (1970), pp. 165–213.

59. *Critique of Judgment*, paragraphs 46–50.

60. On this see Toews, *Hegelianism*, pp. 89 ff.

61. VA, I, p. 48; HA, I, p. 29.

62. *Ibid.* pp. 49–50; p. 30.

63. Ibid.

64. See *Art and Scholasticism*, p. 167; also p. 163.

65. John Hicks, for instance, makes much of this in his philosophy of religion.

66. See *Timaeus* 28d4 ff.

67. Aquinas' brief discussion of beauty in the *Summa Theologiae*, referred to above, takes place in the context of his discussion of the good. Notice

also that Aquinas' discussion of evil in relation to the whole (*S.T.* q 47–49) is also in relation to the distinction and multiplicity of things finite. Aquinas' assertion of the perfection of the order of the universe might be seen as a tremendous glorification of the goodness of created *manyness* (q. 47, *respondeo*). See the theme of positive appearance below in Hegel's aesthetics. In both the search for the unity of the whole is not intended *reductively*. Rather the opposite.

68. A.N. Whitehead, *Adventure of Ideas* (New York: Macmillan, 1967), pp. 334 ff. Note also how "appearance" in Whitehead can have the positive transfigurational role found in Hegel's view of aesthetic appearance below. Thus Whitehead says: "In other words, 'appearance' is the effect of the activity of the mental pole, whereby the qualities and coordinations of the given physical world undergo transformation. It results from the fusion of the ideal with the actual — the light that never was, on sea or land." *Adventure of Ideas*, p. 270.

69. Of course, the precise character of Hegel's reconciliation with the actual was, and is, an explosive issue, with profound political overtones which made Hegel's own disciples wonder whether we here just deal with a quietist acceptance or rationalization of the established Prussian order. The present emphasis on aesthetic transfiguration cannot be construed quietistically. Toews in *Hegelianism* explores the ambiguities of the issue thoroughly with respect to the different attitudes of Hegel's followers. Relevantly to our aesthetic concerns he notes (p. 120): "This accommodationist stance attained its most extreme and enthusiastic expression in a notorious book by the Königsberg Hegelian Karl Friedrich Ferdinand Sietze in which the Prussian state was described as "a gigantic harp tuned in the garden of God in order to lead the world chorale."

70. Gilles Deleuze, *Nietzsche and Philosophy*.

71. Kant is very clearly aware of the power of art to transpose the ugly — "the Furies, diseases, devastations of war, and the like . . . " while yet preserving aesthetic delight (*Critique of Judgment*, par. 48). One experience only he excludes, namely *disgust* — though we might in fact ask whether in the post-Hegelian, post-Nietzschean context, it is just this experience that challenges art. Hegel would sympathize with Schiller's view, in relation to ancient images of death, that "death is not so aesthetic" (*Aber, ihr Herren, der Tod is so asthetisch doch nicht*) (see Hatfield, op. cit., p. 30). Yet his aesthetics, like his philosophy generally, insist on the genuine confrontation and grappling with death. On this see J. Choron, *Death and Western Thought*, Ch. 18.

Insofar as Hegel tries to incorporate the infinite and the negative in his view of beauty, Hegel speaks of what other thinkers, like Kant and Schopenhauer, for instance, call the sublime. Hegel's predeliction for beauty is tied to his respect for the classical Greek ideal of formed, aesthetic wholeness. What he sees as symbolical and romantic art is evidently more related to the sublime, in that both of these imply a certain disproportion between the self and otherness, spirit and sensuousness, inwardness and exteriority. Symbolical art, in Hegel's usage, points to the sublimity of externality in the majesty of nature or in overwhelming human constructions like the Pyramids. Romantic art points us to an inward sublime, the abyss of infinite interiority of (for Hegel) Christian and modern man. Hegel's "Apollonianism" comes out again in his guarded response to these different disproportions.

72. See VA, I, pp. 13, 70; also II, 237–39; HA, I, p. 46; also p. 607. Hegel quotes Terence (not quite correctly) in the first citation, and in the second speaks of Humanus as the new holy of holies in Romantic art. As should be clear from Chapter Three, I argue against interpreting this in exclusively humanistic terms. For an interpretation which is very sensitive to the religious dimension of Hegel's aesthetics but which perhaps tilts more towards the humanistic, see Martin Donougho, "Remarks on 'Humanus heisst der Heilige . . . '". Hegel-Studien, 17 (1982), pp. 214–25.

73. Not incidentally Hegel's high praise for Shakespeare is to be found in almost the last words of the Aesthetics: " . . . the modern world has developed a type of comedy which is truly comical and truly poetic. Here once again the keynote is good humor, assured and careless gaiety despite all failure and misfortune, exuberance and the audacity of a fundamentally happy craziness, folly and idiosyncrasy in general. Consequently there is presented here once more (in a deeper wealth and inwardness of humor) whether in wider or narrower circles of society, in a subject matter whether important or trivial, what Aristophanes achieved to perfection in his field in Greece. As a brilliant example of this sort of thing I will name Shakespeare once again, in conclusion, but without going into detail." VA, III, p. 512; HA, II, pp. 1235–36. See Anne Paolucci, "Bradley and Hegel on Shakespeare," Comparative Literature, 16 (1964), pp. 211–25.

74. On this in connection with Hegel's attitude and death, see Choron, op. cit. p. 154. The theme of transfiguration is perhaps connected with the experience of quasi-religious conversion undergone by, it seems, many of Hegel's followers (see Toews, op. cit., pp. 85; 90; 91; 93). In some cases, for instance Wilhelm Vatke (see Toews p. 91), we have almost a Dionysian intoxication with the Hegelian concept, sounding somewhat like an empty afflatus, also strangely reminiscent of the megalomaniacal hyperbole of the mad Nietzsche. On Hegel and Nietzsche see Leon Rosenstein, "Metaphysical

Foundations of the Theories of Tragedy in Hegel and Nietzsche," *Journal of Aesthetics and Art Criticism*, 28 (1970), pp. 521–33.

75. Heidegger, *Nietzsche*, I, p. 209.

76. Friedrich Nietzsche, *The Will to Power*, p. 427.

77. *Will to Power*, p. 422.

78. See *Will to Power*, pp. 450–51.

79. *Will to Power*, p. 427.

80. This ambiguity is reflected in the splitting of Hegel's heirs between the accommodationists, the reformers and the revolutionaries. We have a perhaps humorous aspect of how Hegel's legacy was carried into the future in Forster's funeral speech at Hegel's burial: No new Emperor would succeed the philosophical Alexander, rather "the Satraps would divide the orphaned provinces among themselves." As Toews (op. cit. p. 204) remarks, Forster seemed innocent of the possibility that the Satraps would soon be at each other's throats in the battle for inheritance. See also (ibid.) Toews' remarks regarding Rosenkranz's play about Minerva's perturbation at the philosophical anarchy after Hegel's death — nobody gets Hegel's inheritance!

81. On Hegel's attitude to Dutch painting see VA, II, pp. 225 ff.; HA, I, pp. 597 ff. See also Paul Tillich *Theology of Culture* (New York: Oxford Press, 1959), Ch. VI "Protestantism and Artistic Style," where he remarks (p. 75) in connection with contemporary symbols of the cross and resurrection (he mentions *Guernica*) that to express conflict is already to go beyond it, to express meaninglessness is already to transcend it. This reminds us of general Hegelian strategy where to plot a limit is already to pass beyond it. In a recent article, Henry Harris, "The Resurrection of Art," *The Owl of Minerva*, vol. 16, no. 1, Fall 1984, pp. 5–20, argues for the continued importance of beauty in Hegel and after Hegel. Earlier I cited Picasso's *Guernica* as an instance of art creatively seizing the opportunity of disunity. Harris gives a very perceptive interpretation of *Guernica* (pp. 17–19).

82. See Choron, op. cit., p. 155.

83. Ibid.; his silent pointing, it seems, was in response to Mrs. Hegel's questioning him about his belief in immortality, as recounted by a former student.

84. See the introduction to this present study on this question of dialectic, ambiguity, and the possibility of a "double" interpretation or reading.

Bibliography

Abrams, M.H. *The Mirror and the Lamp.* New York: Oxford University Press, 1953.

———. *Natural Supernaturalism.* New York: Norton, 1971.

Altieri, Charles. *Act and Quality: A Theory of Literary Meaning and Humanistic Understanding.* Amherst: University of Massachusetts Press, 1981.

Arato, A. and Beghardt, E. (eds.). *The Essential Frankfurt School Reader.* New York: Urizen Books, 1978.

Aron, R. *The Opium of the Intellectuals.* trans T. Kilmartin. New York: Norton, 1962.

Aronson, R. *Jean-Paul Sartre — Philosophy in the World.* London: New Left Books, 1980.

Barfield, Owen. *Poetic Diction.* London: Faber and Faber, 1928.

Barzun, Jacques. *Classic, Romantic and Modern.* Garden City: Doubleday, 1961.

Bernstein, Richard. "Why Hegel Now?" *Review of Metaphysics,* XXXI, 1, September, 1977, 29–60.

Bloom, H. "The Breaking of Form." *Deconstruction and Criticism.* G. Hartman, ed. New York: Seabury Press, 1979.

Bubner, R. "Hegel's Aesthetics — Yesterday and Today." *Art and Logic in Hegel's Philosophy.* W. Steinkraus and K. Schmitz, eds. New Jersey: Humanities Press, 1980, 15–33.

Bullough, Edward. "'Psychical' distance as a factor in Art and as an Aesthetic Principle." *British Journal of Psychology*, V, 2, (1912), 87–118.

Bunjay, Stephen. *Beauty and Truth: A Study of Hegel's Aesthetics*. Oxford: Oxford University Press, 1984.

Burbidge, John. *On Hegel's Logic: Fragments of a Commentary*. Atlantic Highlands: Humanities Press, 1981.

Butler, E.M. *The Tyranny of Greece over Germany*. Boston: Beacon Press, 1958.

Carter, Curtis. "A Re-examination of the 'Death of Art' Interpretation of Hegel's Aesthetics." *Art and Logic in Hegel's Philosophy*. W. Steinkraus and K. Schmitz, eds. New Jersey: Humanities Press, 1980, 83–100.

Chiodi, Pietro. *Sartre and Marxism*. trans. K. Soper. Atlantic Highlands: Humanities Press, 1976.

Choron, Jacques. *Death and Western Thought*. New York: Collier, 1963.

Christensen, D. (ed.). *Hegel and the Philosophy of Religion*. The Hague: Nijhoff, 1970.

Collingwood, R.G. *The Principles of Art*. Oxford: Clarendon Press, 1938.

Cooper, Barry. *The End of History: An Essay on Modern Hegelianism*. Toronto: University of Toronto Press, 1984.

Croce, B. *Aesthetics as Science of Expression and General Linguistic*. trans. Douglas Ainslie. London: Macmillan, 1922.

Cullen, Bernard. *Hegel's Social and Political Thought: An Introduction*. New York: St. Martin's Press, 1979.

Descombes, Vincent. *Modern French Philosophy*. New York: Cambridge University Press, 1980.

Deleuze, Gilles. *Nietzsche and Philosophy*. trans. H. Tomlinson. New York: Columbia University Press, 1983.

Derrida, Jacques. "White Mythology: Metaphor in the Text of Philosophy." *New Literary History*, VI, Autumn 1974, 5–74.

_____. *Writing and Difference*. trans. A. Bass. Chicago: University of Chicago Press, 1978.

_____. *Glas*. Paris: Galilee, 1974.

_____. "Le puits et la pyramide. Introduction à la semiologie de Hegel." *Hegel et la pensée moderne*." J. d'Hondt, ed. Paris: P.U.F. 1970, 27–83.

_____. *Of Grammatology*, trans. G. Spivak. Baltimore: Johns Hopkins University Press, 1976.

Desmond, William. "Collingwood, Imagination and Epistemology." *Philosophical Studies* (Ireland), 24 (1976), 82–103.

_____. Hegel, Philosophy and Worship." *CITHARA*, 19:1 (1979), 3–20.

_____. "Augustine's *Confessions*: On Desire, Conversion and Reflection." *Irish Theological Quarterly*, 47:1 (1980), 224–33.

_____. Review of *Art and Logic in Hegel's Philosophy. The Owl of Minerva*, 12, 4, June 1981, 7–9

_____. "The Child in Nietzsche's Menagerie." *SEMINAR*, V, 1981, 40–44.

_____. "Hegel, History and Philosophical Contemporaneity." *Filosofia Oggi*, IV:2 (1981), 211–26.

_____. "Hegel and the Problem of Religious Representation." *Philosophical Studies* (Ireland) 30 (1984), 9–22.

d'Hondt, J. (ed.) *Hegel et la pensée moderne*. Paris: P.U.F., 1970.

di Giovanni, George. "Burbidge and Hegel on the Logic." *The Owl of Minerva*, 14, 1, September 1982, 4–5.

Donougho, Martin. "The Cunning of Odysseus: A Theme in Hegel, Lukács and Adorno." *Philosophy and Social Criticism*, 1981, 13–43.

_____. "The Semiotics of Hegel." *CLIO*, 11, 4, 1982, 414–30.

_____. "Remarks on 'Humanus heisst der Heilige . . .'" *Hegel-Studien*, 17, (1982), 214–225.

Donoghue, Denis. "Deconstructing Deconstruction." *New York Review of Books*. 12 June, 1980, 37–41.

Eagleton, Terry. *Marxism and Literary Criticism*. Berkeley: California University Press, 1976.

Eliot, T.S. *Selected Prose*. New York: Harcourt Brace Jovanovich, 1975.

Empson, William. *Seven Types of Ambiguity*. Harmondsworth: Penguin Books, 1962.

Fackenheim, E. *The Religious Dimension in Hegel's Thought*. Bloomington: Indiana University Press, 1967.

Findlay, J.N. *Hegel: A Reexamination*. New York: Humanities Press, 1958.

Foucault, M. *The Order of Things*. New York: Random House, 1970.

Flaccus, Louis William. *Artists and Thinkers*. Freeport, New York: Books for Libraries Press, 1967.

Flay, Joseph C. *Hegel's Quest for Certainty*. Albany: State University of New York Press, 1984.

Gadamer, Hans-Georg. *Truth and Method*. trans. G. Barden and J. Cumming. New York: Seabury Press, 1975.

_____. *Hegel's Dialectic*. trans. P. C. Smith. New Haven: Yale, 1976.

_____. *Reason in the Age of Science*. trans. F.G. Lawrence. Cambridge: MIT Press, 1981.

Geraets, T. "The Impossibility of Philosophy . . . and its Realization." *The Owl of Minerva*, 16, 1, Fall 1984, 31–38.

Gibson, A. Boyce. *Muse and Thinker*. Harmondsworth: Penguin Books, 1972.

Gill, Eric. *Art*. London: The Bodley Head, 1934.

Graff, Gerald. *Literature against Itself: Literary Ideas in Modern Society*. Chicago: Chicago University Press, 1979.

Haering, Theodor. *Hegel: Sein Wollen und sein Werk*. Leipzig: B.G. Teubner, 1929.

Harries, Karsten. "Hegel on the Future of Art." *Review of Metaphysics*, 27 (1973–74), 677–96.

Harris, H.S. *Hegel's Development: Towards the Sunlight, 1770–1801*. Oxford: Clarendon Press, 1972.

_____. *Hegel's Development: Night Thoughts (Jena 1801–1806)*. Oxford: Clarendon Press, 1983.

_____. "The Resurrection of Art." *The Owl of Minerva*, 16, 1, Fall 1984, 5–20.

Hartmann, G. (ed.) *Deconstruction and Criticism*. New York: Seabury Press, 1979.

Hartmann, Klaus. "Hegel: A Non-Metaphysical View." in *Hegel: A Collection of Critical Essays*. A. MacIntyre, ed. New York: Doubleday, 1972.

Hartshorne, Charles. *Insights and Oversights of Great Thinkers: An Evaluation of Western Philosophy*. Albany: State University of New York Press, 1983.

Hatfield, Henry. *Aesthetic Paganism in German Literature.* Cambridge, Mass.: Harvard University Press, 1964.

Hegel, G.W.F. *Werke in zwanzig Banden.* ed. E. Moldenhauer and K.M. Michel. Frankfurt: Suhrkamp, 1970.

_____. *Vorlesungen über die Ästhetik, Werke,* Bande 13–15.

_____. *Hegel's Aesthetics.* trans. T.M. Knox. Oxford: Clarendon Press, 1975.

_____. *Phänomenologie des Geistes.* Hamburg: Felix Meiner, 1952.

_____. *Phenomenology of Spirit.* trans. A.V. Miller. Oxford: Clarendon Press, 1977.

_____. *Wissenschaft der Logik.* Hamburg: Felix Meiner, 1963.

_____. *Science of Logic.* trans. A.V. Miller. New York: Humanities Press, 1969.

_____. *Enzyklopädie der philosophischen Wissenschaften im Grundrisse (1830).* Hamburg: Felix Meiner, 1959.

_____. *Hegel's Philosophy of Mind: Being Part Three of the Encyclopaedia of the Philosophical Sciences.* trans. W. Wallace. Oxford: Oxford University Press, 1971.

_____. *Briefe von und an Hegel.* ed. J. Hoffmeister and R. Flechsig. Hamburg: Felix Meiner, 1952–60.

_____. *Hegel: The Letters.* trans. C. Butler and C. Seiler. Bloomington: Indiana University Press, 1984.

_____. *The Difference between Fichte's and Schelling's System of Philosophy.* trans. H.S. Harris and W. Cerf. Albany: State University of New York Press, 1977.

_____. *The Philosophy of Right.* trans. T.M. Knox. Oxford: Oxford University Press, 1967.

_____. *Die Vernunft in der Geschichte.* ed. J. Hoffmeister. Hamburg: Felix Meiner, 1955.

_____. *The Philosophy of History.* trans. J. Sibree. New York: Dover, 1956.

_____. *Vorlesungen über die Philosophie der Religion.* ed. G. Lasson. Hamburg: Felix Meiner, 1925.

_____. *The Christian Religion.* ed. and trans. Peter Hodgson. Missoula, Montana: Scholars Press, 1979.

_____. *Hegels theologische Jugendschriften.* ed. H. Nohl. Frankfurt: Minerva, 1966.

_____. *On Christianity: Early Theological Writings.* trans. T.M. Knox. Philadelphia: University of Pennsylvania Press, 1971.

Heidegger, Martin. *Nietzsche, Volume I: The Will to Power as Art.* trans. David Krell. New York: Harper and Row, 1979.

_____. *Einführung in die Metaphysik.* Tubingen: Niemeyer, 1953.

_____. *Identity and Difference.* trans. J. Stambaugh. New York: Harper and Row, 1974.

Heller, Eric. *The Artist's Journey into the Interior.* New York: Random House, 1959.

Heller, Peter. *Dialectics and Nihilism.* Amherst: University of Massachusetts Press, 1966.

Henckmann, W. "Bibliographie zur Ästhetik Hegels 1830-1965." *Hegel-Studien,* 5, 1969.

Henrich, Dieter. *Hegel im Kontext.* Frankfurt: Suhrkamp Verlag, 1971.

Hirsch, E.D. *Wordsworth and Schelling: A Typological Study of Romanticism.* New Haven: Yale, 1960.

Hochberg, H. "Albert Camus and the Ethics of Absurdity." *Ethics,* 75, 2, January 1965, 87-102.

Hoffman, Piotr. *The Anatomy of Idealism: Passivity and Activity in Kant, Hegel and Marx.* The Hague: Nijhoff, 1982.

Hoffmeister, J. *Hölderlin und Hegel.* Tübingen: J.C.B. Mohr, 1931.

Hofstadter, Albert. "Art: Death and Transfiguration. A Study of Hegel's Theory of Romanticism." *Review of National Literatures,* 1 (1970), 149-64.

Horn, András. *Kunst und Freiheit: Eine kritsche Interpretation der Hegelschen Ästhetik.* The Hague: Nijhoff, 1969.

Hoy, David C. "The Owl and the Poet: Heidegger's Critique of Hegel." *Boundary,* IV, 2, Winter 1976, 393-410.

Hutchings, P. "The Poetic Particular" *Proceedings of the Fifth International Congress of Aesthetics: Amsterdam, 1964.* The Hague: Mouton, 1968. 690-92.

Kain, Philip. *Schiller, Hegel and Marx: State, Society, and the Aesthetic Ideal of Ancient Greece.* Kingston and Montreal: McGill-Queen's University Press, 1982.

Kaminsky, Jack. *Hegel on Art.* Albany: State University of New York, 1962.

Kainz, Howard. "Hegel's Theory of Aesthetics in the *Phenomenology.*" *Idealistic Studies,* 2 (1972), 81–94.

Kant, I. *Critique of Judgment.* trans with analytical indexes by J.C. Meredith. Oxford: Clarendon Press, 1952.

Karelis, Charles. "Hegel's Concept of Art: An Interpretative Essay." *Hegel's Introduction to Aesthetics.* trans. T.M. Knox. Oxford: Clarendon Press, 1979, xi-lxxvi.

Kaufmann, Walter. *Hegel: Reinterpretation, Texts and Commentary.* New York: Doubleday, 1965.

_____. *Discovering the Mind: Goethe, Kant and Hegel.* New York: McGraw-Hill, 1980.

Kedney, J.S. *Hegel's Aesthetics.* Chicago: Griggs and Co., 1892.

Kermode, F. *The Sense of an Ending: Studies in the Theory of Fiction.* New York: Oxford University Press, 1966.

Kojève, A. *Introduction to the Reading of Hegel.* trans. J. Nichols and A. Bloom. New York: Basic Books, 1969.

Knox, Israel. *The Aesthetic Theories of Kant, Hegel, and Schopenhauer.* New York: Columbia University Press, 1936.

Knox, T.M. "The Puzzle of Hegel's Aesthetics." *Art and Logic in Hegel's Philosophy.* W. Steinkraus and K. Schmitz, eds. New Jersey: Humanities Press, 1980, 1–10.

Kramer, Hilton. *The Age of the Avant-Garde.* New York: Farrar, Straus and Giroux, 1974.

La Capra, Dominick. *A Preface to Sartre.* Ithaca: Cornell University Press, 1978.

Lauer, Quentin, S.J. *Hegel's Concept of God.* Albany: State University of New York Press, 1982.

Lefebvre, Henri. *Dialectical Materialism.* trans. J. Sturrock. London: Jonathan Cape, 1968.

Lichtheim, G. *Lukács*. London: Collins, 1970.

Loewenberg, Jacob. "The Exoteric Approach to Hegel's *Phenomenology*." *Mind*, 43 (1934), 424–45.

Lottman, Herbert. *The Left Bank*. Boston: Houghton Mifflin, 1982.

Löwith, Karl. *From Hegel to Nietzsche*. trans. D.E. Green. New York: Doubleday, 1967.

Lucas, R.S. "A Problem in Hegel's Aesthetics." *Renaissance and Modern Studies*, 4 (1960), 82–118.

McClellan, D. *The Young Hegelians and Karl Marx*. London: Macmillan, 1969.

McCumber, John. "Hegel's Anarchistic Utopia: The Politics of his *Aesthetics*." *Southern Journal of Philosophy*, XXII, No. 2, 203–210.

MacIntyre, A. (ed.) *Hegel: A Collection of Critical Essays*. New York: Doubleday, 1972.

Marcel, Gabriel. *Man Against Mass Society*. trans. G.S. Fraser. South Bend, Indiana: Gateway, N.D.

Marcuse, H. *Eros and Civilization*. Boston: Beacon Press, 1955.

_____. *One Dimensional Man*. Boston: Beacon Press, 1964.

_____. *An Essay on Liberation*. Boston: Beacon Press, 1969.

_____. *Reason and Revolution. Hegel and the Rise of Social Theory*. Boston: Beacon Press, 1960.

Maritain, Jacques. *Art and Scholasticism and the Frontiers of Poetry*. trans. J.W. Evans. South Bend: Notre Dame University Press, 1974.

_____. *Creative Intuition in Art and Poetry*. New York: Pantheon, 1953.

Martine, Brian. *Individuals and Individuality*. Albany: State University of New York Press, 1984.

Meszaros, Istvan. *Marx's Theory of Alienation*. London: Merlin Press, 1970.

Midgeley, M. *Heart and Mind*. New York: St. Martin's Press, 1981.

Mitias, Michael H. "Hegel on the Art Object." *Art and Logic in Hegel's Philosophy*. W. Steinkraus and K. Schmitz, eds. New Jersey: Humanities Press, 1980, 67–75.

Montefiori, Alan. (ed.) *Philosophy in France Today*. New York: Cambridge University Press, 1983.

Mueller, G. *Hegel: The Man, His Vision and Work*. New York: Pageant Press, 1968.

Nietzsche, F. *On the Genealogy of Morals*. trans W. Kaufmann and R.J. Hollingdale. New York: Vintage Books, 1969.

_____. *The Will to Power*. trans. W. Kaufmann and R.J. Hollingdale. New York: Vintage Books, 1967.

_____. *The Use and Abuse of History*. trans. A. Collins. Indianapolis: Bobbs-Merrill, 1949.

O'Brien, G.D. *Hegel on Reason and History*. Chicago: University of Chicago Press, 1975.

Olson, A. "Renunciation and Metaphysics: An Examination of Dialectic in Hölderlin and Hegel during their Frankfurt Period." *Man and World*, 15 (1982), 123–148.

Panofsky, Erwin. *Gothic Architecture and Scholasticism*. New York: Meridian Books, 1958.

Paolucci, Anne. "Bradley and Hegel on Shakespeare." *Comparative Literature*, 16 (1964), 211–25.

Paolucci, Henry. "The Poetics of Aristotle and Hegel." *Review of National Literatures*, 1 (1970), 165–213.

Perkins, Robert, (ed.) *History and System: Hegel's Philosophy of History*. Albany: State University of New York Press, 1984.

Plant, R. *Hegel*. Bloomington: Indiana University Press, 1973.

Pöggeler, O. and Gethmann-Siefert, A. eds. *Kunsterfahrung und Kulturpolitik im Berlin Hegels*. *Hegel-Studien* 22. Bonn: Bouvier Verlag Herbert Grundmann, 1983.

Poggioli, Renato. *The Theory of the Avant-Garde*. trans. G. Fitzgerald. New York: Harper and Row, 1971.

Punter, David. *Blake, Hegel and Dialectic*. Amsterdam: Rudopi, 1982.

Reardon, Bernard. *Hegel's Philosophy of Religion*. New York: Harper and Row, 1977.

Ricouer, Paul. *The Conflict of Interpretations*. trans. K. McLaughlin. Evanston: Northwestern University Press, 1974.

_____. *The Rule of Metaphor.* trans. R. Czerny. Toronto: University of Toronto Press, 1977.

Ritter, J. *Hegel and the French Revolution.* trans. R.D. Winfield. Cambridge, Mass.: MIT Press, 1982.

Rorty, Richard. *Philosophy and the Mirror of Nature.* Princeton: Princeton University Press, 1979.

Rosen, Michael. *Hegel's Dialectic and its Criticism.* New York: Cambridge University Press, 1982.

Rosen, Stanley. *G.W.F. Hegel: An Introduction to the Science of Wisdom.* New Haven: Yale, 1974.

Rosenstein, Leon. "Metaphysical Foundations of the Theories of Tragedy in Hegel and Nietzsche." *The Journal of Aesthetics and Art Criticism,* 28 (1970), 521-33.

Ruhle, J. *Literature and Revolution: A Critical Study of the Writer and Communism in the Twentieth Century.* trans. J. Steinberg. New York: Praeger, 1969.

Santayana, G. *Three Philosophical Poets.* Cambridge, Mass: Harvard University Press, 1910.

Santoro, Liberato. "Hegel's Aesthetics and the 'End of Art'" *Philosophical Studies* (Ireland), XXX, 62-72.

Sartre, J.P. *What is Literature?* trans. B. Frechtman. New York: Philosophical Library, 1949.

Schelling, F. *On University Studies.* ed. and trans. E. Wilkinson and L.A. Willoughboy. Athens, Ohio: Ohio University Press, 1966.

Schiller, Friedrich. *On the Aesthetic Education of Man.* trans. R. Snell. New York: Unger, 1965.

Shapiro, Gary. "Hegel on Implicit and Dialectical Meanings of Poetry." *Art and Logic in Hegel's Philosophy.* W. Steinkraus and K. Schmitz, eds. New Jersey: Humanities Press, 1980, 35-54.

Spanos, W.V. et al. (eds.) *The Question of Textuality.* Bloomington: Indiana University Press, 1982.

Steinkraus, W. "The Place of Art in Hegel's System." *Pakistan Philosophical Journal,* 10 (1972), 41-51.

Stepelevich, Lawrence (ed.). *The Young Hegelians: An Anthology*. New York: Cambridge University Press, 1983.

Steinkraus, W.E. and Schmitz, K. (eds.) *Art and Logic in Hegel's Philosophy*. New Jersey: Humanities Press, 1980.

Taminiaux, Jacques. "La pensée esthétique du jeune Hegel." *Revue Philosophique de Louvain*, 56 (1958), 222–50.

Taylor, Charles. *Hegel*. New York: Cambridge University Press, 1975.

Taylor, Mark C. *Journeys to Selfhood: Hegel and Kierkegaard*. Berkeley: University of California Press, 1980.

Tillich, Paul. *The Religious Situation*. trans. H.R. Niebuhr. New York: Meridian Books, 1956.

_____. *Theology of Culture*. New York: Oxford Press, 1959.

Toews, John. *Hegelianism: The Path Towards Dialectical Humanism, 1805–1841*. New York: Cambridge University Press, 1980.

Van der Leeuw, G. *Sacred and Profane Beauty: The Holy in Art*. trans. D.E. Green. New York: Holt, Rinehart, and Winston, 1963.

Vaught, Carl G. *The Quest for Wholeness*. Albany: State University of New York Press, 1982.

Verene, Donald P. *Hegel's Recollection: A Study of Images in the Phenomenology of Spirit*. Albany: State University of New York Press, 1985.

Walsh, W.H. *An Introduction to the Philosophy of History*. London: Hutchinson, 1951.

Weiss, Paul. *Religion and Art*. Milwaukee: Milwaukee University Press, 1963.

Westphal, Merold. *History and Truth in Hegel's Phenomenology*. New Jersey: Humanities Press, 1979.

_____. "The New Flight of the *Owl* . . ." *The Owl of Minerva*, 15, 1, Fall 1983, 5–11.

_____. "Dialectic and Intersubjectivity." *The Owl of Minerva*, 16, 1, Fall 1984, 39–54.

Wilkens, B.T. *Hegel's Philosophy of History*. Ithaca: Cornell University Press, 1974.

Williamson, Raymond Keith. *Introduction to Hegel's Philosophy of Religion*. Albany: State University of New York Press, 1984.

Wimsatt, W.K. and Beardsley, M.C. *The Verbal Icon: Studies in the Meaning of Poetry.* New York: Noonday Press, 1958.

White, Alan. *Absolute Knowledge: Hegel and the Problem of Metaphysics.* Athens, Ohio: Ohio University Press, 1983.

Whitehead, A.N. *Adventure of Ideas.* New York: Macmillan, 1967.

Index

Abrams, M.H., 122, 126

Absolute: vii–viii, xiii–xviii, 1; absence of, 77–81; as absolving, 99; and beauty, 103–106; art and religion, 35–37; and Romantic Irony, 118–120; Left-Hegelian view, 51–56. See also Absolute Idea, The Ideal

Absolute Idea: 9–12, 31, 87; and radiance of beauty, 139–141, 149; and Romantic Irony, 120; as transcendental, 149. See also Absolute, The Ideal

Absolute Spirit: collapsed into objective spirit, 55–56. See also Absolute, Absolute Idea, The Ideal

Adorno, T., 52

Analysis: and deconstruction, 89–90; and synthesis, 97–100

Analytic philosophy: xix; and contemporary fragmentation, 123

Appearance: and art work, 62; and beauty, 132, 140–141. See also *Schein*, the Sensuous

Apollo, Apollonian: 84–85, 87, 90, 92, 96; domesticated, 154; drowned god, 162–163

Apelles, 17

Aquinas, Thomas, xvii, 105, 130–139, 142–143, 147–149, 152–154

Arabic Mysticism, 42

Aristotle, 1, 3, 12, 26, 61, 63–65, 86, 88, 122, 127, 131, 133, 135, 137, 141, 149

Art: after Hegel, 52–56, 178–179n.3; and history, 59–76; and revolution, 54–56; as aesthetic, 37–40, 50–56; as religious, 40–56, 179n.9

Art work: and concreteness, 21–23; *Phenomenology* and *Logic* as, 29–31, 175n.14, 178n.30

Articulation: and dialectic, 92–96; art and philosophy as, 13, 31–32; art as self-articulation, 8; language and deconstruction, 88–91; of concrete concept, 24; teleology and deconstruction, 80–81

Aufhebung: xix; and art work, 64; and dialectic, 95–96; and difference of art and philosophy, 16; and the ugly, 155–156; and Heideggerian retrieval, 161–162; and Schiller, 173n.3

Augustine, Saint, 43

Ayer, A.J., 148

Barzun, Jacques, 116–118

Baumgarten, A. G., 121

Beauty: xvii; and Marx, 51; and Apollonian, 84; and teleology of

217